The Political Economy of Pension Reform in Central–Eastern Europe

STUDIES IN COMPARATIVE ECONOMIC SYSTEMS

General Editors: Wladimir Andreff, *Professor of Economics at the University Paris I Panthéon Sorbonne and Director of ROSES*; Bruno Dallago, *Associate Professor of Economic Policy and Comparative Economic Systems at the University of Trento and President of EACES*; János Kornai, *Allie S. Freed Professsor of Economics at Harvard University and Permanent Fellow at Collegium Budapest, Institute for Advanced Studies*; and Hans-Jürgen Wagener, *Professor of Economics and Vice-Rector at the European University Viadrina at Frankfurt (Oder)*

Recent developments in different economic systems have presented new challenges to economic theory and policy. Scholars in comparative economic systems have to debate and clarify the nature of the economic system, its place within the economy and the dynamics of its transformation in a comparative perspective.

This series is designed to contribute to the debate and advance knowledge in the field. It provides a forum for original comparative research on the economic system and economic performance including important aspects such as economic institutions and their change, economic actors and policy instruments in the transformation process.

The books published in this series are written by leading international scholars writing in a theoretical or applied way and using either country-specific studies or cross-country comparisons. They show how economic analysis can contribute to understanding and resolving one of the most important questions facing the world at present and in the future.

Titles in this series include:

Struggle and Hope
Essays on Stabilization and Reform in a Post-Socialist Economy
János Kornai

The Transformation of Economic Systems in Central Europe
Herman W. Hoen

The Political Economy of Pension Reform in Central–Eastern Europe
Katharina Müller

The Political Economy of Pension Reform in Central–Eastern Europe

Katharina Müller

Research Fellow
Frankfurt Institute for Transformation Studies
European University Viadrina, Frankfurt (Oder), Germany

STUDIES IN COMPARATIVE ECONOMIC SYSTEMS

Edward Elgar
Cheltenham, UK • Northampton, MA, USA

Published by
Edward Elgar Publishing Limited
Glensanda House
Montpellier Parade
Cheltenham
Glos GL50 1UA
UK

Edward Elgar Publishing, Inc.
136 West Street
Suite 202
Northampton
Massachusetts 01060
USA

A catalogue record for this book
is available from the British Library

Library of Congress Cataloguing in Publication Data

Müller, Katharina, 1967–
    The political economy of pension reform in Central–Eastern Europe
/ Katharina Müller.
    (Studies in comparative economic systems)
    Includes bibliographical references and index.
    1. Old age pensions—Europe, Central. 2. Pensions—Europe, Central.
3. Europe, Central—Social policy.   I. Title. II. Series.
HD7164.7.M85 2000
331.25'22'094309049—dc21   99–44830
                                                              CIP

ISBN 1 84064 238 6

Printed and bound in Great Britain by Biddles Ltd, www.Biddles.co.uk

Contents

Figures

Tables

Abbreviations

AARP   American Association of Retired People

AFJPs   *Administradoras de Fondos de Jubilaciones y Pensiones*; private
           pension funds in Argentina

AFP   *Allmän Folkpension*; Swedish first-tier pension

AFPs   *Administradoras de Fondos de Pensiones*; private pension funds
           in Chile

ATP   *Allmän Tilläggspension*; Swedish second-tier pension

AWS   *Akcja Wyborcza Solidarność*; Solidarity Electoral Action
           (Poland)

cf.   *confer*; compare

CZK   Czech Crowns

ČMKOS   *Českomoravská komora odborových svazů*; Czech trades union
           federation

ČNB   *Česká Národní Banka*; Czech National Bank

ČSSD   *Česká Strana Sociální Demokracie*; Czech Social Democratic
           Party

ČSSZ   *Česká Správa Sociálního Zabezpečení*; Czech social security
           administration

DŽJ   *Důchodci za Životní Jistoty*; Czech Pensioners' Party

EBRD   European Bank for Reconstruction and Development

ECU   European Currency Unit

e.g.   *exempli gratia*; for instance

esp.   especially

ÉT   *Érdekegyeztető Tanács*; Hungarian tripartite council

EU   European Union

FUS   *Fundusz Ubezpieczeń Społecznych*; Polish social insurance fund

GDP	Gross Domestic Product
GNP	Gross National Product
gov't	government
HUF	Hungarian Forint
i.e.	*id est*; that is to say
IBRD	International Bank for Reconstruction and Development
IFF	individually fully-funded
ILO	International Labour Organisation
IMF	International Monetary Fund
ISSA	International Social Security Association
KDU-ČSL	*Křest'anská a demokratická unie – Československá strana lidová*; Czech Christian-Democrat Party
KPEiR	*Krajowa Partia Emerytów i Rencistów*; Polish Pensioners' Party
KRUS	*Kasa Rolniczego Ubezpieczenia Społecznego*; Polish social insurance fund for farmers
KSČM	*Komunistická strana Čech a Moravy*; Czech Communist Party
MoF	Ministry of Finance
MP	Member of Parliament
MSZOSZ	*Magyar Szakszervezetek Országos Szövetsége*; Hungarian trades union federation
n.a.	not available
NDC	notional defined contribution
No.	Number
NSZZ	*Niezależny Samorządny Związek Zawodowy*; independent self-governed trades union (Poland)
ODA	*Občanská demokratická aliance*; Civic Democratic Alliance (Czech Party)
ODS	*Občanská demokratická strana*; Civic Democratic Party (Czech Republic)
OECD	Organisation for Economic Co-operation and Development
OPZZ	*Ogólnopolskie Porozumienie Związków Zawodowych*; Polish trades union federation

p.a.	*per annum*; yearly
PAYG	pay-as-you-go
PF	*Pénztarfelügyelet*; Hungarian supervisory agency for pension funds
PR	public relations
PSL	*Polskie Stronnictwo Ludowe*; Polish Peasant Party
PZU	*Państwowe Zakład Ubezpieczeń*; Polish state insurance company
resp.	respectively
RHSD	*Rada hospodářskej a sociálnej dohody*; Czech tripartite council
SAFP	*Superintendencia de Administradoras de Fondos de Pensiones*; Chilean supervisory agency for pension funds
SEK	Swedish Crowns
SERPS	State Earnings Related Pension Scheme (Great Britain)
SLD	*Sojusz Lewicy Demokratycznej*; Left Democratic Alliance (Polish Party)
stand.	standardised
SZEF	*Szakszervezetek Együttműködési Fóruma*; Hungarian trades union federation
SZOT	*Szakszervezetek Országos Tanácsa*; Hungarian trades union federation
TÁRKI	*Társadalomkutatási Informatikai Egyesülés*; Hungarian research institute
UNFE	*Urząd Nadzoru nad Funduszami Emerytalnymi*; Polish supervisory agency for pension funds
US	United States
USAID	US Agency for International Development
UW	*Unia Wolności*; Freedom Union (Polish Party)
VMB	voluntary mutual benefit
vs.	versus
ZUS	*Zakład Ubezpieczeń Społecznych*; Polish social insurance institute

Acknowledgements

The present volume contains the findings of the research project 'Institutional Change in Social Security: Pension Reforms in Poland, Hungary and the Czech Republic', which was completed in early 1999. It formed part of the multi-disciplinary research programme 'The Transformation of Economic Systems and the Reform of Societies in Central and Eastern Europe', conducted at Frankfurt Institute for Transformation Studies, European University Viadrina, Frankfurt (Oder). This programme involves economists, political scientists, sociologists and jurists, and is funded by the *Deutsche Forschungsgemeinschaft*. Its generous financial support is gratefully acknowledged.

I have accumulated many debts over the three years it has taken me to understand the political economy of pension reform in Central–Eastern Europe. First and foremost, this concerns those Czech, Hungarian and Polish experts and policymakers who have shared their time with me to extensively discuss local pension reform issues. Even though not all of them can be mentioned here, it can safely be maintained that this book could not have been written without these background conversations. I particularly appreciated the detailed comments, helpful information and other forms of support provided by Kálmánné Antal, Mária Augusztinovics, László Csaba, Zsuzsa Ferge, Róbert I. Gál, Krzysztof Hagemejer, Péter Mihályi, János Réti, András Simonovits and Miklós Toldi in Budapest; Miroslav Hiršl, Jana Klimentová, Jiří Král, Martin Mácha, Jiří Rusnok, Ondřej Schneider, Clemens Schütte and Jiří Večerník in Prague; Zofia Czepulis-Rutkowska, Stanisława Golinowska, Łukasz Konopielko, Ryszard Petru, Aleksandra Wiktorow and Irena Wóycicka in Warsaw, and Maciej Żukowski in Poznań. Furthermore, I am grateful to Katja Hujo, Rubén Lo Vuolo, Carmelo Mesa-Lago, Manfred Nitsch and Helmut Schwarzer who made the Latin American pension reforms accessible to me, thus helping me to discover the templates of the 'new pension orthodoxy'. For helpful suggestions I would also like to thank Jan Adam, Wladimir Andreff, Bruno Dallago, Ulrike Götting, Sabine Horstmann, Klaus Müller and Joan Nelson. Moreover, I benefited from the opportunity to discuss my findings with the participants of the May 1999 pension reform workshop in Héviz, organised by the Bremen-based Centre for Social Policy Research.

I would also like to express grateful appreciation to my supervisors at European University Viadrina, Hans-Jürgen Wagener and Hermann Ribhegge, who have supported my efforts without reservation, notwithstanding a very tight time schedule. Throughout the entire three-year project period, I had the fortune of working with very helpful colleagues at the Frankfurt Institute for Transformation Studies. I would like to make special mention of two Viadrina colleagues: Frank Bönker contributed many suggestions, references and stimuli that proved pivotal when my ideas started to take shape. Incessantly, Andreas Ryll provided me with decisive criticism, indispensable support and permanent encouragement, thereby ensuring the successful conclusion of this project. Both have had a strong influence on my way of thinking, even though I probably failed to translate most of their advice into this piece of work. Finally, I would like to express my appreciation to two persons who have greatly enhanced the readability of this volume: Melany Reynolds-Jacobs improved the style of the original draft, while Andreas Paul was in charge of the final appearance of this book.

Frankfurt (Oder), June 1999   Katharina Müller

1.   Introduction

1.1   TRANSFORMATION AND SOCIAL SECURITY IN CENTRAL AND EASTERN EUROPE

Since the late 1980s, the countries of Central and Eastern Europe have witnessed sweeping changes in their economies and societies. Compared with this, the area of social security has long remained exempt from structural change. With the exception of the introduction of unemployment benefits – a reaction to open unemployment, so far unknown in Central and Eastern Europe – the existing social protection systems survived the system change basically unaltered (see Götting 1996). However, it would be erroneous to conclude that there was an underlying consensus regarding the maintenance of the *status quo* in social policy. It is much the opposite: the scope and direction of social sector reforms are more disputed than the measures to be taken in other areas of economic and political transformation, where market economy and democracy are widely accepted blueprints.[1] Controversies include the evaluation of the legacies of the past – i.e. the socialist welfare state – as well as the role of social policy in the transformation process.[2]

Unlike its counterparts in the West, the socialist welfare state included not only protection against the loss of income due to old age, sickness, disability and other contingencies, but also the right to a job, low prices for basic foodstuff, housing, transport and energy, free or subsidised access to education and culture, and a relatively egalitarian income distribution.[3] This guarantee of comprehensive social security enjoyed enduring approval by the population of Central and Eastern Europe (see Ferge 1994).[4] Still, scholarship has been highly critical of the socialist welfare state, although the respective reasoning is diametrically opposed. Neoliberal economists have characterised socialist social policy as 'lavish', 'vastly overextended' (Sachs 1996a: VII, 1996b: 6) and 'premature' (Kornai 1995: 131), given the level of GDP per capita reached by Central and Eastern European countries. They are convinced that past entitlements were too generous to be affordable, contributing decisively to the economic collapse of socialism. By contrast, scholars from the field of social policy have stressed the shortcomings of the socialist welfare state: most social benefits were insufficiently low (Ferge

1

1995) and by no means universally accessible to all citizens, but presupposed officially recognised employment (Standing 1996). The 'undeserving poor' (Ferge 1991: 134) – those regarded as unproductive or disloyal, as well as their families – were excluded from socialist welfare provision.[5] Moreover, the socialist welfare state had a residual character, getting by on the left-overs of the 'productive spheres' (Ferge 1991). Both lincs of argument coincide in their criticism towards the paternalistic, patronising character of the socialist welfare state (e.g. Deacon 1992).[6]

There was further disagreement about the status of social policy within the transformation process.[7] While in the early years of transition, policymakers had assumed that macroeconomic and political reforms were more pressing than a change of the existing set of social security institutions, welfare and distributive issues started to attract greater attention after a wave of election victories of post-communist forces in Central and Eastern Europe, which created worries about a backlash against market-oriented reforms (see Cornia 1996). However, there was considerable discord as to the type of reforms needed in the field of social policy. Some scholars and external advisors suggested disposing of past entitlements as quickly as possible, assuming that the 'system of cradle-to-grave security' implied high fiscal costs, impeded macroeconomic growth, and created negative work and saving incentives (Kopits 1994; Krumm, Milanovic and Walton 1995). 'Decades of spoon-feeding' (Kornai 1997a: 1186) should give way to greater individual sovereignty. They called for a radical restructuring of the existing social net in Central and Eastern Europe, aiming to target scarce resources towards poverty reduction, while embarking on the marketisation and individualisation of additional protection functions (for a critique see Standing 1998).[8]

This residualist strategy has been opposed on the grounds that, while based on sound economic reasons, it fails to take political or social imperatives in transformation countries into account (see ILO-CEET 1995; Standing 1996). They argue that social policy is crucial to buffer the social costs of the restructuring of the economy, and to prevent political opposition to the transformational agenda, as it allows for a compensation of the losers (see Tomann and Scholz 1996).[9] Thus, the question is not whether Central and Eastern European countries can afford a welfare state, but whether they can afford to do without it (see Trapp 1993), considering the high level of expectations based on the dual cognitive references, West European and socialist welfare states (see Offe 1994: 193). Notwithstanding the undisputed need to restructure the existing welfare state institutions (see e.g. Barr 1994b), the importance of social policy for the success and legitimacy of the transformation process should not be underestimated. 'Whereas everybody feels that dependency on the state has to be decreased in the market system, people's trust in the new regime is reinforced to a high degree by the maintenance of social security' (Večerník 1996: 192).

In recent years, the debate on post-socialist social policy has shifted from emergency measures to institutional rebuilding (see Graham 1997). The almost exclusive focus on the social costs of transition, having turned out to be much higher than expected (see Ferge et al. 1995), is giving way to long-term structural concerns.[10] How radically should the design of existing pension, health care and education systems be altered in order to make them compatible with the new market economy environment (see Nelson 1997)?

1.2   THE FOCUS OF THIS STUDY

The present study focuses on a particularly interesting area of post-1989 social policy: the existing old-age security systems and their recent reform. Retirement pension schemes are among the most complex and multi-dimensional arrangements to be found in modern societies. They concern not only social, but also macroeconomic issues and, in accordance with the respective public–private mix, may have an impact on public finance, saving, labour and capital markets (see Arrau and Schmidt-Hebbel 1994). Moreover, the political economy of pension schemes has attracted the attention of scholars, since it results from interactions between various stakeholders, such as pensioners, government, public pension institutions, private pension funds, trades unions and employer organisations. Multiple actors amount to many potential veto players (Tsebelis 1995), making old-age security reform a highly sensitive and politically difficult issue. Furthermore, pension reform is a challenging task because it affects substantial entitlements, and involves difficult trade-offs in terms of goals and values (see Nelson 1998).

The existing public pension systems in some Central and Eastern European countries have undergone fundamental change in recent years. Stimulated by the 'new pension orthodoxy' (Lo Vuolo 1996), mainly transmitted by the World Bank, several transition countries opted for a partial shift to funding, thereby replicating Latin American reform models. 'Privatizing social security is a growth industry ... Simulating the economic impact of privatizing social security is also a growth industry' (Kotlikoff, Smetters and Walliser 1998b: 327). Surprisingly, scholars have been considerably less concerned with explaining the political feasibility of such radical change in retirement provision, although it defies conventional wisdom concerning the politics of pension reform: political scientists, sociologists and economists coincide in stressing the remarkable resilience of existing retirement arrangements.

As the recent reform dynamics in some Central and Eastern European countries exemplifies that partial or full privatisation of old-age security can be accomplished, it calls for fresh research into the political economy of old-age security reform.[11] This study aims to accept this challenge, focusing on the divergent pension reform experiences of Poland and Hungary on the one hand, and the Czech Republic on the other. These three countries exhibit many similarities, not only in terms of the pre-1989 characteristics of their societies and economies, but also with regard to their political and economic consolidation *vis-à-vis* other transition countries. Furthermore, they started from widely identical old-age security systems in 1989. Yet, in recent years, they have opted for markedly different strategies to reform their existing old-age security schemes.

While Poland and Hungary resorted to partial pension privatisation, following Latin American role models, the Czech reform efforts remained well within the boundaries of the Bismarckian–Beveridgean pension traditions. The present study examines the emergence of these different pension reform paths in Central–Eastern Europe, trying to identify the determinants of paradigm choice in the area of old-age security. In particular, it will be asked which structural-institutional and actor-related factors account for radical pension reform. Starting from a comparative-empirical basis, this study is intended as a contribution to the political economy of pension reform, interpreting it as part of a medium-range theory of policy reform.

The focus and approach of the present study are largely unprecedented within the area of comparative research on pension reform. Earlier scholarship has concentrated mainly on West European and North American pension reforms (e.g. Pierson and Weaver 1993; Kohl 1994; Pierson 1994; Taylor-Gooby 1997; Döring 1998). The recent Latin American pension reforms have also been compared extensively (e.g. Banco Nacional de Comercio Exterior 1996; Nitsch and Schwarzer 1996; Institut für Iberoamerika-Kunde 1997; Mesa-Lago 1998; Queisser 1998b; Schwarzer 1998). A North–South comparison of pension system development has been conducted by Williamson and Pampel (1993), which, however, still left East European countries out of consideration. The first East–West comparison of old-age security reforms was presented by Augusztinovics et al. (1997). In some recent studies, Central and Eastern European pension reforms have been analysed within a wider comparative framework of social security reforms in transition (e.g. Cichon 1995; Pestoff 1995b; Brusis 1998; Götting 1998). A recent comparative study of Polish, Hungarian and Czech pension systems (Boller 1997) provides a detailed description and analysis of the local pension systems, while the politics of pension reform are only a marginal issue.

The first comparative-empirical hypotheses regarding the political economy of pension reform in Central–Eastern Europe have been spelt out by

Götting (1998) and Müller (1997c, 1998a, b, e). The most recent contributions to the politics of pension reform include a paper by Nelson (1998), comparing the politics of pension and health care reforms in Hungary and Poland, and a study on the political feasibility of the latest pension privatisations in Poland, Hungary and Kazakhstan, commissioned by the World Bank and conducted by Orenstein (1998a). Concerning the set-up, the present study provides a comparative analysis of different paradigm choices, whereas Nelson and Orenstein consider only country cases where radical pension reforms have been adopted. While the present study largely shares the methodology used by Nelson and Orenstein, its distinctive feature lies in the joint consideration of both actor-related and structural-institutional factors (see below). Moreover, the present study draws on the existing economic and political science approaches to pension reform, as well as on research results from the political economy of policy reform (e.g. Rodrik 1996; Tommasi and Velasco 1996).

It is assumed here that structural factors – notably the financial situation of the existing public retirement schemes and the degree of external debt – largely determine which actors take part in the process of pension reform, as well as their relative strength. Considering the actors' respective cognitive maps (Axelrod 1976) and consequent perception of pension reform alternatives, the resulting actor constellations condition the basic paradigm choice. In a second step, following the interaction of the reform team with other political actors, the details of the specific local arrangements are produced. Hence, the constellations and interactions of actors involved in pension reform are analysed within the relevant structural-institutional context, to account for the political economy of pension reform in Central–Eastern Europe.

Although exciting and rewarding, empirical research in the context of economic and social transformation is a difficult task. Some remaining reservations include the availability and quality of statistical data on old-age security in Central–Eastern Europe, which tend to differ considerably among authors. Instead of using local sources, and in spite of some discrepancies with the latter, I have decided to use the data from Schrooten, Smeeding and Wagner (1999) for all three countries. Having been calculated according to a uniform methodology, they are thought to allow for a cross-country comparison. My outsider's account of the Hungarian, Polish and Czech reform stories merits another caveat, even after extensive conversations with social security experts and policymakers in Budapest, Prague, Warsaw and Poznań.[12]

1.3   A ROAD-MAP

This volume is structured as follows: chapter 2 reviews the main issues of old-age security, as far as they are relevant for the following analysis of Central–Eastern European pension reforms. First of all, the basic design choices for pension systems are summarised, i.e. voluntary vs. mandatory membership, public vs. private management, redistribution vs. insurance, funded vs. pay-as-you-go financing and defined benefits vs. defined contributions. Then, particular country cases relevant for practical pension policy are presented. The final part is on the new pension orthodoxy and its critics. The paradigmatic impact of the former, as transmitted by the influential World Bank document 'Averting the Old Age Crisis. Policies to Protect the Old and Promote Growth' (World Bank 1994a), has been substantial in Central and Eastern Europe.

Chapter 3 contains the theoretical context and methodology of this study. The political economy of pension reform is interpreted here as a broad concept that comprises the existing economic, sociological and political science approaches. Interestingly, these methodologically heterogeneous approaches coincide when it comes to emphasising the inertia of old-age security arrangements. To account for the political feasibility of radical pension reforms, it is therefore deemed necessary to include some insights from the recent literature on the political economy of policy reform. This strand of research deals precisely with the politics of fundamental reforms that had long been considered unlikely by scholars. In the last part of this chapter, I will spell out the conceptual framework of this study, that is mainly inspired by actor-centred institutionalism (see Mayntz and Scharpf 1995). The advantage of this method is that it combines actor-centred and structuralist-institutionalist approaches, long thought to be mutually exclusive, into an integrated framework (Scharpf 1997: 36).

The case-studies on Poland, Hungary and the Czech Republic constitute the empirical centre-piece of this study (chapters 4 to 6). For each of the countries considered a similar structure of analysis is used, to prepare the ground for the subsequent comparative chapter. First, the institutional legacy, post-1989 problem settings and initial measures in old-age security are reviewed, which were mostly of an *ad hoc* type. With regard to second-phase reforms, the policy paths bifurcate: while systemic pension reform, following radical Latin American role models, is undertaken in Hungary and Poland, in the Czech Republic the traditional Bismarckian–Beveridgean paradigm remains unchallenged, resulting in comparatively moderate pension reform measures. I will analyse the respective political processes leading to pension reform, and describe the divergent reform outcomes. Each of the country chapters concludes with a summary of the respective problem settings, relevant actors and paradigm choices in old-age security.

Chapter 7 analyses Central–Eastern European pension reforms from a comparative viewpoint, seeking to explain the divergent paradigm choices made in the three countries under consideration. This includes a comparison of the socialist legacy and the first-phase pension reforms, to take possible path dependencies into consideration. A separate section is devoted to the conceptual and political economy implications of the Argentine-type blueprint chosen by Hungarian and Polish policymakers. Finally, to account for the bifurcation of second-phase reform paths, the interaction between structural settings and actor constellations, as well as the resulting paradigm choices in old-age security are analysed comparatively.

In chapter 8, I will attempt to draw some conclusions about the political economy of pension reform in Central–Eastern Europe, intended as a medium-range contribution to the existing multi-disciplinary body of literature in the field. The main factors influencing institutional choice in the area of old-age security will be identified. Which structural-institutional and actor-related determinants account for radical pension reform, or the absence of it?

NOTES

1. The latest trends in Russia and Belarus exemplify that it would be misleading to assume these aims to be universally shared throughout Central and Eastern Europe.
2. The normative differences underlying this controversy, which concern the appropriate roles and responsibilities of the individual and the state in social security, are rarely made explicit. For an exception cf. the dispute between Zsuzsa Ferge and János Kornai in Hungary (e.g. Kornai 1996, 1997b; Ferge 1996, 1997a, b).
3. See Adam (1991). For a detailed account on the socialist welfare state and its transformation see Götting (1998).
4. Adam (1991: 2) interpreted the socialist welfare system as part of a tacit social contract between the regime and the people in Central and Eastern Europe: 'In my opinion, people have committed themselves to accept the regime and not to revolt against it ... In return, the government offers a package of rights and benefits which can be denoted as socialist.'
5. The term 'undeserving poor' is, in fact, a 19th century euphemism, as indicated by Standing (1998: 10).
6. Ferge (1991: 134) maintains that Central and Eastern European citizens did not acquire 'social rights', but were allotted 'social gifts' by the State. However, this does not seem to hold in all areas of socialist social security, since Tomeš (1994b: 6) speaks of 'legal entitlements', particularly when it comes to acquired pension claims.
7. While Cornia (1996) claims that social policy has been neglected during the early years of transition, Graham (1997: 397) points out that 'in the absence of a sound macroeconomic policy framework, no social welfare reform is likely to succeed'. The sequencing of social policy as a first- or second-phase reform issue is also discussed by Wagener (1999).
8. 'In transition countries, the primary objective ... should be to provide minimal benefits for survival to the growing number of truly vulnerable households.' (Chu and Gupta 1996: 19)
9. See Poganietz (1997) for a discussion of compensation payments in a transition economy.

10. For differing opinions on the social costs of transition see, e.g., Milanovic (1993); Danecki (1994); Adam (1996); Graham (1996); Nelson (1997); Szamuely (1997).
11. It is well known that Latin America exhibits further examples of pension privatisation (see subchapter 2.3). Fundamental reforms may even occur in Western industrialised countries, a case in point being the radical pension reform recently passed in Sweden, the welfare state's stronghold (see subchapter 2.2).
12. Between 1996 and 1999, I have conducted over eighty background interviews with local experts. While proving pivotal for the understanding of the reform dynamics in the three countries considered, these interviews are not directly quoted in the present study.

2. Reforming Old-Age Security: Design Choices and Policy Blueprints

2.1 BASIC POLICY CHOICES FOR OLD-AGE PENSION SCHEMES

The design of old-age security schemes differs widely across the world, and neither economists nor social policy experts are unanimous about the first-best combination of relevant design features. Besides the much discussed choice of the financing method – full funding versus pay-as-you-go – other features of old-age security schemes are equally important in determining their overall economic and social impact. While some retirement pension schemes are mainly designed to allow for a smoothing of individual income over the life cycle, thus stressing the insurance aspect, others aim to provide adequate retirement incomes for all, implying considerable redistribution. Pension schemes can be publicly or privately managed, membership may be mandatory or voluntary, and there are defined benefit and defined contribution plans. In the following, the main design choices for pension systems are briefly reviewed.[1]

Mandatory vs. Voluntary Membership

Among the rationales for forcing individuals to participate in a pension scheme, individual myopia and insurance market failure stand out.[2] Due to short-sightedness or deliberate free-riding, some individuals make no provision for their old age (see Feldstein 1998). By imposing costs on the taxpayers later on, this behaviour is likely to generate externalities that mandatory old-age insurance sets out to avoid. Adverse selection may make voluntary insurance against the risks of longevity and disability unavailable, while compulsion enables a pooling solution (see Kotlikoff 1989; Barr 1992). The level of mandatory coverage determines how much space remains for voluntary pension schemes. Voluntary old-age security, supplementing the benefits from compulsory schemes, can be provided by employer-sponsored occupational schemes, private pension funds, personal savings or individual life insurance. Informal support from family members may be an additional source of income in old age, based on an implicit and unenforceable inter-generational contract (see World Bank 1994a: 49–65).

Public vs. Private Management

At first the public–private dichotomy might not seem meaningful, as a mix of public and private providers of old-age security exists in almost all countries (see Rose 1989). However, the respective roles of market and state in the provision of retirement pensions differ considerably from one country to another. In this sense, it is particularly relevant whether state or market run the mandatory pension business, which tends to be the most significant part of old-age security in quantitative terms because of its compulsory nature.[3] From the broadly recognised need for a mandatory pension scheme it does not necessarily follow that the latter has to be publicly run.[4] The government can limit its role to enforcing individual participation in a private pension scheme, while taking over some additional regulatory and supervisory functions.

However, if policymakers decide to redistribute income from high to low lifetime earners via the pension system (see below), part of it would have to be publicly run. Moreover, it should be noted that private pension providers cannot supply insurance against severe depression, capital market risks and unanticipated inflation after retirement. Private pension schemes also tend to be more expensive to administer, since they often involve a large number of suppliers, entailing fewer economies of scale (see Heinrich et al. 1996). Public old-age schemes, on the other hand, have been accused of being subject to political interference (see Diamond 1997). Frequent changes of entitlement rules may create a credibility problem *vis-à-vis* the contributors to the scheme (see Breyer 1996; Holzmann 1997b).

Insurance vs. Redistribution

In insurance arrangements providing old-age benefits pensions are actuarially related to the amount of past premiums paid by the insured. An old-age scheme is said to be actuarially fair when there are no net gains from participating in the scheme, i.e. when the present value of payouts equals the present value of lifetime contributions for all retirement ages and cohorts (see Börsch-Supan 1997: 201).

Alternatively, policymakers can decide to integrate elements of redistribution. Instead of preserving status differentials, they may seek to equalise old-age income. Similarly, interruptions of the contribution record due to child-raising, higher education and unemployment may be compensated for. Three different types of redistribution stand out (Barr 1993a: 225–6): redistribution from rich to poor usually results from a non-actuarial pension formula. However, differential mortality implies a partial offsetting of this redistributive bias. Redistribution from men to women occurs when the contribution–benefit link is the same for both sexes, even though female life expectancy is higher. This effect is increased when the retirement age for women is lower than that of men. Redistribution from young to old occurs when, in a pay-as-you-go scheme, a generation as a whole receives more than the sum of its past contributions.

Funded vs. Pay-As-You-Go Financing

While pay-as-you-go (PAYG) implies that current outlays on pension benefits are paid out of current revenues from pension contributions, thus calling for inter-generational solidarity as a necessary precondition, in individually fully-funded (IFF) schemes the insured accumulates a fund over the entire working life, which is converted into an annuity upon retirement.[5] The controversy on the appropriate financing method started over 100 years ago and has received extensive coverage in economic literature.[6] In order to compare the advantages and drawbacks of both financing methods, their respective effects on saving and growth, labour and capital markets, as well as their allocative and dynamic efficiency have been broadly discussed.[7] While the extensive literature is inconclusive both theoretically and empirically, the current mainstream within economic scholarship argues in favour of a switch to funding, implying considerable transition costs (see subchapter 2.4).

Defined Benefits vs. Defined Contributions

In defined benefit plans, pensions are based on a prescribed formula (e.g. the number of years in service, the final salary), providing a guarantee of replacement ratios. In contrast, defined contribution plans pay out pensions according to the size of accumulated pension contributions plus the investment returns yielded by them over the decades, ensuring actuarial fairness (see Davis 1998: 12–15). These arrangements differ *inter alia* with regard to the bearer of the long-term risks of investment, inflation, longevity and disability. In the case of defined contribution plans pensioners themselves are burdened with these risks.[8]

Notional defined contribution (NDC) plans are an interim solution, employed in many of the latest pension reforms, designed to increase the transparency and the contribution–benefit link of existing PAYG schemes. Although capital accumulation is only virtual in these schemes, NDC plans can be interpreted as mimicking IFF schemes, since individual benefit levels depend exclusively on past contributions, recorded in notional individualised accounts, and their virtual rate of return (see Holzmann 1997a, b; James 1998; Rutkowski 1998).[9]

Designing an Old-Age Security System

The implicit social contract, and the prevailing attitudes towards the appropriate roles and responsibilities of the individual and the state in old-age provision, are of crucial importance when a fully-fledged national pension system is set up from the 'menu' presented above. Not all combinations of the design features reviewed above are technically feasible, e.g. defined contribution plans are by definition fully funded. However, there is considerably more diversity in the design of pension schemes than is conventionally assumed. Substantial intra-generational redistribution is no inherent design feature of mandatory public PAYG systems. On the other hand, voluntary or mandatory fully-funded schemes entailing a strict contribution–benefit link are generally associated with private management, comprising occupational and personal funded pension schemes.[10] Funded schemes can, however, also be publicly managed (e.g. the national provident funds in Malaysia and Singapore; see Heller 1998). Finally, not all of the design choices listed above are mutually exclusive, as most national pension systems are multi-tiered.

In the next two sections, some prominent role models of pension reform are presented. As the economic and distributional effects of pension systems depend on specific combinations of the parameters spelt out above, particular country cases become important in practical pension policy. First, the traditional West European pension blueprints – Bismarck and Beveridge – and the latest reform trends are reviewed, followed by the radical Latin American pension reforms in subchapter 2.3.

Here, the idea is to provide a rough outline of the respective combination of design features without attempting a comprehensive evaluation of the historical evolution, strengths, shortcomings and political-economy implications of these role models. Rather, this chapter seeks to give an overview of the perceived paradigmatic 'menu' in Central–Eastern Europe.

Concerning the selection of the country cases, I have limited myself to the role models perceived as relevant by the policymakers in Hungary, Poland and the Czech Republic. For this reason, both the US Social Security system and the provident funds in South East Asia have been left out of this review. The final part of this chapter is on the new pension orthodoxy, whose impact has been substantial in Central and Eastern Europe. The chapter ends with a review of the international controversy triggered by the recent privatisation proposals, and reflected in the local pension reform discussions in Poland, Hungary and the Czech Republic. Although some of the prominent controversies within economic scholarship are touched upon in subchapter 2.4, the other subchapters deliberately follow a social administration or social policy approach (see Hill 1990): it is assumed that Central–Eastern European policymakers perceive the state of the economic pension reform discussion only indirectly, via ready-made reform blueprints that are tried and tested, exemplifying traditional insights or recent concerns.

2.2   WEST EUROPEAN MODELS: BISMARCK, BEVERIDGE AND BEYOND

Across Western Europe, the design of old-age security systems varies widely (for an overview see GVG 1994; Steinmeyer 1996). Here, the focus will be on the two traditional West European pension paradigms, the Bismarckian and the Beveridgean model (see Döring 1998). These concepts overlap with the 'conservative-corporatist' and 'social democratic-universalistic' regime types in Esping-Andersen's prominent classification (1990: 85–7).[11] Additionally, recent reform trends are reviewed, notably the interesting Swedish case. In this subchapter, the main focus will be on the mandatory tiers of old-age security, while the existing voluntary pension schemes are only briefly touched upon.

Bismarck vs. Beveridge

The Bismarckian tradition derived from the pioneering social insurance system introduced by the German Chancellor Bismarck in the 1880s. To appease the arising socialist movement (see Wilde 1981), old-age and disability pensions were set up in 1889, following health insurance (1883) and accident insurance (1884). The Beveridgean conception, on the other hand, goes back to 1942, when William Beveridge published his report on 'Social Insurance and Allied Services', in which he coined his famous objective: 'freedom from want'.[12] In the Beveridge report the problem of adequate income support in old age is considered to be particularly relevant (see Beveridge 1942: 90). The concepts of both Beveridgean and Bismarckian old-age security underwent some changes in meaning over the decades.[13] Below, an outline of the current understanding of these models is presented (see Table 2.1), before turning to some exemplifying country cases.

The Bismarckian model is a contribution-financed insurance scheme mainly focusing on dependent employees. It aims at the maintenance of the accustomed living standard of the insured. In comparison, the Beveridgean model boils down to a tax-transfer system, designed to protect all citizens against old-age poverty. While in the former earnings-related scheme pension benefit levels are related to individual contribution history, the latter provides flat-rate benefits, either universally or on a means-tested basis. Both systems are publicly managed, but, in the Bismarckian system, representatives of trades unions and employers' associations are involved in decision-making. The Bismarckian and Beveridgean schemes follow a different systemic logic, but are not mutually exclusive when combined in a two-tiered pension system, with Beveridgean-style old-age benefits paid out by the first tier, and a second tier following the Bismarckian principles. Depending on the benefit level provided by them, they leave some space for supplementary private old-age provision, mainly occupational schemes, personal savings plans or individual life insurance contracts (see Reynaud 1995: 51–4).

Table 2.1   The Bismarckian and the Beveridgean models of old-age security

	Bismarckian model	Beveridgean model
Objective	income maintenance	prevention of poverty
Benefits	earnings-related	flat-rate
Eligibility	contribution record	residence or need
Financing	contributions	taxation
Administration	tripartite	public

Source: Based on Bonoli (1997: 357).

In spite of some deviations from the ideal-typical blueprints, the Swedish case might provide an example for such a combination of both principles in one national pension system (see Kohl 1994; Kruse 1997). In this country, the introduction of a 'Beveridgean' universal basic pension scheme was initiated as early as 1913 (see Alber 1987). The current old-age security system in Sweden consists of two mandatory tiers, a basic flat-rate scheme and a supplementary earnings-related scheme.[14] The total of contributions to be paid to both tiers amounts to 18.86 per cent of gross wage for employers and 1.0 per cent for employees (1998). Both the first and the second tier are publicly managed and, jointly, enable the maintenance of the accustomed living standard. The first-tier AFP pension, *Allmän Folkpension*, in force since 1948, provides a living minimum for all Swedish residents at the age of 65 or older, without means-testing and independently of any previous or current gainful employment. It is financed from taxes and from employers' contributions. The second-tier ATP pension, *Allmän Tilläggspension*, introduced in 1960, is an insurance scheme mandatory for all gainfully employed Swedes between 16 and 64 years of age. It is financed from employers' and employees contributions. However, the existing contribution–benefit link is relatively weak, since only the best 15 years are taken into account. Interestingly, the ATP tier managed to accumulate substantial reserves during the first decades of its existence: the National Pension Insurance Fund amounted to SEK 715 billion (approx. US$ 91 billion) in 1997, yielding considerable investment returns. Since the early 1980s, the ATP tier has functioned mainly on a PAYG basis, paying current benefits out of the incoming contributions, without obtaining further surpluses. A third, voluntary tier consists of four different occupational pension plans (see Kohl 1994; Wadensjö 1996) and of private savings.[15]

There is no country in today's Western Europe that relies on a Beveridgean old-age scheme as the only mandatory tier of old-age security. By contrast, a monolithic Bismarckian scheme is to be found in many countries, not least of all in its birthplace, Germany. It will be outlined here, since it exemplifies a more faithful version of the Bismarckian principle than the Swedish ATP tier.

Germany's statutory pension insurance (*Gesetzliche Rentenversicherung*), a public PAYG scheme, is mandatory for blue- and white-collar workers, as well as for certain groups of self-employed (see Queisser 1996; Döring 1997; Schmähl 1999).[16] The retirement age for men is 65; women can currently retire at the age of 60, to be increased to 65 until 2004. Additionally, one has to fulfil a minimum of five contribution years to be entitled to an old-age pension. The contribution rate – that amounted to 20.3 per cent of gross wage in 1998 – is shared equally between employers and employees. An additional source of financing is provided by the federal grant, designed to cover the costs of recognising some non-contributory periods (e.g. child-raising, military service and higher education) – the so-called 'non-insurance-related benefits'.

The German point system for benefit calculation implies a relatively strict contribution–benefit link, following the principle of equivalence among age cohorts: with their contribution payments, the insured acquire pension entitlements, assessed in relation to nationwide average earnings in the same period of time. The insured acquires one earnings point for each calendar year in which his/her individual earnings are exactly equal to the average gross earnings of all employees. As the total of earnings points provides the basis for benefit calculation, pension levels are closely related to the entire contribution history. Additionally, the timing of retirement is reflected in the benefit level, although the reduction is below an actuarially fair rate (Schmähl 1999: 103): early retirees suffer a reduction of the total value of their earnings points, and vice versa for late retirees. Current pension benefits are annually adjusted to the development of average net earnings. The so-called 'standard pensioner' – a standard which many Germans fall short of – receives 70 per cent of present average net earnings, after accumulating 45 earnings points.[17]

It should be noted that Germany also claims to have a three-tier system of old-age security (Schmähl 1999: 92–3).[18] Besides the mandatory public PAYG tier described above, there are two supplementary voluntary tiers: a second tier, consisting of occupational pension plans for public and private sector employees (see Davis 1995; Deutsche Bank Research 1998), and a third pillar, comprising private savings for old age.

Mainstream Pension Reform Trends in Western Europe

Although the crisis of the welfare state had been much discussed in the advanced industrialised countries since the 1970s, the policy of retrenchment in West European social security turned out to be surprisingly moderate (see Esping-Andersen 1996: 10). Mainstream pension reform policy in West European countries was limited to parametric changes within the public PAYG scheme (see Döring 1998), e.g. an extension of working life, cutbacks of benefit levels and a strengthening of the contribution–benefit link. Furthermore, the financing of benefits was partially shifted from contributions to taxes, in order to lower wage costs in the face of economic globalisation. It should be noted that the rapid increase of the contribution rate resulted from long periods of high unemployment, that tended to undermine the financing base of social insurance systems linked to gainful employment.[19]

Partial Privatisation: The Swedish Reform

Sweden provides a prominent exception to the rule that pension reforms in Western Europe were generally aiming to improve the feasibility of the existing public PAYG schemes *without* considering the introduction of mandatory private IFF elements.[20] The pre-reform old-age security system in Sweden with its basic flat-rate tier (AFP) and supplementary earnings-related scheme (ATP) has been described above. The recent Swedish reform, approved by parliament in June of 1998, implies a remarkable change in the public–private mix in Swedish old-age security.[21] After four years of parliamentary discussion (see Kruse 1997; Persson 1998a), a political majority for a fundamental old-age security reform was won: the first-tier AFP pension will be replaced by a means-tested, tax-financed minimum pension from 2001, and the second, ATP tier will be partially substituted by private pension funds. For those Swedes born between 1938 and 1953, the transition is gradual, but those born in 1954 and after will receive pensions entirely according to the new rules.[22] Pension entitlements acquired under the pre-reform system will be recognised, albeit with the application of the new rules, which includes crediting part of these entitlements to the newly established pension fund accounts. The political feasibility of the fundamental Swedish reform will not be discussed here. It should be noted, however, that the existence of the well-endowed National Pension Insurance Fund allows for a partial shift to funding without a double burdening of the transitional generation (Persson 1998a: 181).

In the future, the total contribution rate of 18.5 per cent of gross wage, half of which will probably be paid by employers, will be divided in the following way: 16 percentage points will go to the PAYG scheme, and the remaining 2.5 percentage points will be accumulated in a private pension fund. Each individual will thus have two accounts where his/her contributions will be registered: a public NDC account (see subchapter 2.1), annually adjusted to average income growth, and a private defined contribution account with a private pension fund, yielding actual investment returns. Entitlement rules within the PAYG pillar will be tightened considerably: instead of the best 15 years, life-time income will determine the benefit level. Accumulated pension entitlements will then be divided by the remaining life expectancy at retirement. Furthermore, the introduction of a flexible retirement age implies that it is impossible to retire before the age of 61, and that later retirement increases the prospective pension benefits considerably. Even if years of child-raising and military service are considered as 'notional income', the reformed PAYG system will largely mimic an actuarial, funded scheme (Persson 1998b). The introduction of NDC accounts and a quasi-actuarial pension formula in the public tier was developed by Swedish reformers, but pioneered by Latvia in 1996 (see Fox 1997; Vanovska and Velde 1997; Bite 1998; James 1998).[23]

As a rule, however, the existing pension arrangements in Western industrialised countries were subject to cautious retrenchment policy (see Pierson 1996). A fundamental transformation from the state to the market as the main provider of old-age security seems to be out of the question. Contrary to this, many Latin American countries have opted for full or partial pension privatisation. In the following section, this radical paradigm change in old-age security will be reviewed.

2.3   LATIN AMERICAN PRECEDENTS FOR PENSION PRIVATISATION

A Prehistory of the Recent Reforms

The origins of old-age security schemes in Latin America date back to the beginning of this century.[24] A few decades after mandatory old-age insurance had been introduced in Germany, the 'Bismarckian model' (see subchapter 2.2) became very popular in Latin America.[25] Coverage and benefits in the so-called pioneer countries were gradually extended from powerful pressure groups such as state employees – the military, civil servants, teachers – and the well-paid 'labour aristocracy', i.e. those employed in transport, energy, banking, communications etc., to politically weaker groups, notably agricultural workers and domestic servants (see Mesa-Lago 1978, 1991). The favourable age structure of the insured population as well as the progressive integration of new contribution groups into the pension schemes provided for a comfortable financial basis during the first decades of their existence.

Still, public pension schemes in Latin America suffered from a number of serious shortcomings (see Mesa-Lago 1993; Hujo 1999): a weak contribution–benefit link coincided with generous entitlement conditions and replacement rates, even for early retirement and invalidity benefits. Consequently, contribution rates as well as state subsidies were elevated, while, simultaneously, evasion and underreporting of income increased. Furthermore, the existing old-age security systems were highly fragmented and consisted of multiple funds, each with different legislation and management, benefits and contribution rates. They reflected regressive stratification, creating problems of equality between different groups of insured and costly administration. Last but not least, the most vulnerable groups of the population, particularly the informal sector workers, were generally excluded from the existing social insurance schemes linked with formal, dependent employment (see Mesa-Lago 1992).

In the 1980s, the economic crisis, followed by stabilisation and adjustment plans, greatly diminished public resources for social policy, just when the need for compensatory state measures in the context of recession and the social costs of adjustment became most pressing (see Mesa-Lago 1996, 1997a). Investment of social security funds in public bonds, rendering negative real interest rates, led to a decapitalisation of pension reserves in a context of mounting inflation.[26] At the same time, pension programmes in the pioneer countries became mature and reached the limits of coverage expansion. In many countries of the region, the real value of pension benefits was almost completely eroded by inflation. In others, public social security institutions even defaulted on their pension liabilities, failing to pay out retirement benefits altogether. Hence, pension reform had turned into a pressing issue.

The Way Towards the Paradigm Change

Chile was the first country in Latin America to enact a radical departure from the Bismarckian paradigm by privatising its pension system.[27] In 1981, in the context of a neoliberal ideology and the extraordinary powers of the Pinochet dictatorship, the existing public PAYG system was replaced by a compulsory IFF scheme administered by private pension funds (see below for details). At first, the Chilean reform seemed to remain the bold experiment of an autocratic regime, with little attraction for democratic policymakers. From the early 1990s onwards, however, when a democratic government had taken over from the long-standing Pinochet dictatorship in Chile, reference to the Chilean pension reform became 'politically palatable' (Mesa-Lago 1997b: 498). The so-called 'Chilean model' evolved as a reform paradigm for Latin America and beyond.

In recent years, a number of Latin American countries have implemented variations of the substitutive 'Chilean model', most of them under democratic regimes (see Nitsch and Schwarzer 1996; Schwarzer 1998). The reforms in the region are usually divided into three main groups (see Mesa-Lago and Kleinjans 1997; Mesa-Lago 1998).

1. *The substitutive model* The former public system is closed down and replaced by a private IFF system. Examples are Bolivia (1997), El Salvador (1997) and Mexico (1997).
2. *The parallel model* A private IFF system is introduced as an alternative to the public system (reformed or not), resulting in the coexistence and competition of two parallel systems. Examples are Peru (1993) and Colombia (1994).
3. *The mixed model* A newly created private IFF component on a mandatory basis complements the reformed public system. Examples are Argentina (1994) and Uruguay (1996).

Common to all of these 'second-generation' reforms (Queisser 1995, 1998b) is the introduction of a mandatory private pension fund tier, that either competes with, substitutes or complements the public PAYG scheme. In the following sections, I will review the 'Chilean model' and its most interesting variation, the 'Argentine model' (for a comparison of basic pension fund characteristics in Chile and Argentina see Table 2.2). The Argentine pension reform experience has been of special relevance to both Hungarian and Polish policymakers (see below).

The 'Chilean Model'

In 1981, Chile was the first country in the world to switch from a public PAYG pension system to a multi-pillar scheme in which the lion's share of old-age security falls to private, IFF pension funds (*Administradoras de Fondos de Pensiones*, or AFPs). Queisser (1993: 127) points out that the significance of the Chilean case does not consist in developing a substantially new concept for old-age security, but in putting existing neoliberal reform proposals into practice, thereby establishing a precedent. 'Chilean-style' pension privatisation has also been proposed as a major reform option for pension systems in Central and Eastern Europe.[28] So far, Kazakhstan has been the only country in the region to follow this advice verbatim (Rutkowski 1998).

In the new Chilean pension system, a publicly run first pillar pays out tax-financed social assistance pensions to a limited number of elderly persons in need, who have contributed not at all or less than 20 years to the pension insurance.[29] The first pillar is absolutely insufficient, as social assistance pensions are artificially limited to 300,000 persons, and correspond to only 10.5 per cent of the average wage. The second pillar consists of funded private pension funds. These AFPs collect the mandatory contributions that are being paid to them by Chilean employees – 10 per cent of gross wage, plus 2.5–3.5 per cent, divided between the AFPs' commission and a premium for disability-survivors insurance. The AFPs are expected to invest the accumulated funds profitably over the decades, following specific investment rules set by the state supervisory agency, SAFP (*Superintendencia de Administradoras de Fondos de Pensiones*). The amount of future pensions depends on the rate of return to pension assets and on the lifetime earnings profile of the insured (defined contribution plan). Furthermore, life expectancy factors by gender and the number, age and life expectancy of the insured's dependants are taken into account in the actuarial calculus (Arenas de Mesa 1997: 13). Pensions are generally paid out by the AFPs when the retirement age of 60/65 (women/men) is reached. Early retirement is possible when the insured's accumulated funds exceed a certain threshold. Pensioners that meet a minimum of 20 contribution years, but receive less than a minimum pension level, are entitled to a top-up from the state budget. A third pillar encourages voluntary savings to provide for old age.

The new private IFF system, mandatory for new entrants to the labour market, substitutes the former public PAYG scheme, to be phased out in the medium term. Those already insured with the old system at the time of reform were free to enter the new system or stay in the old, public scheme. The government issued so-called 'recognition bonds' to cover acquired pension entitlements of those switching to the funded system (see subchapter 2.4 for more details). The privileged pension schemes of the armed forces and the police remained untouched – which does not come as a surprise given that the reform was carried through under a military dictatorship.

The advocates of the 'Chilean model' claim that the switch to a private, funded scheme increased long-term saving and, thus also, investment, resulting in a greatly improved growth performance. Moreover, the role of government in old-age security was effectively restricted, so the argument goes, allowing for a reduction in public spending (see, e.g., World Bank 1994a; Fougerolles 1996). Notwithstanding many objections to these high hopes, part of which will be discussed in subchapter 2.4, the 'Chilean model' has stimulated pension reform all over the world (see Standing 1998: 9).

The 'Argentine Model'

When Argentina introduced a fundamental reform of its pension system in 1994, inspired by the Chilean example, it aroused considerable interest.[30] Being the first Latin American country to replicate the substitutive private 'Chilean model' under a pluralistic regime, it created another precedent: the 'lesson of the Argentine reform is that it is possible to implement radical pension reform through the democratic process' (Vittas 1995: 3), not only in an authoritarian context. However, political pluralism had an impact on the reform design: instead of the substitutive Chilean pension system, Argentina ended up with a pension reform of a mixed type (see Schulthess and Demarco 1996; Hujo 1999).

The new Argentine pension system combines a sweeping reform of the public PAYG system with the introduction of mainly privately managed pension funds (*Administradoras de Fondos de Jubilaciones y Pensiones*, or AFJPs).[31] The insured can decide to redirect part of their pension contributions to one of the AFJPs, thereby choosing the mixed pension path and participating in two mandatory, earnings-related schemes simultaneously. Alternatively, they can opt to remain in the public PAYG system, thus choosing the public pension path. This choice is also open to new entrants to the labour market. According to the decision made by the insured, their contribution (11 per cent of gross wage) is directed towards the public pension scheme or to a AFJP. The corresponding employers' contribution (now 16, later 12 per cent) will be used to finance the public scheme, preserving some remains of the inter-generational contract. Retirement age was raised to 60/65 (women/men).

*Table 2.2   Basic characteristics of Chilean and Argentine pension funds,
1995*

Characteristics	Chilean pension funds	Argentine pension funds
Acronym	AFP	AFJP
Existing since	1981	1994
Management	private	mainly private
Relation to public pension scheme	substitutive	complementary
Membership in pension funds	mandatory for new entrants to the labour market	optional
Financing	IFF	IFF
Affiliates to pension funds (in % of all insured)	82.0	72.9
Number of funds	13	18
Affiliates of 3 largest funds (in % of total affiliates)	68.6	50.1
Affiliates that contribute regularly (in % of total affiliates)	56.1	49.1
Total assets, in million US$ (% of GDP)	32,900 (44.1)	8,800 (2.8)
Real rate of return p.a.	11.7	16.7

Source: Based on Queisser (1998).

Post-reform pension benefits will consist of three components, that differ
according to the choice made by the insured. When opting for the public
pension path, the insured will be entitled to (1) a universal basic pension, (2)
a compensatory pension, that covers their pre-reform pension entitlements,
and (3) an additional pension fed by pension claims accumulated between the
1994 pension reform and retirement. If the insured choose the mixed pension

path, they will also be entitled to the first two components handed out by the public old-age security system. However, instead of the third, the PAYG-financed additional pension, they receive a so-called 'ordinary pension' from their AFJP, on a strictly actuarial basis. It should be noted that the receipt of all public retirement benefits – universal basic pension, compensatory pension, additional pension – presupposes a minimum of 30 contributory years. These strict entitlement conditions, particularly difficult to meet for women, the unemployed and informal sector workers, obviously provide an incentive for the mixed scheme, where benefits resulting from individual capital accumulation are guaranteed regardless of the number of contributory years.

When the new Argentine pension system came into force after a political bargaining process of two years (see Isuani and San Martino 1995), it exhibited a number of political compromises (see Arenas de Mesa and Bertranou 1997; Hujo 1999). For the purpose of the present study, four departures from the 'Chilean model' are considered most important (see Table 2.3), as they have political and fiscal implications which will be discussed later on (see subchapter 7.2):

Table 2.3   Selected features of the Chilean and Argentine pension reforms

Characteristics	Chilean reform (1981)	Argentine reform (1994)
Opting-out of mandatory pension fund tier	complete opting-out is possible	only partial opting-out is possible
Employers' contribution	abolished when switching to IFF tier	maintained to finance first tier
Building up of mandatory pension fund tier	fast	slow
Treatment of acquired pension claims	interest-bearing recognition bonds	compensatory pension

Source: Based on Müller (1998a).

First, the public scheme is only partially replaced by the newly created mandatory pension fund tier, while a complete opting-out of public old-age security, as in Chile, is impossible. Second, employers' contributions are maintained to finance the obligations of the public scheme, even if the respective employee chooses the IFF tier. Thus, the fiscal burden resulting from the partial regime change from PAYG to IFF financing is lowered. Third, the mandatory pension fund tier is being built up more slowly than in Chile, as it is only complementing the public tier and nobody is obliged to enter it. Fourth, contrary to the Chilean precedent, where interest-bearing recognition bonds had been handed out, the Argentine reformers opted for a compensatory pension arrangement to cover the acquired pension entitlements, resulting in a lower fiscal burden because interest payments are avoided. More importantly, implicit public pension debt is not made explicit right away, but only step by step.

2.4   THE NEW PENSION ORTHODOXY AND ITS CRITICS

The Harbingers

In the context of ageing populations, financially troubled public PAYG schemes and a much-discussed crisis of the welfare state in industrialised countries, the Latin American pension privatisations outlined above had an impact on experts and policymakers far beyond the region (see Esping-Andersen 1996). However, the ground for a paradigm change in old-age security had long been prepared by conservative critics of the welfare state (see Queisser 1993: 104–14): Friedrich A. Hayek, Milton Friedman, Gordon Tullock, Martin Feldstein, Peter Ferrara and others denounced the 'perversity, futility and jeopardy' of public welfare provision (Hirschman 1991). The debate on the economic effects of the US Social Security system intensified in the 1970s and 1980s (see Thompson 1983).[32] Concerned with the construction of a majority coalition to phase out the Social Security retirement programme, the conservatives used an 'excellent political strategy for framing the policy debate' (Kingson and Williamson 1996: 28).[33] And indeed, the terms of the prevailing discourse have shifted: as remarked by Schmähl (1998: 193), today's mainstream within economic scholarship argues in favour of replacing the existing public PAYG systems with private IFF schemes. The most frequently mentioned advantages expected of such paradigm change are a rise in saving and efficiency improvements on both the financial and the labour market, leading to an increase in long-term growth (see, e.g., Sachs and Warner 1996; Corsetti and Schmidt-Hebbel 1997).

The starting-point for the advocates of pension privatisation is the fact that 'Aaron's rule', i.e.

$$m+g > r$$

– the well-known condition for the superiority of PAYG schemes (Aaron 1966) – is reversed in the light of ageing populations: then, the rate of return, *r*, yielded by IFF schemes on the capital market, exceeds the rate of return implicit in PAYG schemes, which amounts to *m+g*, with *m* = population growth rate and *g* = growth rate of average wage (see Davis 1995).

While the former is a macroeconomic line of argument, similar considerations have been applied to the microeconomic level (see Feldstein 1998): hypothetical rate of return differentials between public PAYG and private IFF schemes have been calculated by relating the flow of lifetime contributions of an individual to the flow of his/her expected pension benefits, computing the rate of return that equalises the present values of both flows (see Börsch-Supan 1998: 145–7). For the case of Germany, the implicit rate of return of the PAYG system (below 3 per cent) compared unfavourably to the real rate of return yielded on the financial market (5.9 per cent).[34] In another approach, the respective contribution rates necessary to achieve the same benefit level in both systems have been calculated, concluding that a private IFF scheme would enable a lowering of pension contributions by one-third (Siebert 1998: 23–4). 'If this worker had a choice *de novo* between the PAYG and the funded system, he quite clearly would "opt out" into a funded system' (Börsch-Supan 1998: 148).

However, this hypothetical choice does not tell the whole story, since any shift from a PAYG to a IFF system entails considerable transition costs, stemming from the pension entitlements acquired by contributors to the PAYG scheme: implicit public pension debt is made explicit because of the change in the financing method. 'Privatization can offer substantial long-run economic gains. But those gains are not free, nor are they immediate' (Kotlikoff, Smetters and Walliser 1998a: 140). The most recent contributions by advocates of pension privatisation focus on the possible design of a Pareto-improving transition, mostly modelled on the US Social Security system.[35] It is disputed whether a transition to funding can be Pareto-improving in a pension system with a close contribution–benefit link, such as the German one (see Breyer 1996; Fenge 1997; Hirte and Weber 1997; Homburg 1997).[36]

While originally not contained in the so-called 'Washington Consensus' (Williamson 1990, 1998), systemic reform of old-age security schemes has become part and parcel of this neoliberal reform package by now.[37] In Latin America, it concluded the era of the populist welfare state, that used to hand out social benefits to privileged interest groups in return for political support (see Touraine 1989: 415). Instead, the lion's share of social security is delegated to private institutions, who are supposed to be more efficient providers of individual welfare, while assigning a merely subsidiary role to the state, limiting its tasks to poverty reduction and pension fund supervision (see Nitsch and Schwarzer 1996; Hujo 1997). A research report of the World Bank, published in 1994 to establish the guiding criteria of the organisation's pension policy, attracted considerable attention world-wide and may be considered to be the best-known exemplification of what has become the 'new pension orthodoxy' (Lo Vuolo 1996; own translation), as well as its major propagating mechanism.[38]

The World Bank's 'Averting the Old Age Crisis'

Publicised throughout the world, the report 'Averting the Old Age Crisis' (World Bank 1994a) intends to address a global problem with a universal strategy modelled not only on social policy considerations but also on macroeconomic desiderata, as indicated by its keynote subtitle 'Policies to Protect the Old <u>and</u> Promote Growth'.[39] Regarding the hierarchy of these objectives, the World Bank's leading pension expert, Estelle James, makes it clear that the multi-pillar model should be introduced mainly because of efficiency and growth considerations, referring to a better provision of old-age security as a mere 'secondary argument' (James 1997: 16).

'The graying of the world's population' is the crisis scenario anticipated in the Bank's report (World Bank 1994a: 27). Declining birth-rates and medical advances have triggered population ageing world-wide, implying that the system dependency ratios of PAYG pension schemes – the number of pensioners divided by the number of contributors – are rising steadily. Consequently, increased contribution rates, a higher pension age and/or lower old-age benefits are inevitable if the financial stability of PAYG systems is to be restored. While this set of problems is neither new nor disputed, the Bank's resulting policy prescriptions were not received with unanimity (see below).

The World Bank claims that the existing public pension schemes on a PAYG basis 'have spun out of control in middle- and high-income countries' (p. 1). Their inherent weaknesses allegedly include its single-pillar character, a weak contribution-benefit link, labour market distortions and its proneness to political manipulation. Furthermore, rising pension expenditures are held responsible for mounting fiscal deficits, inflation and cuts in social spending, e.g. in health and education (pp. 11–14, 234–7). Public pension schemes are also considered unable to face the demographic challenge without obstructing economic growth by means of high contribution rates. As 'government-backed pensions have proved both unsustainable and very difficult to reform' (p. xiii), the only way out of the pension crisis is, according to the World Bank, a multi-pillar system, visibly though not admittedly modelled on the Chilean precedent (see Figure 2.1).[40] The redistributive, publicly managed first pillar, designed to alleviate old-age poverty, pays out some kind of basic pension (means-tested, flat rate or minimum pension guarantee). The second pillar consists of mandatory, private schemes (personal or occupational arrangements), based on individualised defined contribution plans with a strict actuarial relationship between individual contributions and pension benefits. Voluntary savings for old age are referred to as third pillar (pp. 15–16).

Mandatory publicly managed pillar	Mandatory privately managed pillar	Voluntary privately managed pillar	
Redistributive plus co-insurance	Savings plus co-insurance	Savings plus co-insurance	objectives
Means-tested, minimum pension guarantee, or flat	Personal savings plan or occupational plan	Personal savings plan or occupational plan	form
PAYG tax-financed	IFF contribution-financed	fully funded contribution-financed	financing

Source: World Bank (1994a: 15); modified. Please note that the underlying insurance concept differs from the one introduced in subchapter 2.1.

Figure 2.1   The World Bank's three-pillar model

The World Bank claims that among the advantages of its pension concept are the following (pp. 239–54): the new public-private mix allows for risk diversification across different financial and managerial sources. Government involvement in old-age security is decreased, the role of the market strengthened. As benefits are actuarially tied to contributions in the private pension fund pillar, transparency increases and incentives for contribution evasion are reduced. The introduction of a mandatory funded tier is expected to boost long-term saving, capital market deepening and growth (p. 254).

The Bank holds that in Eastern Europe, Chilean-style pension privatisation would imply special psychological and political advantages: 'These choices would signal the government's intention to transfer responsibility to individuals for their own well-being … and establish a constituency for macroeconomic stability, financial sector reform, and enterprise privatization' (p. 286).[41] The Bank emphasises the universal character of its pension reform concept, and urges policymakers in industrial and developing countries to get down to this 'best way for most countries' (p. 292).

First- and Second-Best Reform Paths

Where fundamental pension reform as proposed above is not attainable right away, the Bank recommends 'tactical design and sequencing' (World Bank 1997: 151). This can be exemplified via the mixed pension reform path chosen in Argentina.[42] From the World Bank's point of view, the new Argentine pension system is clearly second-best in terms of efficiency. One of the Bank's pension experts has called the mixed reform outcome in Argentina a 'diluted' version of the 'Chilean model' (Vittas 1995: 6–7). Full replication of the new pension orthodoxy's radical reform agenda would have included, on the one hand, downgrading any existing public PAYG tier to the limited goal of poverty reduction and, on the other, entrusting the private, funded tier with the whole of the mandatory earnings-related pension business. However, the 'optimal sequencing from an efficiency standpoint may not be politically feasible' (World Bank 1997: 153). In this case, it is recommended that policymakers resort to a gradual phasing-out of the public scheme, while at the same time moving from partial to full privatisation of old-age security.[43] In this sense, the parallel and mixed reform paths followed by a number of Latin American countries may be interpreted as entailing a hidden agenda, being mere interim solutions to facilitate a Chilean-type reform path – 'a two-stage strategy to circumvent resistance' (World Bank 1997: 153).

Preparing the Political Ground

'There is little point in arguing over the nuances of theoretical plans if the political dynamics are not altered' (Butler and Germanis 1983: 556). Advocates of pension privatisation have long been aware that tactical design choices are not all it takes to make radical reform politically feasible. As early as 1983, a strategy for phasing-out the US Social Security system was published, focusing on the preparation of the political ground for its privatisation.[44] While contemporaries expressed their scepticism about the political viability of this plan (see Flowers 1983), this early advice largely anticipates the strategies employed by today's pension privatisation advocates in Latin America, Eastern Europe and elsewhere. Interestingly, these suggestions coincide to a great extent with the insights of the subsequent literature on both the politics of retrenchment and the political economy of policy reform (see subchapters 3.2 and 3.3). The Butler–Germanis plan is also a rare document in that it reveals the tactics of the radical reformers in great detail. Therefore its most important elements will be summarised below.

First of all, Butler and Germanis suggest tackling pro-Social Security interest groups. This includes calming current pensioners, the 'most powerful element of the coalition that opposes structural reform' (Butler and Germanis

1983: 549), assuring them that their benefits will be paid in full. Other political supporters of Social Security are to be divided by 'methods of neutralizing, buying out, or winning over' (p.552).

Second, the authors seek to bring about a policy-induced change in public opinion. Via an 'education campaign' (p.551), the 'myth' that Social Security is an insurance programme financed by contributions, while providing an earned annuity, is to be exposed (p.550). The idea of this campaign would be to erode the notion of legitimacy of claims. At the same time, it should be made clear how unfavourably Social Security compares with a private scheme. To achieve this, individual accounts, as well as annual statements of payments and expected pension benefits, are to be introduced into the public scheme (p.554).[45]

Third, Butler and Germanis suggest phasing in private retirement provision by encouraging individual opting-out of Social Security (p.551). By so doing, they aim to construct a coalition that will gain directly from pension privatisation, such as banks, insurance companies, the business community and those privately insured, and will thus form its 'natural constituency' (p.551).

Butler and Germanis stress that apart from this political strategy, a financial crisis in the Social Security scheme is another necessary precondition to achieve radical pension reform (pp.548, 556). The role of crises – real or artificially constructed – in fostering political change has been highlighted by the literature on the political economy of policy reform.

Critics of the 'New Pension Orthodoxy'

The International Labour Organisation (ILO) and the International Social Security Association (ISSA) are the new pension orthodoxy's most prominent opponents in the global pension reform arena.[46] In paradigmatic terms, the confrontation is between neoliberal individualism and the Bismarckian–Beveridgean welfare state tradition (see subchapter 2.2). Underlying this international debate are fundamental normative differences as to the appropriate roles of market and state in social security, as well as to the extent to which individuals are able to determine their own economic well-being (Turner 1998: V).

After comparing ILO and World Bank three-pillar pension reform proposals, Mesa-Lago (1996: 88) concludes that the design of the first and third tier is very similar in both cases – as a matter of fact, hardly anybody would oppose any type of minimum pension guarantee or voluntary savings. Thus the main controversy concerns the mandatory second tier, that pays out the lion's share of the pension benefits in most cases.

The transition from a public PAYG system to an old-age security scheme mainly based on private pension funds, as suggested by the new pension orthodoxy, boils down to a risky strategy for future pensioners (Beattie and McGillivray 1995): since the amount of future old-age benefits is linked to rates of return to pension assets, the investment risk has to be borne by the insured. In many parts of the world, high inflation rates threaten to erode accumulated pension capital in real terms – a risk that cannot be insured by a private pension fund scheme. Insufficient investment opportunities might amount to another drawback: pension funds are not expected to diversify their investment portfolio globally, but rather to invest the accumulated pension capital on the local financial market, in order to close the 'savings gap' asserted by the new pension orthodoxy (e.g. World Bank 1994a: 93; Fontaine 1997). To achieve this end, a restrictive portfolio regulation has been used.[47] However, on emerging markets the domestic supply of financial instruments with a suitable risk–return profile might be limited.

Recent forecasts by Mueller (1998) for the US counter the new pension orthodoxy's assumption that private pension funds guarantee higher benefits than public PAYG schemes. A transition to funding does not automatically shield old-age security schemes against the demographic risk (see Barr 1993a; Bovenberg 1998). The recent crises in South East Asia and Russia have made it clear that, in times of globalisation, local capital markets, particularly in developing and transition countries, are fully exposed to major financial market crashes elsewhere. The Mexico crisis alone had left the Chilean pension funds with annual losses of 2.5 per cent in 1995 (Arrau 1998), thus reducing the accumulated pension capital in real terms. Furthermore, Bosworth and Burtless (1998: 53–4) have pointed out that global efforts to expand domestic capital formation via a privatisation of old-age security are likely to result in diminishing returns to capital.

Moreover, the critics of the new pension orthodoxy have questioned the assumption that the transition to a private IFF scheme necessarily lowers contribution evasion. They point to the Chilean case where over 40 per cent of affiliates fail to contribute regularly to the pension funds (see Table 2.2), particularly those with low, erratic incomes. Concerns also extend to the prospective benefit level: in Chile, an average wage-earner with 36 contribution years – an excellent profile in Latin America – would only achieve a replacement rate of 35 per cent.[48] Furthermore, there are doubts as to the administrative efficiency of the Chilean system: administrative costs are high, mainly due to excessive marketing costs, which amount to 30–40 per cent of operating costs.[49] The fact that 70 per cent of the insured are affiliated to the three major AFPs might well point to an oligopolistic structure (see Mesa-Lago 1997b).

Table 2.4   Responsiveness of PAYG and IFF schemes to main risks

	Public PAYG schemes	Private IFF schemes
Macroeconomic Risks		
Output shocks	lower revenue, but effects on individuals can be mitigated	possible effects on financing which cannot be mitigated
Unemployment	lower revenue, but effects on individuals can be mitigated	no effect on financing, but affected individuals receive lower future benefits
Low wage growth	lower revenue, but effects on individuals can be mitigated	no effect on financing and current benefit level
Financial crisis (depression, war, hyperinflation, natural disaster)	possible lower revenue, but effects on individuals can be mitigated	accumulated stock reduced or even eliminated
Low rates of return	no direct effects on financing and benefits	no effects on financing but lower benefits
Demographic Risks		
Higher dependency ratio	deteriorating finances	no direct effects on financing and benefits
Smaller labour force	higher wages and future benefits	lower returns and future benefit levels
Political Risks		
Contract change	relatively easy	difficult
Responsiveness to fiscal situation	high	low

Source: Holzmann (1997a: 9); modified.

A switch from PAYG to IFF financing implies high transition costs: Obtaining political support for the privatisation of old-age security presupposes the recognition of pension entitlements acquired under the former PAYG system.[50] Usually, this results in a double burden on the transitional generations, who have to contribute to their own retirement plans, while also paying for current pension obligations (see Gonzalez 1996).[51] In Chile, the government issued the so-called 'recognition bonds' to cover acquired pension entitlements of those switching to the funded system. Recognition bonds are indexed to inflation, earn 4 per cent annual interest and become due when their bearers retire. As implicit liabilities are being transformed into explicit ones, the pension-induced strain on the public budget is by no means relieved. To cover existing pension claims, the Chilean government issued debt bonds that were held mainly by the newly created private pension funds (see Nitsch and Schwarzer 1996). In the first 10 years of the new system there was a reform-related pension deficit of 4.0 per cent of GNP p.a., which over-compensated extra personal savings stemming from the IFF pension scheme (2.4 per cent p.a.).[52] According to a forecast by Arrau (1992), the reform-related pension deficit will only disappear in 2020, that is, 40 years after the pension reform in Chile. This suggests that, in the short and medium run, the Chilean regime change is resulting neither in reduced public spending nor in increased national savings (see Schulz-Weidner 1996). Hence, no extra growth effects can possibly be attributed to the Chilean switch to a private, funded pension system (see Holzmann 1996; Mesa-Lago 1997b).

Apart from the empirical questioning of the chain of causation used by the World Bank, which relates the introduction of private pension funds to higher savings, hence to increased investment and ultimately to an improved growth performance (see Schmidt-Hebbel, Servén and Solimano 1996; Mackenzie, Gerson and Cuevas 1997), it should be noted that there is also a long-standing theoretical controversy about each of the three links in this argument, as pointed out by Barr (1993b), Singh (1995) and Ribhegge (1999).

Are parametric reforms of public PAYG systems a viable option, or is pension privatisation the only way? While the underlying assumption of the World Bank's 'Averting the Old Age Crisis' is that private, funded schemes are inherently superior to public PAYG pension systems, critics of the new pension orthodoxy do not share this view: in their opinion, many of the existing public PAYG systems function efficiently without being on the brink of collapse. The introduction of a strict contribution–benefit link, an extreme case being an NDC plan, could greatly improve transparency in unfunded schemes and improve acceptance by the insured without the need to privatise old-age security (see Schulz-Weidner 1996: 168). With some degree of parametric adaptation, the existing PAYG schemes will be able to face the demographic challenge (see Becker-Neetz 1995; Cichon 1997). 'Ageing should not be used as an excuse to discredit and consequentially dismantle the existing social protection systems, in order to replace them by systems which serve a different purpose' (Cichon 1995: 14).[53] In view of the danger that macroeconomic considerations crowd out social policy objectives when it comes to pension reform (Queisser 1993; Schmähl 1998), there is a need to clarify the values at stake (Kingson and Williamson 1996).

In the following, I will abandon the debate on the desirability of full or partial privatisation of old-age security and turn to the question that this study centres on: in which circumstances can the radical reform proposals of the new pension orthodoxy be expected to be politically feasible?

NOTES

1. Here, I am largely following the taxonomy in World Bank (1994a: 73–96), Börsch-Supan (1997: 201) and Davis (1998). For other approaches to the basic issues of old-age security see, e.g., Schmähl (1981), Mesa-Lago (1996: 75–8) and Turner (1998: 7–10).
2. See Lundholm (1991) for a comprehensive analysis of compulsory social insurance.
3. Concepts of 'welfare triangles', depicting the roles of state, community and market in welfare provision proportionately (see Pestoff 1995a, 1998), seem to miss this point by presenting a distorted account in quantitative terms.
4. See Friedman (1972) for a contemporary critique of compulsory old-age insurance. It should be noted that 80 years ago, compulsory public pension schemes were broadly considered as 'un-American', 'socialistic' and 'undemocratic' in the US (Weaver 1983: 368).
5. Beyond the simple PAYG–FF dichotomy, partial funding – generally taking the form of scaled premium systems – can be considered an interim option. Under this financing method, that combines some features of PAYG with collective capitalisation, reserves are built up over a given period, e.g. 10 years, to cover expected pension liabilities. Meanwhile, they are invested on the capital market (see Mesa-Lago 1996: 76).
6. For the German discussion, Manow (1998) gives an interesting account of the changing perception of secure pension financing over the decades.
7. It is beyond the scope of this study to give a detailed account of the long-standing PAYG–IFF debate. (for an overview see Barr 1994a; Fenge 1997; Hemming 1998; Siebert 1998; Eatwell 1999; Ribhegge 1999; Thompson 1999). However, some of the arguments will be taken up in subchapter 2.4.
8. 'This means essentially that welfare states (or companies) are withdrawing their commitment to benefit *adequacy*' (Esping-Andersen 1996: 26).
9. These 'notional rates of return' boil down to an indexation of the virtual pension capital to the growth in GDP, average wages or prices (see Holzmann 1997a: 6).
10. For a discussion of the strengths and weaknesses of occupational vs. personal funded pensions see Davis (1998: 10–12). In this study, the latter are being referred to as IFF schemes.
11. Esping-Andersen (1990: 85–7) distinguishes three types of pension arrangements: the conservative-corporatist regime type (Austria, France, Germany and Italy) is based on a publicly-run insurance scheme that preserves status differentials, while the market plays only a marginal role. In the liberal-residualist regime type (Switzerland) private provision of old-age benefits tends to prevail. The social democratic-universalistic regime type (Scandinavia, Netherlands) creates population-wide pension rights that tend to equalise old-age income on a comparatively high level. Earlier typologies include the works of Titmuss (1974), Mishra (1977) and Korpi (1980). See Bonoli (1997) and Götting and Lessenich (1998) for recent attempts to provide alternative classification patterns. In this study, I will not follow Esping-Andersen's classification, as the demarcations underlying his definition of the public–private mix in old-age security are not convincing (see Esping-Andersen 1990: 81).

12. For retrospectives on the Beveridge report see Baldwin and Falkingham (1994); Hills, Ditch and Glennerster (1994); Johnson and Falkingham (1994).
13. The Bismarckian pension system had originally been set up as a fully-funded scheme, but was replaced by a PAYG scheme in the post-war decades, in view of the devastating effects of both the hyperinflation of the 1920s and of World War II on the capital stock (see Börsch-Supan 1997: 207).
14. See below for the most recent reform of the Swedish pension scheme.
15. These collectively agreed benefits are compulsory for all employers who are members of the Swedish Employers' Confederation.
16. For a critique of the current German pension system see Börsch-Supan (1998).
17. According to the so-called 'Pension reform 1999', the standard pension level was to be reduced from 70 to 64 per cent of present average net earnings until 2030. This was to be accomplished by the integration of a demographic factor into the pension formula, reflecting the increasing life expectancy of those over 65 (see Deutsche Rentenversicherung 1998; Schmähl 1999). However, the newly elected German government suspended this gradual lowering of the pension level for the years 1999 and 2000 (see Handelsblatt 1998: 5).
18. The German taxonomy of tiers differs from the convention in the recent international pension reform debate (see subchapter 2.4).
19. For different approaches to the political economy of West European pension reforms see subchapter 3.2.
20. To some extent, Britain is another exception to this rule. Still, the privatisation of the second tier (State Earnings Related Pension Scheme, or SERPS) has been more cautious than in the Swedish case, being based on voluntary opting-out. See Johnson and Rake (1997), Disney (1998); Disney and Johnson (1998).
21. For details on the Swedish reform see Ministry of Health and Social Affairs (1998); Working Group (1998).
22. Those born in 1938 will receive four-twentieths of their pension according to the new rules and sixteen-twentieths according to the old rules. The share of the new system is gradually increased until it reaches nineteen-twentieths for those born in 1953 (with the proportion of the old system amounting to one-twentieth).
23. The Latvian quasi-actuarial pension formula is as simple as $P = C/E$, with $P =$ annual pension, $C =$ pension contributions accumulated by the insured, yielding a notional rate of return equal to the growth rate of wages, and $E =$ remaining life-expectancy at the time of retirement (see Vanovska and Velde 1997). As to the parallels between the Swedish and Latvian reforms, it should be noted that a Swedish advisor assisted pension reform in Latvia (see Schmähl 1998).
24. The following two sections draw heavily on Hujo (1999: 122–5).
25. Mesa-Lago (1991) refers to Chile, Uruguay, Argentina, Cuba and Brazil as pioneer countries in introducing pension schemes. He distinguishes two further groups: the intermediate countries (first pension programmes introduced in the 1930s and 1940s) such as Peru, Bolivia, Mexico and Colombia, and the latecomer countries (first pension plans in the 1950s and 1960s), some Central American and Caribbean countries.
26. Most Latin American pension systems were based on the scaled premium system, i.e. partial funding (Mesa-Lago 1993); see note 5 above.
27. For analyses of the Chilean pension reform see Queisser (1993); Schulz-Weidner (1996); Arenas de Mesa (1997); Mesa-Lago and Arenas de Mesa (1997); Edwards (1998).
28. See Holzmann (1994), World Bank (1994a), Sachs (1995), Fougerolles (1996); as well as local proposals in individual Central and Eastern European countries (e.g. Topiński and Wiśniewski 1991). For a critique of a potential replication of the 'Chilean model' in Central and Eastern Europe see Nitsch (1996) and Müller (1997b).
29. Here, the terminology proposed by the World Bank is used, referring to a publicly managed, PAYG tier as first pillar, to a mandatory, privately run IFF tier as second pillar, and to a voluntary, privately run IFF pillar as third pillar. Throughout this volume I will mostly use the more adequate term 'tier' instead of 'pillar'.
30. See, e.g., Nobel laureate Gary S. Becker, who pointed to the 'social security lesson from Argentina' (1996: 9).

31. At present there is only one public pension fund, managed by *Banco Nación*, a state bank. Recently, the privatisation of *Banco Nación* has started to be under discussion, so the only public AFJP might be privatised soon (see Hujo 1999).
32. For more recent contributions to this debate see Baker (1996), Diamond, Lindeman and Young (1996), Jones (1996), Kotlikoff (1996), Mitchell and Quinn (1996), Myers (1996), Tanner (1996), Williamson (1997).
33. In 1983, the ultra-conservative Cato Institute even published a strategy of 'guerrilla warfare against both the current Social Security system and the coalition that supports it' (Butler and Germanis 1983: 552). See below for details.
34. For a critique of this type of calculations see Ribhegge (1990) and Mitchell and Zeldes (1996). The latter point to the fact that part of the higher rate of return in private schemes must be considered a premium for higher risk.
35. See, e.g., Arrau and Schmidt-Hebbel (1993); Feldstein (1995, 1998); Gonzalez (1996); Homburg (1997); Kotlikoff, Smetters and Walliser (1998b). These analyses are based on an inter-generational interpretation of the Pareto criterion.
36. Ribhegge (1998) doubts that the Pareto criterion is useful for social policy analysis, as it disregards distributional aims. On Pareto-optimal redistribution see Hochman and Rodgers (1969).
37. The term 'Washington Consensus' was coined by John Williamson (1990) and comprises a set of market-oriented economic policy measures agreed upon 'by all serious economists' (Williamson 1993: 1334). For some reflections on a new 'post-Washington consensus' see Kołodko (1999).
38. While appropriate on an international level, this label does not apply to all national discussions, a case in point being Germany, where the 'orthodoxy' still defends PAYG.
39. The title of the World Bank report can be considered to be an allusion to Peter Ferrara's early proposal to phase out the US PAYG system: 'Social Security: Averting the Crisis' (1982).
40. In an earlier document by the Bank's pension expert Dimitri Vittas (1993), different country experiences were combined in a best-practice structure. The suggested blueprint – which differs markedly from the Bank's 1994 panacea – drew explicitly on the old-age security systems of Chile, Switzerland and Singapore.
41. See Fougerolles, who expects that pension privatisation will reduce the conflict between capital and labour, since 'individuals have a direct and visible stake in the reformed, free-market economy – they are investors' (1996: 93).
42. The World Bank itself has chosen the Peruvian example, where a parallel pension reform path had been implemented, to illustrate its 'tactical sequencing' advice (World Bank 1997: 153). Yet the Peruvian case, characterised by an authoritarian reform context, is not deemed particularly instructive for the purpose of the present analysis, which focuses on pension reforms conducted under democratic conditions.
43. 'Allow participants to opt out of public scheme, then phase it out' (World Bank 1997: 145).
44. The authors are Stuart Butler and Peter Germanis, representatives of the Heritage Foundation, a conservative think-tank.
45. The latest efforts to introduce NDC plans (see subchapter 2.1) in a number of countries, including Latvia, Sweden, Italy and Poland, can be interpreted as an intent to operationalise this suggestion: 'The NDC approach appropriates the vocabulary of funded individual accounts and uses it to define PAYG promises ... This extra transparency helps both policy-makers and the public to understand the trade-offs inherent in any PAYG arrangement' (Holzmann 1997a: 6).
46. See Iyer (1993) for the outline of an ILO pension proposal. Beattie and McGillivray (1995), representatives of ILO and ISSA, respectively, have formulated a comprehensive critique of the World Bank's pension reform concept. For a detailed reply see James (1996).
47. Only recently, the ceiling for foreign instruments was raised from 3 to 9 per cent of the Chilean pension funds' portfolio (Arenas de Mesa 1997: 34–35).
48. Key to these kinds of calculations is, of course, the assumption on interest rate trends. Here, an average real interest rate of 3 per cent has been assumed (see Schulz-Weidner 1996: 171–2).

49. Administrative costs of AFPs make up 15-30 per cent of annual contributions, being much higher than in many public pension systems (see Diamond 1994).
50. See Butler and Germanis (1983). Some representatives of the new pension orthodoxy have doubted that an explicit compensation for past entitlements is necessary in all cases (see e.g. Feldstein 1996: 12; Sachs and Warner 1996: 49).
51. In Chile, the old system is left with only 16 per cent of those insured, but 96 per cent of pensioners (see Mesa-Lago 1997b). The old public pension system will only disappear when all its beneficiaries have died.
52. See Arrau (1992), Queisser (1993), Nitsch and Schwarzer (1996).
53. Similarly Queisser (1998b: 15): 'The overriding objective of pension reforms, regardless of the model proposed, must be the improvement of retirement income security … A policy measure that has a positive impact on … other areas but fails to improve the provision of pensions, should not be given the label of pension reform.'

3. Approaching the Political Economy of Pension Reform

3.1 ON THE POLITICAL FEASIBILITY OF RADICAL PENSION REFORMS

The previous chapter has shown that the international economic mainstream is largely unanimous about the need to privatise the existing public PAYG schemes. This new consensus is corroborated by semantic observations: according to mainstream discourse, only pension *privatisation* is considered to deserve the label 'reform', or 'real reform' (see e.g. Browning 1983; Sachs and Warner 1996; Góra and Rutkowski 1998), while less radical approaches are viewed as mere 'patching up' (Feldstein 1996; Börsch-Supan 1998).[1] This is in accordance with Ribhegge's (1998) observation that the term 'reform' is, ultimately, crypto-normative.

Still, the political viability of such a radical reform step is quite a different matter, as stated by the new pension orthodoxy's harbingers: '[N]o amount of logic will overcome an unfavorable coalition of interest groups' (Butler and Germanis 1983: 556). When Feldstein, after arguing for a transition to funding, stresses that 'the key missing ingredient now is the political will to impose the short-run costs that would produce such large long-run benefits' (Feldstein 1998: 314), he pays some attention to the political preconditions of radical pension reform. Still, in order to understand the political economy of pension reform, the commitment of policymakers is certainly not the only relevant aspect.[2]

Pension systems have long been considered particularly difficult to reform, as they tend to create powerful clienteles (see e.g. Olson 1965; Browning 1983).[3] This is particularly true for PAYG systems that build up long-term expectations, being hard to reverse (see Davis 1998: 3). Pensioners constitute a substantial part of the electorate, and amount to the largest single-issue constituency in many countries, while their power is thought to increase as population ageing proceeds (Butler and Germanis 1983; Börsch-Supan 1998). The elderly are also viewed sympathetically by other voters, who may perceive themselves as being indirectly hurt by cutbacks, providing for a large blame-generating potential of pension reforms (Pierson and Weaver 1993: 115).

On the basis of three Central–Eastern European cases, this study attempts to shed light on the political feasibility of the radical reform proposals of the new pension orthodoxy. When is a pension reform 'radical'? Reforms within public PAYG schemes – e.g. a higher retirement age, a downward adjustment of benefits – have often been perceived as drastic by current and future beneficiaries, provoking considerable protest. Even so, in the context of this study, I will use the term 'radical pension reform' only to denote the partial or full privatisation of existing public old-age security (similarly Weaver 1983; Pierson 1996).[4] Such a reform is radical because it implies a fundamental paradigmatic departure from the previous pension system, that is two-fold: a departure from collective to individual provision for old age, as well as from the state to the market as the main supplier of retirement pensions. The 'paradigm shift' (Holzmann 1997a: 6) inherent in radical pension reform therefore amounts to a substantial rewrite of the underlying social contract, which does usually not occur in the case of a mere change of the entitlement conditions.

Can radical pension reform be expected to be politically feasible? Conventional wisdom has it that 'any pronounced challenge to the basic structure of the [pension] system is equivalent to political suicide' (Buchanan 1983: 340). 'It never pays to eliminate the [PAYG] system, regardless of how poor the return becomes' (Weaver 1983: 365). Obstacles to pension privatisation include the substantial transition costs resulting from a shift from PAYG to funding, engendering fiscal and distributional issues. To mitigate the heavy double burden of taxation on the transitional generation, that may otherwise well oppose radical reform (see Barreto de Oliveira 1997: 59), the use of temporary debt financing has been advocated (see James 1998: 285).[5] Recent research directed towards the design of a Pareto-improving transition to funding has sometimes mistaken such a reform path, based on elaborate compensation schemes, for a politically feasible one (e.g. Hirte and Weber 1997: 304), whereas in practical politics, Pareto-inferior institutional arrangements may survive for a long time (see Buchanan 1983; Ribhegge 1998), e.g. because of uncertainty regarding the identities of gainers and losers (see Fernandez and Rodrik 1998).[6]

Furthermore, established institutional arrangements in the area of welfare provision are thought to be hard to change because they involve substantial economic, social, cognitive and normative investment and adaptation efforts, turning into sunk costs when these institutions undergo radical change (see Pierson 1994; Götting 1998: 38). This argument may well be applied to radical pension reform, amounting not only to a fundamental paradigmatic departure from the previous system of old-age provision, but also to a fundamental change in the existing institutional framework.

·Hence it comes as no surprise that the existing works on the political economy of pension reform, by political scientists, sociologists and economists, coincide in their scepticism of the idea that policymakers will engage in fundamental pension reform steps (see subchapter 3.2). The first country to privatise its PAYG system, Chile, was long seen as an isolated case, while the feasibility of the radical pension reform was explained by the repressive, authoritarian character of the Pinochet regime (see e.g. Mesa-Lago 1998: 626). Yet the recent pension reform dynamics has shown that full or partial pension privatisation can also be accomplished under democratic regimes. This suggests a need for fresh research into the political economy of pension reform to explain under which circumstances such a move is politically feasible. The recent literature on the political economy of policy reform provides some interesting insights into the political viability of radical reforms (see subchapter 3.3). In subchapter 3.4 the conceptual framework of this study will be spelt out.

3.2   EXISTING APPROACHES TO THE POLITICS OF PENSION REFORM

The challenging issue of old-age security and its reform has triggered an extensive body of multi-disciplinary literature.[7] Social policy researchers have not limited themselves to a comparative analysis of the institutional characteristics of existing retirement schemes. Beyond such a static approach, some scholars have taken up a dynamic perspective, intrigued to find out which factors account for the development and transformation of old-age security arrangements, focusing on pension reform as an ongoing process. Economists as well as political scientists and sociologists have contributed to this strand of research, following methodologically distinct approaches. In the following, the existing contributions to the political economy of pension reform will be surveyed.

Contributions by Political Scientists and Sociologists

When analysing pension policy, political scientists and sociologists have long resorted to general theories of welfare state development.[8] Following the taxonomy drawn up by Williamson and Pampel (1993), five different approaches can be distinguished: the industrialism perspective, the social-democratic perspective, the neo-marxist perspective, the neo-pluralist perspective and the state-centred perspective.[9] These theories, that have traditionally been considered as competing and mutually exclusive, differ *inter alia* in that some of them – the industrialism and the neo-marxist perspectives – stress the impact of functional imperatives, or structures, while others – notably the social-democratic and the neo-pluralist perspectives – focus on the role of political forces, or actors, in shaping the development and transformation of old-age security arrangements (see Esping-Andersen 1990: 13–16). A common feature of all these theories, developed in the pre-retrenchment era, is that they seek to explain the expansion of social security in general, and public retirement programmes in particular.

A departure from such conventional sociological and political science approaches to the development and transformation of social security is marked by the recent work of Paul Pierson and his collaborators, who shifted the analytical focus to the 'new politics of the welfare state', i.e. from the expansion of social security to its cutback. This trend in social policy followed the much-discussed crisis of the welfare state since the end of the post-war economic boom in the 1970s, and was first advocated by conservative governments, such as the Reagan and Thatcher administrations, that 'viewed retrenchment not as necessary evil but as necessary good' (Pierson 1994: 1). Pierson defines retrenchment as 'policy changes that either cut social expenditure, restructure welfare state programs to conform more closely to the residual welfare state model, or alter the political environment in ways that enhance the probability of such outcomes in the future' (Pierson 1994: 17).[10]

Pierson maintains that recent efforts to roll back social security follow an entirely different logic – and thus political strategy – from welfare state expansion. The transformation of political coalitions, constituencies and bargaining strategies calls for a new framework of analysis: 'Retrenchment is not simply the mirror image of welfare state expansion' (Pierson 1996: 156). As a matter of fact, however, Pierson's departure from traditional theories of welfare state development is not complete: to some extent his analysis takes up the methodological framework of the neo-pluralist and state-centred perspectives, as the following paragraphs will unmistakably show.

In spite of the conspicuous 'paradigm breakdown' (Myles and Pierson 1997: 1), welfare state adaptation has so far been modest (Esping-Andersen 1996; Pierson 1996).[11] This comes as no surprise, since policies of retrenchment are essentially unpopular, unlike the expansion of social benefits that enabled political credit claiming. A welfare state roll-back has short-term costs that are highly visible, concentrated and immediate, while its benefits are more long-term, contingent and diffuse (Pierson and Weaver 1993).[12] This implies that electoral ambitions and policy preferences of retrenchment advocates are likely to clash.[13] Downward adjustments in social programmes will therefore only be undertaken when the resulting political costs can be kept down.[14] Thus, the new politics of the welfare state amounts to efforts at 'blame avoidance' (Weaver 1986).

Focusing on Western Europe and North America, Pierson and Weaver (1993) and Pierson (1994, 1996) have analysed how unpopular, politically risky cutbacks in the existing old-age security scheme can be carried through. Basically, policymakers try to minimise the political costs of retrenchment by resorting to division, compensation and obfuscation strategies (see Pierson 1994: 19–24), i.e. playing off one group of beneficiaries against another, compensating politically crucial groups for lost benefits and lowering the visibility of cutbacks, e.g. by manipulating indexation mechanisms or by increasing the complexity of reforms.[15] In addition, looking for a broad consensus on reform may help to spread the blame (Pierson 1996: 147). However, the success of political strategies to minimise the political costs of retrenchment depends very much on the specific political context in which they are implemented. In the following, a number of aspects that influence the political feasibility of retrenchment strategies will be highlighted.

Three potential centres of opposition to pension cutbacks were identified: the grey lobby, consisting of beneficiaries themselves; organised labour, identifying retirement benefits as part of the 'social wage'; and some political parties, mainly social democrats with a strong political commitment to the welfare state. Yet political resources available to these opponents to downward adjustments in retirement programmes are by no means determinative of pension reform outcomes (Pierson and Weaver 1993: 142).

The design of political institutions seems to have an ambivalent impact on the scope for a welfare state roll-back: concentrated power has a greater capacity to act, but less leeway to diffuse blame, while the contrary is true when there are many institutional veto points (Immergut 1992).[16] However, new institutional arrangements, such as pension reform commissions, can be devised to facilitate loss-imposing agreements. Concerning electoral cycles, it is argued that most retrenchment initiatives are carried through soon after an election. Pension cutbacks are unlikely to be pursued shortly before elections, when the hazards of accountability are high (Pierson and Weaver 1993).

Fiscal crises can facilitate downward adjustments in social programmes, since retrenchment may be framed as an 'effort to save the welfare state rather than destroy it' (Pierson 1996: 177).[17] However, Pierson and Weaver (1993: 141) found that economic pressures, measured in terms of general fiscal imbalances or as the share of pension expenditures in particular, were insufficient to explain pension reform outcomes in the country cases under consideration. While the affordability of current pension spending levels clearly was an issue in the local political debates, the size of budget deficits and the timing of loss impositions were in no way connected. The far-reaching British pension reform of 1986 was even carried through when there were no fiscal problems at all, thereby 'resolving a problem that did not exist' (Taylor-Gooby 1997: 16). This example from Thatcherite Britain confirms that not only a changed context but also a change in the goals and values of policymakers has an impact on the pension reform agenda (see Pierson 1994: 8).

Finally, the political success of retrenchment strategies depends crucially on earlier policy choices and the 'policy feedback' resulting from them: 'Existing policies can set the agenda for change ... by narrowing the range of feasible alternatives' (Pierson and Weaver 1993: 146).[18] It is suggested that public PAYG schemes, once in place, create a path dependence and lock in policymakers (see Pierson 1996: 175; Siebert 1998: 27).[19] In particular, this argument is raised for Bismarckian, contribution-financed schemes that create commitments based on earned entitlements as they mature. With the political costs of change exceeding the costs of continuity, public retirement schemes are thought to be 'notoriously resistant to radical reform' (Pierson 1996: 176).

Contributions by Economists

Economists' contributions to the political economy of old-age security systems have sought to explain the rationale of political support for an institutional arrangement that the economic mainstream considers harmful to most people in the long run. 'The key to understanding this paradox is the fact that with a pay-as-you-go system it is always in the interests of older persons to continue or to expand the system' (Browning 1983: 382). Because of its heavy *status quo* bias, this strand of economic research has been appropriately denoted as the 'political economy of unfunded public pension schemes' (Breyer 1998: 273).

Economic approaches to the political economy of pension reform are usually based on relatively abstract public choice models (for an overview see Breyer 1990, 1994, 1997).[20] Public pension systems are treated as a distributional zero-sum game among generational cohorts, in which a trade-off exists between workers' contributions and retirees' benefits (see Weizsäcker 1990: 491).[21] Most authors take the Browning (1975) model of once-and-for-all majority voting on the level of social security contributions as their point of reference. As the median voter will most probably be an older worker or even a pensioner, his/her preferred contribution rate and benefit level are higher than the socially efficient ones, resulting in a public pension system that is essentially oversized and has a built-in tendency to ever-continuing expansion (see Homburg 1988).

Acceptance of the PAYG system is expected to remain high, even if its implicit rate of return falls below the corresponding rate in a fully-funded scheme. This apparently paradoxical result can be explained by the high percentage of voters within or close to retirement age, who profit from the maintenance of the unfunded old-age scheme, while future generations do not have any political clout. 'Society can become locked into perpetuating this chain-letter type of arrangement – no one wants to stop the process when he gets near the payoff' (Browning 1983: 382).

Marquardt and Peters (1998) maintain that the process of population ageing even tends to stabilise the PAYG system politically, although a rising proportion of elderly voters results in a decreasing birth rate, thereby diminishing the implicit rate of return of the PAYG schemes, making it less attractive. Yet, at the same time, due to the ever larger number of voters benefiting from the *status quo*, support for the existing old-age scheme increases, reflected in a higher contribution rate. The authors have called this phenomenon 'collective madness'. However, objections have been raised both to this label and to the underlying reasoning (see Breyer 1996; Breyer and Stolte 1999).[22] Breyer and Stolte (1999: 84) have pointed out that the effect of population ageing on the pension system is indeterminate in median-voter models.[23]

Since Browning's classic paper (1975), the median-voter models used to analyse the political economy of PAYG schemes have been refined to include, e.g., repeated voting, altruism and family size (see Breyer 1994: 64), but are still subject to criticism (see e.g. Drost 1997: 90). Obviously, the notion of direct democracy underlying the median voter model is counterfactual: '[I]n many Western democracies ... decisions are taken without consultation of the voters ... So, it can be expected that not merely the interests of the median voters count' (Verbon, Leers and Meijdam 1998: 361). Therefore, some political economists have resorted to models of representative democracy, assuming that politicians maximise a weighted sum of the utility functions of a representative worker and a representative pensioner (see Verbon 1986), or, alternatively, that both the working-age and the retired generations are granted a veto position by politicians (see Hansson and Stuart 1989). Yet most of these contributions coincide with the median-voter analyses in that they stress the stability and expansion of PAYG schemes (see Breyer 1994 for a survey). It was only recently that a few papers went off the beaten track of the political economy of unfunded pension schemes by considering the possibility of downward adjusted benefit levels or even a transition to funding. Two examples will be presented below.

Breyer and Stolte (1999) seek to explore the observable fact that, in the light of population ageing, politicians resort not only to increases of the contribution rate but also to benefit cuts, thus putting the burden of demographic change upon both the young and the old. Traditional median-voter models fail to explain such reform measures that harm the interests of the elderly. Breyer and Stolte (1999: 86) assume that the majority of the

electorate consists of older voters who maximise their utility under
constraints, i.e. the reaction of the minority – younger workers with the power
to vary their labour supply – to their decisions. They find that a shrinking
worker–pensioner ratio results both in a fall of the benefit level per pensioner
and in a rise of the contribution rate (Breyer and Stolte 1999: 89).

Verbon, Leers and Meijdam (1998) analyse whether a transition to funding
is politically feasible, following a process of population ageing in a
representative democracy. Somewhat counter-intuitively, they find that
systemic reform is more likely to occur if the elderly are relatively
influential.[24] Pensioners and older workers might be so successful in
achieving an expansion of the existing PAYG scheme that, subsequently, the
adverse economic consequences of the latter may dominate the political
pressures against shrinking the public PAYG system. However, the authors
themselves stress that their conclusions are far from being unambiguous, and
that a transition to funding becomes even more unlikely when political power
is endogenised (see Verbon, Leers and Meijdam 1998: 368).

Resilient Old-Age Schemes?

In all, the contributions by economists, political scientists and sociologists
surveyed in this subchapter, in spite of their differences in methodology and
theoretical objectives, show one interesting similarity, which is probably due
to their exclusive focus on Western industrialised countries: most authors
seek to explain the expansion of the welfare state or emphasise the
remarkable resistance of social security arrangements to substantial
downward adjustments. By now, a conspicuous conflict between the
theoretical predictions and the observable facts has arisen, as conceded by
Breyer and Stolte (1999: 80). Those authors who *do* focus on the political
viability of cutbacks consider only cautious retrenchment: when Pierson and
Weaver (1993) explore how moderate cutbacks of public retirement schemes
can be made politically feasible, or Breyer and Stolte (1999) seek to find out
why the burden of demographic change is shared between the young and the
elderly, a radical reform of old-age security is ruled out. However, this is
contrary to the observable evidence in some East European and many Latin
American countries.

3.3   INSIGHTS FROM THE POLITICAL ECONOMY OF
POLICY REFORM

The previous subchapter has shown that the existing literature on pension
reform emphasises the inertia of old-age security arrangements, a result that is

increasingly becoming counterfactual. The limited scope of earlier scholarship thus calls for a broadening of the methodological horizons of this study. In order to approach the political feasibility of radical pension reforms, some findings on the political economy of policy reform will be included in the present analysis. This multi-disciplinary strand of research seems particularly relevant for the present study, since it has come up with some explanations concerning the political viability of radical, market-oriented reforms, that had long been precluded by conventional wisdom, assuming selfish, rent-maximising bureaucrats and obstructionist vested interests (see Rodrik 1993; Williamson 1994a).[25]

Early contributions to the political economy of policy reform compared failed and successful reform efforts, centring on the politics of structural adjustment programmes and market-oriented reforms in developing countries (e.g. Bery 1990; Whitehead 1990; Krueger 1993). Its focus of attention was soon to be extended to Central and Eastern Europe, but also to OECD countries (e.g. Williamson 1994b). Here, I will not attempt to give a fully-fledged survey of this growing body of literature, that includes works by political scientists and economists, coming up with different methodologies: while some authors hold that the only practical approach is a comparative one, based on case-studies, others have attempted a formalisation of the underlying explanatory models (for a review see Rodrik 1996; Tommasi and Velasco 1996; Sturzenegger and Tommasi 1998b; Bönker 1999).

Why does a fundamental change of agenda occur in the first place? Some scholars have stressed the importance of 'vigorous political leadership' (Sachs 1994: 503). Courageous, extraordinarily committed individuals (see Harberger 1993) – often market-oriented economists-as-politicians (see Williamson 1994a) – and their ability to communicate a coherent vision of the 'promised land' ahead might prove crucial for radical reform (see Balcerowicz 1994; Rodrik 1994). However, the existence of these agenda setters against powerful interest groups can certainly not be considered sufficient to guarantee success (see Williamson and Haggard 1994; Tommasi and Velasco 1996).

Another line of argument focuses on the influence of the international financial institutions, which has been reviewed from various angles. To start with, the simultaneous application of similar blueprints across countries – sometimes referred to as 'Washington consensus' – suggests a common international transmission mechanism of ideas (see Stallings 1994: 46). On many occasions, the IMF and the World Bank have acted as vital catalysts for an agenda entailing fundamental change (see Toye 1994). Their conditionalities may be interpreted as extra leverage given to reform-minded policymakers (see Sachs 1994; Williamson 1994a). Even if the involvement of the international financial institutions bears the risk of backlash effects as far as local politicians are concerned, who may be accused of 'kow-towing to Washington', it also amounts to a proven mechanism of blame avoidance for unpopular policy measures (see Haggard and Webb 1993).[26]

A frequently raised argument for the explanation of radical change is a preceding crisis (see Sturzenegger and Tommasi 1998a: 9–15).[27] While standard economic theory holds that welfare is maximised in a context of minimal distortions, scholars of the political economy of policy reform have pointed to the 'benefit of crises' (Drazen and Grilli 1993). Situations of perceived emergency can induce contending political groups to agree upon unpopular, painful measures. Crises can facilitate the destruction of political coalitions that had blocked reform, breaking a previously existing stalemate and putting the economy on a welfare-superior path (see Drazen and Grilli 1993; Williamson 1994a; Haggard and Kaufman 1995).[28] However, the 'benefit of crises' hypothesis has not met with unanimity among scholars of the political economy of policy reform.[29] While difficult to quantify, it has even been criticised as tautological: 'That policy reform should follow crisis, then, is no more surprising than smoke following fire' (Rodrik 1996: 27). Other critics have highlighted that an economic crisis will usually be associated with a lack of resources to compensate the losers of the reform. While some scholars hold that crises may only amount to an opportunity to introduce *ad hoc* stabilisation measures (see Haggard and Webb 1993; Nelson 1994; World Bank 1997), others have shown that crises may indeed bring about deep institutional reforms (see Wagener 1997).

Losers of radical reform measures amount to potentially powerful *ex ante* obstacles. Yet, democratic regimes differ with regard to their respective capability of filtering discontent. Hence, many analyses of the political economy of policy reform consider the design of political institutions, such as the electoral and party system, and institutional veto points. A fragmented party system and dysfunctional intermediary institutions will contribute to the 'unfiltered' expression of political discontent. The situation in Central–Eastern European countries has been characterised by an institutional vacuum, that results from largely discredited trades unions and 'old' parties, providing policymakers with the necessary leeway to proceed with radical restructuring without meeting strong opposition (see Bönker 1995: 192). At the same time, governments setting out to implement reforms that generated extraordinary demands for state initiative and efficiency faced a weak, delegitimised and ill-equipped state apparatus (see Nelson 1994).

While so far the focus has been on constraints and chances inherent in the reform context, I will now turn to an aspect that is more directly under the reformers' control: the design of the reform strategy (see Haggard and Webb 1993; Rodrik 1993). There has been much discussion about the appropriate timing, speed, bundling and tactical sequencing of fundamental reforms (see

Sturzenegger and Tommasi 1998a: 16–22). The issue extends beyond the well-known 'shock therapy vs. gradualism' controversy (see Dewatripont and Roland 1998; Wei 1998). Big bang strategies might render reforms irreversible before substantial opposition can build up (see Sachs 1994). Yet there are also plausible arguments for strategic sequencing (see Martinelli and Tommasi 1998). When not all reforms are tackled at once, but the most promising ones are given priority, demonstration effects may be produced and political support created, as benefits are visible early in the process (see Nelson 1994; World Bank 1997). An appropriate packaging and design, including compensation of groups adversely affected, is crucial for the feasibility of radical reforms, because it might allow for a bypassing of vested interests and division of the opposition. Reform design bears a direct impact on the cost profile, or 'redistributional calculus' of radical reforms (World Bank 1997: 146).

Even if the allocation of costs is relevant for the viability of reforms, it has to be pointed out that high social costs will not necessarily be obstructive to radical reforms. This can be due to a lack of political voice and power of those affected (see Tommasi and Velasco 1996). But it is also the interpretation of reform costs and the consequential crediting of blame that matters (see Bönker 1995: 189–90). In particular, distributional implications of large policy changes may be tolerated when a newly elected government succeeds in attributing them to the previous regime, a phenomenon denoted as 'honeymoon effect' (see Williamson 1994a). This effect is enforced when the previous regime has spent a long time in office and when the situation is perceived as being critical (Haggard and Webb 1993; Rodrik 1994). For both reasons, there was a special window of opportunity for sweeping reforms after the 1989 regime change in Central–Eastern Europe, although not in all transition countries was it long enough to enable second-stage institutional reforms before 'reform fatigue' (Bruno 1993) set in. From the honeymoon hypothesis it can be inversely concluded that radical reforms are less likely to succeed shortly before elections.[30]

Obviously, not all of these stylised findings apply equally in all countries and for each area of economic reform likewise. However, in the context of the present study they can be expected to provide useful insights regarding the political feasibility of radical pension reforms, and will thus be integrated into the conceptual framework outlined below.

3.4   THE CONCEPTUAL FRAMEWORK OF THIS STUDY

The General Approach

This study seeks to shed light on the political economy of pension reform in Central–Eastern Europe. Political economy is a 'powerful but elusive term' (Janoski and Hicks 1994: 365), meaning different things to different authors.[31] Among today's economists, a political-economy approach is often equated with a public choice perspective (see e.g. Olson 1983: 355). Yet the current strand of research auto-denominated as political economy is much broader than that (for an overview see Staniland 1985). Among scholars of the political economy of reform, this concept denotes a focus on political-economic interactions (e.g. Krueger 1993; Rodrik 1996). Here, I will follow the latter understanding when approaching the political economy of pension reform, focusing on the old-age policy choices of individual and collective actors under economic, political and institutional constraints.

As pointed out by Sturzenegger and Tommasi (1998a: 1), '[e]conomists have always been better at telling policymakers what to do than at explaining why policymakers do what they do'. The preceding subchapters have provided a survey of existing approaches to the political economy of pension reform. This study will take up some of the earlier findings of political scientists and sociologists, as far as they prove useful to explain pension reform *after* the 'golden age' of the welfare state. As the focus of the present study is on radical pension reforms, considered as unlikely by earlier scholars, insights from the political economy of policy reform will complement the analysis. Compared with this, the economic approaches to pension reform appear less appropriate for the kind of empirical-comparative analysis to be conducted in the present study. The two most important reasons for this assessment will be spelt out in the following.

First, the analysis of pension reforms in Central–Eastern Europe cannot abstract from the fact that the latter have been conducted under conditions of economic and political transformation. Where government and intermediate political actors are muddling through the turmoil of systemic change, there is obviously no 'politics as usual', calling for a careful choice of the conceptual framework to examine these reforms. Balcerowicz (1994: 177) has pointed out that, during the 'period of extraordinary politics', standard public-choice theory is inapplicable, mainly because political institutions are in a state of flux. In the absence of stable preferences, let alone established political institutions, highly aggregated analytical tools, such as the ones used in median-voter models and other approaches to the political economy of unfunded public pension schemes, are deemed ill-suited. In a transformational setting, the concrete interactions within the political system cannot be disregarded altogether, but have to be brought back into the analysis.

Second, when analysing policymakers' institutional choice between publicly run PAYG systems and privately managed, fully-funded schemes, the issue is more complex than the distributional zero-sum game assumed by conventional contributions to the political economy of pension reform (see Holzmann 1997b: 3). Such an approach may be appropriate for the analysis of reforms within existing PAYG schemes, aimed at expansion or retrenchment of the latter, but fails to grasp a major aspect of the paradigm choice involved in the PAYG vs. IFF issue: the strengths and drawbacks effectively associated with the public or private management of a pension system in a given local context. Not only in Central–Eastern Europe has opposition against a privatisation of old-age security often been voiced by individuals and groups who would not be affected by such a change in a tangible distributional way, but who reject such a policy measure on the basis of their value-judgements on the role of the individual and the state. Pierson (1994: 8) has stressed a similar point in the case of retrenchment, maintaining that pension reform may partly be triggered by modified goals and values of policymakers, a case in point being conservative governments. This cognitive aspect can only be taken into account when political actors with their respective policy preferences are explicitly included in the analysis. In the case of the Central–Eastern European countries analysed below, party ideologies seem to have been less important. Yet the actors' social policy orientations, shaped by either the new pension orthodoxy or the Bismarckian–Beveridgean pension traditions (see subchapters 2.4 and 2.2), have had a considerable impact on the paradigmatic outcome of Central–Eastern European pension reforms.

All in all, the impact and leeway of those political actors who make up the 'menu', generate the agenda and shape the reform design have to be brought back into the analysis. Furthermore, it is crucial to explicitly consider local contextual constraints to the policy choice mechanism. I have chosen to use the comparative-empirical insights provided by three case-studies as a starting-point for medium-range conclusions on the political economy of radical pension reform, thereby following Merton's call to 'create small families of empirically verified theorems', a necessary complement to the development of total systems of theory (Merton 1948: 165).[32]

Actor-Centred Institutionalism

As noted in subchapter 3.2, many previous analyses of welfare state development and pension reform followed either a structuralist-institutionalist or an actor-centred approach (see Esping-Andersen 1990: 12–18). Thereby, this strand of research reflected largely the 'classical' schism within social sciences, that also extended to the research efforts on the political economy of transitions (see Merkel 1994), torn between macro-approaches that have been criticised for their teleological overtones, and actor-centred analyses, rejected as being largely descriptive (see Bos 1994).

Following some recent calls for an integration of both perspectives by providing the old structural-functionalist paradigm with an actor-related micro-foundation (see Overbye 1994; Haggard and Kaufman 1995; Wiesenthal 1996), the present research effort is largely inspired by a methodology that combines actor-centred and structuralist-institutionalist approaches into an integrated framework: the heuristics of actor-centred institutionalism, developed by Mayntz and Scharpf (1995), and further specified by Scharpf (1997). Given the assumed relevance of both structural setting and actor constellations for pension reform outcomes, this approach, seeking to overcome the prevailing analytical dichotomy (Mayntz and Scharpf 1995: 46), is deemed particularly suitable.

'What is gained by this fusion of paradigms is a better "goodness of fit" between theoretical perspectives and the observed reality of political interaction that is driven by the interactive strategies of purposive actors operating within institutional settings that, at the same time, enable and constrain these strategies' (Scharpf 1997: 36). Similar intents to combine actor-centred and structuralist-institutionalist perspectives have been made by other scholars under different labels: 'actor-system dynamics' (Burns, Baumgartner and Deville 1985); 'situational-structural framework' (Zürn 1992); 'institutional analysis and development' (Ostrom, Gardner and Walker 1994); 'constrained-choice approach' (Wiesenthal 1995: 35).

The actor-centred institutionalist approach has not yet been employed to analyse pension reform dynamics. However, this heuristics proved to be useful for the examination of many other policy areas.[33] In the following, an attempt is made to provide a brief summary of the basic explanatory framework of actor-centred institutionalism (see Figure 3.1), albeit without following the game-theoretical interpretation and extension of the heuristics of actor-centred institutionalism in Scharpf (1997).[34] I will now define the terms 'actors', 'actor constellations', 'modes of interaction' and 'structural-institutional context'.[35]

The first step to explain past policy processes and their respective outcomes is the identification of relevant *actors*, whose choices will ultimately lead to the policy outcome under consideration. They may be individual, corporate or collective, and are characterised by specific action resources, perceptions and preferences. Action resources, including personal properties, physical resources or privileged access to information, enable actors to influence a policy outcome and are, to a great extent, determined by the prevailing institutional rules. The actors' perceptions and preferences decide on their specific action orientation. Some of these are rather stable, others may be influenced by learning or persuasion. They influence the actors' evaluation of the *status quo* and the desirability of a certain course of action.

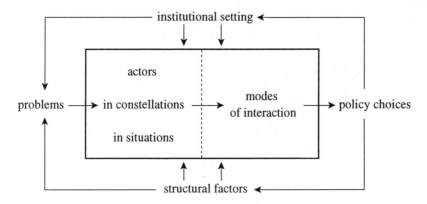

Sources: Mayntz and Scharpf (1995: 45); Scharpf (1997: 44); own modifications.

Figure 3.1   Actor-centred institutionalism: The basic explanatory framework

Individual, corporate or collective actors will not proceed in a political vacuum, merely based on their own action resources, perceptions and preferences. Their interaction with other relevant actors will be analysed in a two-stage approach, that will proceed from a static picture to dynamic interaction. In the first place, policy outcomes are shaped by *actor constellations*, involving all actors participating in the respective political process, as well as their strategy options and strategic preferences. A given constellation, then, enables a variety of *modes of interaction*, e.g. non-cooperative, co-operative and hierarchical ones.[36] The actual policy outcome will be determined by both the specific actor constellation and the respective mode of interaction.

Beyond its focus on political actors and their dynamics, interaction-oriented policy research in the present analytical framework will also pay attention to the *structural-institutional context* in which the political process takes place. It is important to note that neither institutional setting nor structural factors are thought to actually determine a particular policy outcome. Rather, this contextual setting is assumed to stimulate, enable or restrict the strategy options available to the actors involved. It may also shape the actors' perception of the *status quo* and the action that needs to be taken.

But political actors may also shape institutional rules, and their policy decisions have an impact on the structural environment (see Figure 3.1) – hence, the relationship between actors and the respective contextual setting is mutually interdependent.[37]

This brief review of the heuristics of actor-centred institutionalism will be followed by a specification of the main issues and hypotheses of this study, thereby referring to some of the insights of the politics of retrenchment and the political economy of policy reform. Subsequently, the relevant political actors and the structural-institutional setting will be identified. In a final subsection, I will spell out my selection of country cases.

Issues and Hypotheses

As noted above, conventional wisdom among scholars of the political economy of pension reform considers a fundamental regime change in old-age security to be highly unlikely. Contrary to this, the present study seeks to explain the feasibility of these radical pension reforms, focusing on the different cases of Poland and Hungary on the one hand, and the Czech Republic on the other. While the former countries did resort to partial pension privatisation, following Latin American role models, the reform efforts of the latter remained well within the boundaries of the Bismarckian–Beveridgean pension traditions. The present study provides a comparative analysis of these divergent pension reform paths, trying to identify the factors determining paradigm choice in the area of old-age security. In particular, it will be asked which structural-institutional and actor-related factors enable radical pension reform, propagated by the new pension orthodoxy (see subchapter 2.4).

Here, it is assumed that it is the constellation of political actors, shaped by a given structural-institutional setting, that determines paradigm choice in old-age security. This hypothesis is fundamental to the present study and can be specified as follows: structural and institutional factors condition largely which actors become involved in the process of pension reform, as well as their relative strength. Given the actors' respective cognitive maps (Axelrod 1976) and their consequent perception of pension reform alternatives, the constellation of relevant actors defines the basic paradigmatic outcome. The details of the specific local arrangements are produced in the subsequent interaction process with secondary actors.

Consequently, for radical pension reform to become feasible, those actors inclined towards pension privatisation – the Ministry of Finance and the World Bank – must have stakes and leverage in the local reform process, thereby outweighing the Ministry of Labour with its typical preference for the Bismarckian–Beveridgean paradigms. The relative strength of 'privatisation advocates' within a given set of pension reform actors is largely determined by the respective structural-institutional setting, notably the financial situation of the existing public PAYG schemes and the degree of external debt. Hence, the paradigm choices made in the three countries under consideration will be explained by an analysis of the constellations and interaction of pension reform actors within the relevant structural-institutional context.

Once the basic paradigm choice is made, reform strategies become important, as stressed by both the contributions to the politics of retrenchment and to the political economy of policy reform, as well as the new pension orthodoxy itself. As to the timing of pension reform, both retrenchment and radical reforms are thought unlikely issues to be pursued shortly before elections, when the hazards of accountability are high. Regarding reform design, policymakers trying to pursue retrenchment efforts may minimise the concomitant political costs, *inter alia*, by lowering the visibility of cutbacks, e.g. by manipulating indexation mechanisms or by increasing the complexity of reforms. In the case of radical pension reforms, the importance of tactical sequencing has been stressed, an example being the recommendation to combine partial pension privatisation with a gradual phasing-out of the public scheme, to facilitate full privatisation in a second step. Strategic bundling and unbundling is also an issue in pension reform design.

Relevant Political Actors

The political economy of pension schemes is considered to be the result of multiple interactions between various stakeholders, making old-age security reform a highly sensitive and politically difficult issue, as they amount to many potential veto players (Tsebelis 1995).[38] In this study, I assume that the main actors shaping old-age security in Central–Eastern Europe are two portfolios within government, the Welfare and Finance Ministries. An important external actor, the World Bank, complements the list of major actors in the local pension reform arena.

At first glance, it might seem surprising that the Ministry of Finance is considered a potentially important actor in pension reform – a genuine social policy area. Here, I follow a point stressed by Alber (1996) that departs from the narrow concepts of political costs underlying both Pierson's analyses of retrenchment and the median-voter models used by economists. Apart from the 'need-satisfaction interests' of current and future pensioners, the 'cost-containment interests of contributors, taxpayers and business investors' have to be taken into account as well (Alber 1996: 16). Once it is accepted that policymakers are always exposed to both types of pressures, with the latter being particularly pronounced when fiscal crises loom ahead, the Ministry of Finance enters the analysis as a potential actor, embodying this second kind of pressure (see Alber 1996: 18).[39]

Following the reasoning in subchapter 2.4, the World Bank, with its well-known stance in favour of a privatisation of old-age security, is considered to be a potentially influential external actor in Central–Eastern European pension reform (see Deacon and Hulse 1997; Mouton 1998). The World Bank's leverage is partially determined by its stakes as an important creditor in many transition countries. However, the Bank's impact is not limited to binding conditionalities resulting from its own financial involvement. Rather, it is the general level of external indebtedness that matters, as the IMF and the World Bank 'have been used by the international financial community as a sort of beacon to shed light on economic prospects' (Zecchini 1995: 125). When their recommendations are disregarded by local governments, alternative sources of market financing can usually not be relied upon. Hence, it can be expected that the more severe the external debt problem in a given country is, the greater the leverage of the World Bank will be.[40] For the Central–Eastern European cases considered, it is assumed that the Bank's influence in the pension reform issue is exerted not so much through conditionalities but first and foremost as an agenda setter or, rather, agenda shifter in the local pension reform debate.[41] Channels to support ongoing pension reforms include an expert-based knowledge transfer and, last but not least, loans to strengthen the existing reform capacities (see Holzmann 1997a: 12), a potentially attractive assistance package for local policymakers.[42]

Secondary internal actors that may influence the details of the local pension reform outcome, but not the basic paradigm choice, are trades unions, employers' and pensioners' associations, the self-government of social insurance bodies, local financial institutions and watchdog institutions such as constitutional courts and ombudspeople. It has been pointed out that a developed system of intermediate institutions can relieve the strain on public policy, as it assumes mediating functions, and secures consent.[43] However, in the Central–Eastern European context of political and economic transformation, the influence of intermediate political actors is considerably smaller than in Western industrialised countries with their entrenched vested interests. In post-socialist Central–Eastern Europe, intermediate actors have long been absent or weak (see Hausner, Pedersen and Ronit 1995; Stykow 1996), and thus the region has been denominated as 'associational wasteland' (Offe 1993: 15). Consequently, Central–Eastern European policymakers had considerable room for manœuvre in the area of social policy, enabling largely autonomous policy choices, based on the advice of internal and external experts (Götting 1998: 280–1; Mouton 1998: 25).

The Structural-Institutional Setting

The strength, strategic capacity and leeway of the relevant political actors is, to a great extent, shaped by the contextual setting. Furthermore, it stimulates or restricts the perception of available options by local actors (see Mayntz and Scharpf 1995: 58–60). The respective policy context is therefore explicitly included in my empirical-comparative analysis of pension reform in Central–Eastern Europe. The following aspects of the structural-institutional setting will be considered (see Götting 1998: 30–41):

Economic context This aspect includes the general economic setting, notably the level of external indebtedness. The financial situation of the existing old-age security systems is another important aspect. Fiscal bottle-necks restrict the government's scope for action, but may also facilitate pro-cyclical retrenchment policies or even fundamental structural changes. Hence, scholars of both the politics of retrenchment and the political economy of policy reform have developed 'benefit of crises' hypotheses that will be of pivotal importance in the following chapters.

Institutional legacies Earlier scholarship on welfare state development has stressed the importance of existing institutional arrangements for future reform paths (policy feedback or path dependence).[44] Lock-in effects, that push up opportunity costs in the case of institutional change, result from multiple investment decisions and adaptation efforts to the *status quo* by individuals. As regards PAYG old-age security schemes, such effects can be produced by past pension claims acquired by a large part of the population. These entitlements have to be acknowledged in the case of a transition to an IFF scheme, even by a dictatorship such as Pinochet's in Chile, or after the overall regime change in Central and Eastern Europe, amounting to a historic turning-point.

Design of political institutions Both the contributions to the politics of retrenchment and to the political economy of policy reform have stressed the importance of the design of political institutions. The formal structure of the political system may influence the relative strength of government and potential opponents of reform.[45] Veto points, built into the political system, provide a particular group with strategic opportunities and potential political impact (see Immergut 1992: 8). It has been pointed out above that strong governments do not always embark on radical reform, as concentrated authority is tantamount to concentrated responsibility, providing little chance of blame avoidance (Pierson 1996). Finally, new institutional arrangements, such as special pension reform commissions, may help to circumvent existing opposition to reform.

Selection of Country Cases

It has been suggested that Eastern Europe may have turned into a 'testing ground for the future of social policy elsewhere in the industrialised world' (Deacon and Hulse 1997: 41). Hence, the pension reform paths followed in this region may prove significant for scholars and policymakers elsewhere (see Overbye 1994; Queisser 1998a). For the comparative-empirical part of the present study, three Central–Eastern European countries have been selected, to allow for a comparative analysis of two different pension reform paths – one of them radical, the other one rather conventional.

Hungary, Poland and the Czech Republic exhibit many similarities, not only in terms of the pre-1989 characteristics of their socialist societies and centrally planned economies, but also with regard to their post-socialist political and economic consolidation, that has been extraordinarily successful compared with other East European transition countries (for selected economic indicators see Tables 7.4–7.6). Other resemblances include a similar cultural heritage, national independence before 1989 and a far-reaching orientation towards the European Union (see Bönker 1997: 2).

As to old-age security, all three countries share a common legacy of Bismarckian pension systems in the interwar period, and have experienced a similar reorganisation of their old-age insurance schemes during communist rule. Consequently, they started from widely identical old-age security systems in 1989. According to theories of path dependence, this homogeneous legacy might have been expected to lock in Polish, Hungarian and Czech policymakers in a similar way (see Pierson 1996: 175; Siebert 1998: 27).

However, a closer look at the policy environment that pension reformers are subject to reveals important differences between Poland and Hungary on the one hand, and the Czech Republic on the other. The three countries differ particularly with regard to the financial situation of the existing public PAYG schemes (see Tables 4.4, 5.4 and 6.4) and the degree of external debt (see Tables 7.4–7.6). According to the above reasoning, these structural factors are thought to condition local actor constellations in pension reform that, in turn, are assumed to determine the respective paradigmatic outcomes.

Hence, it is consistent with our basic explanatory framework that Polish, Hungarian and Czech policymakers opted for markedly different strategies to reform their existing old-age security schemes.[46] In Poland and Hungary, the existing public PAYG schemes have been complemented by a mandatory private IFF pillar, amounting to partial privatisation of old-age security. In the Czech Republic, pension reforms followed a less radical pattern: the existing public PAYG scheme remains the only mandatory pillar of old-age security, but has been thoroughly reformed.

In the following chapters, I will give separate accounts of the Hungarian, Polish and Czech pension reforms, before assessing common features and differences among the cases considered and before, finally, venturing medium-range conclusions on the political economy of radical pension reform.

NOTES

1. For a reverse linguistic usage cf. Peters (1990: 104): 'Reform vs. privatisation'. On the 'semantics of problem-solving' see Hirschman (1963: 247–9).
2. See Williamson (1994a) for an analysis of the relationship between committed 'technopols', i.e. market-oriented economists in key policymaking positions, and the circumstances that will help them implement their agenda.
3. In some countries, the elderly are a well-organised lobby group. This is particularly true for the US: the 'American Association of Retired People' (AARP), set up in 1958, has 28 million members and a staff of 1,300 (Pierson 1994: 3).
4. In Central–Eastern Europe, the term 'systemic reform' has been coined to indicate radical pension reform (see e.g. Klimentová 1997a: 2). In Latin America, this type of pension reform is called 'structural reform' (see Mesa-Lago 1998).
5. However, as indicated by Börsch-Supan (1997: 204), interest payments would have to be covered by taxing the transitional generation.
6. Fernandez and Rodrik (1998: 73) have pointed out that '[a]ny such transfer scheme may be time-inconsistent, providing incentives to the *ex post* majority to renege on the agreement'. On time-consistency of credible commitments see Dixit (1996: 145).
7. See e.g. Stropnik (1997) for an overview on current issues in old-age security, that includes contributions by economists, mathematicians, sociologists, gerontologists and social workers.
8. Many attempts have been made to classify the abundant literature on welfare state development, e.g. Gough (1989); Esping-Andersen (1990: 9–18); Williamson and Pampel (1993); Ragin (1994); Pierson (1996: 147–53).
9. The industrialism perspective interprets the evolution of the welfare state as a response to economic development (see e.g. Wilensky 1975, 1976). According to the social-democratic perspective (see e.g. Myles 1984; Esping-Andersen 1985), social welfare spending reflects working-class pressure, exerted by organised labour and leftist political parties. In the neo-marxist perspective (see e.g. O'Connor 1973; Gough 1979), social security is considered an instrument of social control, designed by the ruling class to co-opt labour and diminish pressures for a more radical redistribution of economic resources. The neo-pluralist perspective interprets social policy as the result of competition between multiple interest groups (see e.g. Olson 1965; Janowitz 1976). The state-centred perspective (see e.g. Skocpol 1985; Skocpol and Amenta 1986) entails several different approaches that coincide in stressing the social policy impact of the state as an autonomous agent, not just as a transmission belt of political interest groups or classes.
10. Pierson also differentiates between 'systemic' and 'programmatic retrenchment' (Pierson 1994: 15), but this taxonomy is not followed in the present study, as the labels are not in line with the current linguistic usage in the pension reform arena described above.
11. Esping-Andersen (1996: 2) has called this a '*welfare state* failure: that is, the edifice of social protection in many countries is "frozen" in a past socio-economic order that no longer obtains, rendering it incapable of responding adequately to new risks and needs' (emphasis by G.E.-A.). For a different view see Taylor-Gooby (1997), who argues that Esping-Andersen's assessment fails to take into account observable social policy innovations.
12. For a general criticism of this 'asymmetry hypothesis' cf. Rodrik (1996: 29–30).

13. It is assumed that voters have a 'negativity bias', being more aware of losses than of equivalent gains (Weaver 1986).
14. Alber (1996: 16) has criticised Pierson's concept of political costs for being one-dimensional: '[N]ot only cutbacks but also the preservation of benefit levels have political costs ... democratic policy makers would be ill-advised to only consider the political costs of curtailments. Instead, they must try to satisfy voter *and* business interests (i.e. consider pressures via the voice and the exit mechanism)' (emphasis by J.A.). I will return to this criticism in subchapter 3.4.
15. According to Washington lobbyists, reforms are 'less likely to generate a popular outcry if television reporters cannot explain the implications of the new policies in fifteen seconds' (Pierson 1994: 21).
16. Immergut (1992: 27) defines veto points as 'points of strategic uncertainty where decisions may be overturned', depending both on constitutional rules and electoral results.
17. See subchapter 3.3 below for a discussion of the 'benefit of crises' hypothesis.
18. On the concept of 'policy feedback' see Esping-Andersen (1985) and Pierson (1993). It is maintained that the effects of earlier social policy decisions not only influence the patterns of interest-group formation but also processes of social learning, shaping the cognitive processes of political actors. Finally, they may result in long-term commitments, creating lock-in situations in which the costs of changing the *status quo* become very high, inhibiting exit from a current policy path (see Pierson 1994: 39–50).
19. On path dependence see Stark (1992: 21): 'Actors who seek to move in new directions find that their choices are constrained by the existing set of institutional resources. Institutions limit the field of action ... [but] also favor the perception and selection of some strategies over others'. This concept draws on the findings of David (1985), Arthur (1989) and North (1990); for a critical discussion of its applicability to transformation research see Beyer and Wielgohs (1999).
20. For the purposes of the present study, it is deemed sufficient to present the results of these models, without providing the reader with details on the technical set-up and underlying assumptions. The existing contributions to the political economy of unfunded public pension schemes are based exclusively on models of direct and indirect democracy, while failing to take into account both the pressure of interest groups and the influence of bureaucrats. For an exception cf. Congleton and Shughart (1990).
21. Strictly speaking, this strand of literature refers to workers' *taxes*, assuming a weak contribution–benefit link in the pension system under consideration. This notion does not hold, e.g., for the German case.
22. Breyer and Stolte (1999: 84–5) stress that it is self-evident that a drop in the birth rate must be followed by an increase in the contribution rate or a fall in the benefit level – to restore the pension system's budget equation.
23. When the age of the median voter increases, the contribution rate tends to rise. But a decreasing population growth rate reduces the implicit rate of return in the PAYG system, thereby making a smaller contribution rate preferable. These two opposite effects result in an indeterminate total outcome (Breyer and Stolte 1999: 84).
24. This is contrary to the above-mentioned findings of Marquardt and Peters (1998), also based on the median-voter approach.
25. For a survey of existing contributions on the 'dynamics of deterioration' – in absence of much-needed reforms – see Rodrik (1996: 12–17, 21–5); Tommasi and Velasco (1996: 192–7).
26. See Rodrik (1994: 30–31) for a critical view of the alleged positive impact of foreign aid and concomitant conditionality on reform.
27. For an early discussion of 'crisis as an ingredient of reform' see Hirschman (1963: 260–4).
28. See Drazen and Grilli (1993) for a formalisation of the argument that crises may be welfare-improving.
29. 'Indeed, the objective identification of a crisis is no easier in the heady days of the Washington consensus than it was in the bad old days of those endless neo-Marxist debates about "the crisis"' (Toye 1994: 41).

30. For a discussion of earlier works on the theory of political business cycles see Haggard and Webb (1993: 148–9).
31. Reference to the term 'political economy' can be traced back to the 18th century, when it was the old name for 'economics'. Thereafter, Marxist analysis was conducted under this title, whereas, since the 1960s, the Chicago school seems to have 'appropriated' the term (see Groenewegen 1991: 560).
32. A similar argument, defending a careful case-study methodology against over-theorised 'short-cuts to the understanding of multifarious reality', has been raised by Hirschman (1970: 329).
33. Actor-centred institutionalism has been used to analyse health care reforms (Döhler and Manow 1995), infrastructure development (Mayntz and Schneider 1995), research activities (Schimank 1995), self-organisation and self-co-ordination in policy networks (Lütz 1995; Scharpf and Mohr 1997), non-coordinated collective action (Schimank and Wasem 1995), international standardisation and technological co-ordination (Genschel 1995; Grande 1995; Werle 1995) and institutional learning in German reunification (Czada 1995).
34. Game-theoretic modelling is precluded in the transformational context, that generates substantial uncertainties about the initial situation and the 'rules of the game'. Moreover, it is highly demanding in terms of the observability of the latter.
35. The following paragraphs draw heavily on Mayntz and Scharpf (1995: 43–64); Scharpf (1997: 43–9).
36. This study will not attempt an in-depth analysis of the actual modes of interaction occurring in the case-studies under consideration, as they did not prove accessible to an outside observer.
37. This dynamic interpretation of actor-centred institutionalism is particularly relevant in the context of political and economic transformation, where the policy environment is in flux.
38. According to Tsebelis (1995: 289), veto players are individual or collective actors whose agreement is required for a change of the *status quo*.
39. Please note the potential link to the 'benefit of crises' hypothesis discussed above (see subchapter 3.3).
40. The role of both Western models and external assistance – among other external determinants in East European transitions – has been stressed by Bönker (1994). See subchapter 3.3 for a general discussion of the role of the international financial institutions as catalysts for radical change.
41. The first concept has been developed by McKelvey (1976) for a direct democracy model in which the agenda setter can bring about the desired result of voting by determining the number and order of the voting rounds. Here, I will employ this term in a broader sense. Compared to this, agenda shifting is the power to intervene at critical moments, defining models which then go unquestioned for years to come (see Jacoby 1998: 18).
42. A leading pension expert of the Bank has referred to this crucial involvement, somewhat cautiously, as 'the creation of an awareness of the issues among the politicians and the population at large', or – even more flowery but still plain – as 'sowing the seeds' for pension reform (Holzmann 1997a: 12).
43. If intermediate institutions, on the contrary, lack power, representation and competence, they may prove obstructive (see Wiesenthal 1993, 1996).
44. The terms 'path dependence' and 'policy feedback' appear to be used synonymously by some authors; see subchapter 3.2.
45. See Bönker (1997) for an effort to distinguish and measure critical variables of government strength in Poland, Hungary and the Czech Republic.
46. For an analysis of pension policy in Poland, Hungary and the Czech Republic see Müller (1997a, 1998b, d, e, 1999a, b).

4.   Pension Reform in Hungary

4.1   THE LEGACY:
RETIREMENT SCHEMES BEFORE 1989

Social insurance has a long tradition in Hungary, dating back to the end of the last century. A mandatory health insurance for workers was introduced as early as 1891, rendering Hungary one of the European pioneers in the area of social insurance.[1] Civil servants were the first group to receive old-age protection. Their pension scheme, set up in 1912, was financed from the state budget and did not contain any insurance elements. It was not until 1928 that mandatory old-age provision for blue- and white-collar workers was legislated in Hungary, largely following the Bismarckian model (see Ferge 1991; Czibere 1998). The obligatory insurance of workers and employees against invalidity, old age and death came into effect on 1 January 1929. The system was self-governed, of a defined-benefit type and paid out pensions consisting of a flat-rate part and an earnings-related part.[2] Contributions were split between employers and employees, and the retirement age was 65 for both sexes (see Bod 1995b: 175–6). Coverage, however, amounted only to 31 per cent of the population in 1938 (Boller 1997: 264), since the pension system was mainly targeted at urban labour, while the entire rural workforce was excluded from old-age insurance.[3] Hungary's early pension system operated on a collectively fully-funded basis, investing in shares, state bonds and urban real estate, until it collapsed in 1944–46, after the funds' property had largely been destroyed during World War II, with the remaining reserves devaluated by post-war hyperinflation (see Bod 1995b: 176).

Notwithstanding the breakdown of the early fully-funded pension schemes, Hungary's post-war policymakers were willing to acknowledge the accrued pension entitlements. Inescapably, this decision implied that the 1949 pension reform, passed by the newly established communist regime, involved a shift to PAYG financing. In addition, benefit levels were lowered considerably, the contribution–benefit link was abolished and the three separate schemes for workers, employees and civil servants were unified. Contributions were to be paid exclusively by employers, and the pension system was integrated into the central budget (see Augusztinovics 1993: 307; Bod 1995b: 176–7). In the

1950s, the pension scheme underwent further changes. The self-governing bodies, that had been ruling the Hungarian social insurance since its inception, were abolished in 1950. Instead, the Communist Party's 'transmission belt', the Central Council of Trades Unions (*Szakszervezetek Országos Tanácsa*, or SZOT), was entrusted with the administration of the scheme.[4] In 1954, a 3 per cent employees' contribution was introduced, that added to the 4 per cent employers' contribution already in place.[5] Retirement age was lowered to 60 for men and 55 for women, while the number of qualifying years was raised. Similarly to the pre-World War II benefit rules, old-age pensions were two-part, consisting of a base pension, connected to last earnings, and an earnings-related part, related to the number of employment years.

It was not until 1961 that old-age security was provided to members of agricultural co-operatives, by then almost the entire rural population.[6] This helped to bring about a significant increase in coverage: it doubled from 47.3 in 1950 to 96.6 in 1965 (Augusztinovics 1993: 309).[7] The expansion of the Hungarian pension system was completed by Law No. II of 1975, which further unified and standardised old-age provision by granting the agricultural workforce the same entitlement conditions as urban labour. The aim of this law was to bring about 'uniform pension conditions for all strata and in all respects' (Ministry of Finance 1982: 21). The pension formula was modified, converting the two-part retirement benefit into a single amount, with entry pensions reflecting both the years of employment and the level of previous earnings. After 42 years of employment, the maximum replacement rate was reached: retirement benefits then equalled 75 per cent of earnings over the last three years. Augusztinovics (1993: 309) states that 'the relatively high level of benefits [was] generally appreciated at that time'.[8]

Due to the pension scheme's integration into the central budget, the opportunity to accumulate the considerable surplus from the early years of coverage expansion for later periods was missed (see Bod 1995b: 180). Then, the maturing retirement scheme would have called for such reserves (see the rising system dependency ratios in Table 4.1).[9] Apart from this systemic dynamics, the general deterioration of economic conditions after 1978 induced a covert downward adjustment of absolute and relative benefit levels. In the context of mounting inflation, the gradual erosion of the real value of pensions was brought about by two means (Augusztinovics 1993: 310).[10] First, previous earnings used in benefit calculation were not adjusted to inflation. Second, in 1982 degression in entry pensions was introduced, yet without adjusting the nominal limits of the brackets over time. As nominal wages increased in the inflationary process, ever larger portions of previous earnings fell into higher income brackets, until even low and medium earners suffered considerable losses in their entry pensions.

Additionally, the bulk of current pension payments was reduced by under-compensating for inflation: between 1975 and 1988, current pensions were increased by a meagre 2 per cent p.a. and additional *ad hoc* corrections. Only minimum pensions were fully adjusted to inflation, but barely sufficed to cover the subsistence level (see Simonovits 1997: 57–60). When benefits started to erode from the mid-1970s onwards, around one-fifth of pensioners supplemented their old-age benefit by resorting to paid work, creating a 'reserve army of labour' that was officially sanctioned (see Maltby 1994: 144–6; Széman 1995: 333).

Table 4.1   The Hungarian pension system, 1950–1985: selected indicators

Indicators	1950	1955	1960	1965	1970	1975	1980	1985
Insured in % of population in active age	37	52	65	76	82	84	82	85
Pensioners in % of population in pension age	39	38	43	59	56	71	83	93
System dependency ratio[a]	28.0	22.0	24.0	33.0	29.8	36.0	43.0	50.4
Replacement ratio[b]	21.5	24.9	32.4	32.3	35.7	46.8	54.9	54.9
Pension expenditures in % of GDP	n.a.	n.a.	2.5	3.6	3.9	5.6	7.8	8.9

Notes: [a] pensioners in % of contributors
[b] average pension in % of average wage

Sources: Bod (1995b: 178–80); Simonovits (1997: 61).

All efforts to erode benefits in real terms fell short of offsetting the effects of the maturation of the Hungarian old-age scheme, reflected in high coverage and rising system dependency ratios. Hence, pension expenditures continued to rise, reaching 7.8 per cent of GDP in 1980 and 8.9 per cent in 1985 (see Table 4.1). During the 1980s, there was a growing consensus that pension reform was inevitable: '[I]t was an open secret ... that the pension system was obsolete, parsimonious, incomplete and unsustainable at the same time, full of iniquities and inconsistencies' (Ferge 1997c: 2). Yet early recommendations, prepared by the Institute of Sociology of the Hungarian Academy of Sciences, were locked away.[11] In 1987, even the Central Committee of the Hungarian Communist Party acknowledged the need for fundamental reforms in the area of social insurance (see Brusis 1992: 530). Still, no comprehensive blueprint for pension reform was adopted until soon after the systemic change (see Augusztinovics 1993: 309).

4.2 OLD-AGE SECURITY IN TRANSFORMATION: INITIAL MEASURES

Transformation and Old-Age Security

While pension reform had already been on the agenda in the last years of Hungary's communist regime, the perceived urgency of such a reform was reinforced when economic transformation aggravated the financial strain on the existing retirement system.[12] Not only did the number of employed Hungarians fall by 25.0 per cent between 1989 and 1996 – in the same period the number of pensioners rose by 22.4 per cent (see Table 4.2). Among the latter, the ranks of old-age pensioners increased below average with 19.0 per cent, while the number of disability pensioners jumped by 49.5 per cent, as eligibility criteria for this benefit were fairly liberal (see Czúcz 1993: 748).[13] This suggests that the existing pension system was largely used in lieu of the unemployment scheme, to absorb those affected by the restructuring of the state enterprise sector (see CCET 1995: 99).

As the number of contributors to the pension scheme plummeted while the number of beneficiaries continued to increase, the system dependency ratio rose from 51.4 (1989) to 83.9 per cent (1996). The resulting financial crisis of the Hungarian pension scheme – revenues fell permanently short of expenditures (see Table 4.4) – is reflected in a rising ratio of pension expenditures to GDP between 1989 and 1994. Tables 4.2 and 4.3 show that demographic trends did not add to the financial imbalances of the Hungarian pension system, as the old-age dependency ratio remained largely unchanged since the late 1980s.[14]

The following sections will focus on the early measures taken by the subsequent democratically elected governments to change the existing Hungarian old-age security scheme in terms of its organisation, financing, eligibility and benefits. A final section will be devoted to the introduction of supplementary old-age schemes, the so-called voluntary mutual benefit funds, in 1994.

Table 4.2   Population, employed and pensioners: Hungary, 1989–1996

	1989	1990	1991	1992	1993	1994	1995	1996
Population (millions)	10.4	10.4	10.4	10.3	10.3	10.3	10.2	10.2
20–59 years old (thousands)	5,664	5,518	5,508	5,499	5,496	5,498	5,534	5,581
60+ years old (thousands)	1,982	1,960	1,970	1,980	1,984	1,986	1,986	1,985
Employed (thousands)	4,823	4,795	4,669	4,242	3,867	3,701	3,636	3,615
Pensioners (thousands)	2,477	2,556	2,680	2,798	2,870	2,935	2,983	3,032
Old-age pensioners (thousands)	1,371	1,462	1,516	1,546	1,569	1,593	1,604	1,632
Disability pensioners (thousands)	502	543	575	639	665	696	724	750

Source: Based on Schrooten, Smeeding and Wagner (1999).

Organisation

The first step towards a change in organisation and administration of old-age security in post-communist Hungary had actually been taken in the very last years of the previous regime: the Social Insurance Fund was separated from the state budget and turned into an autonomous body from 1 January 1989, to achieve more transparency and accountability in social insurance expenditures (see Ferge 1991: 141; CCET 1995: 20). The Social Insurance Fund was also to be self-governed, such as before World War II, but the respective regulations were postponed until the former monopoly of SZOT had been broken and a more democratic, decentralised trades union structure gradually emerged (see Ferge 1999: 232).[15] Finally, Law 84 of 1991 was passed, that regulated self-governing in social insurance to enable the participation of both contributors and beneficiaries of the pension and health insurance. Furthermore, self-government was aimed at ensuring that the Pension Fund would not be misused for the 'alleviation of the day-to-day hardships faced by the central state budget' (Bod 1995b: 181).

Table 4.3   The Hungarian pension system, 1989–1996: selected indicators

Indicators	1989	1990	1991	1992	1993	1994	1995	1996
Old-age dependency ratio[a]	35.0	35.5	35.8	36.0	36.1	36.1	35.9	35.6
System dependency ratio[b]	51.4	53.3	57.4	66.0	74.2	79.3	82.0	83.9
Replacement ratio[c]	63.3	63.8	64.0	60.8	57.4	54.8	57.9	56.7
Pension expenditures in % of GDP	9.1	9.7	10.5	10.6	11.1	11.5	10.6	9.9

Notes: [a] 60+ years old in % of 20–59 years old
              [b] pensioners in % of contributors
              [c] average pension in % of average wage

Source: Based on Schrooten, Smeeding and Wagner (1999).

The self-government of the pension fund was made up of 60 delegates, 24 of which were representatives of employers' organisations, 32 elected trade union representatives and the remaining 4 delegates of the National Chamber of Retired Persons (see Bagdy 1995: 40). The nationwide elections to the self-governing bodies were held in May 1993, bringing about a landslide victory of the National Confederation of Hungarian Trades Unions (*Magyar Szakszervezetek Országos Szövetsége*, or MSZOSZ), the successor organisation to SZOT and political ally of the Hungarian Socialist Party (Sell 1998b: 114). On the pension insurance list, MSZOSZ gained 50.1 per cent of all votes (Ladó 1995: 328). Board members had been elected in 1993 for a four-year term. However, instead of holding fresh elections to the self-governing bodies of social insurance in 1997, trades unions decided that seats should be allocated to the different federations in pre-assigned proportions (see Orenstein 1998a: 32; Sell 1998a).

Today, the reintroduction of self-government seems to have been a failed experiment: in summer 1998, the newly elected conservative government stripped the social insurance funds of their self-governing bodies (see Ferge 1999). This may come as no surprise, considering the vociferous role played by the Pension Fund's self-government in the pension reform debate (see subchapter 4.3). The self-government had been vested with unusually broad policymaking authority, unparalleled in any OECD country, resulting in a conflict with the government's formulation of pension policy (see CCET

1995: 99; Czúcz and Pintér 1996: 17). On the other hand, allegations of embezzlement of funds and corruption had severely undermined the legitimacy of the Health Fund's self-governing body.

Financing

From 1990 onwards non-insurance expenses – such as family allowances and provisions related to unemployment and political rehabilitation – were gradually moved from the old-age scheme to the state budget. This process, aimed at strengthening the insurance principle and yet to be completed, is known as the 'purification of the profile' (Czúcz and Pintér 1996: 17) or 'cleansing of social insurance' (Ferge 1999: 232).

Table 4.4   The Hungarian Pension Fund, 1993–1996 (in per cent of GDP)

	1993	1994	1995	1996
Revenues	9.2	8.8	9.0	8.2
Expenditures*	9.4	9.4	9.3	8.6
Balance	−0.2	−0.6	−0.3	−0.4

Note: * Please note that pension expenditure data differ from the ones given in Table 4.3. This discrepancy is not explained by the authors.

Source: Based on Schrooten, Smeeding and Wagner (1999).

In 1992, the Social Insurance Fund was dissolved into the financially autonomous, extra-budgetary Pension and Health Funds, while the split of lump-sum contributions into a pension and a health insurance part completed the process of separating the different branches of social security financially. Standardised pension contributions amounted to 26.5 per cent of standardised gross wage in 1997 (employees: 5.2 per cent; employers 21.3 per cent).[16] Since the start of economic transformation in Hungary, poor tax compliance has become widespread (see CCET 1995: 24–5). Hence, the level of outstanding pension contributions has increased dramatically, amounting to over 20 per cent of total pension expenditures in 1996 (Czúcz and Pintér 1996: 15). The Pension Fund's persistent deficit (see Table 4.4) is covered by the government budget.[17]

As early as 1991, the Hungarian Parliament had adopted a decision aimed at improving the financial situation of the social security funds by awarding them HUF 300 billion of – yet to be privatised – state assets, or well over 10 per cent of GDP. A possible rationale for this move has been explained in

Bod (1995b: 180): since the pension scheme had been integrated into the central budget during the post-war decades, the Hungarian state-owned or co-operative property can be interpreted as partially reflecting the 'implicit reserves' built up during the maturation of the PAYG system. Hence it was argued that the former should be used to cover the existing pension entitlements.[18] However, the scheduled transfer of state assets was postponed time and again, until it was hardly operational because the privatisation of state property had been largely concluded.[19]

Eligibility and Benefits

In 1991, the Hungarian Parliament decided to increase the retirement age, which had remained at its post-war level of age 60 for men and age 55 for women. However, the relevant legislation followed only with considerable delay, due to the strong resistance of trades unions. The general public also opposed this move: a survey conducted in May–June 1995 found that 94 per cent of those questioned rejected a higher retirement age (TÁRKI 1995: 8–9).[20] After years of failed attempts to enact the raising of the retirement age, Act No. LIX/1996 finally specified a gradual increase to 60 for both sexes until 2004, and to 62 until 2008 (see Boller 1997: 292–3; Gál 1996: 6).

Early retirement of the elderly unemployed is possible under the 'Pre-pension Programme', while the 'Early Retirement Programme' is directed at employees of firms in financial difficulties. Interestingly, these programmes do not burden the Pension Fund. Rather, the Pre-pension Programme is financed by the 'Solidarity Fund', funded by employees' and employers' contributions, while the Early Retirement Programme is financed from the 'Employment Fund', funded by the general budget, by privatisation proceeds and by employers, who are required to cover part of the costs of their own employees' early retirement. As both funds are limited in size, not everyone who is eligible may receive these benefits (see CCET 1995; Széman 1995).[21]

The vesting period to become eligible for a regular old-age pension was raised from 10 to 20 qualifying years. These include non-contributory years, such as periods of military service, university studies, maternity and sickness allowance. Furthermore, a partial pension was introduced for insured with a minimum of 10 qualifying years (15 years as of 1993). Most former branch privileges have been abolished, except for workers in hazardous occupations, who may still retire early, and for the military (see Götting 1998: 160–1).

Benefit calculation is intricate, highly redistributive and only loosely linked to previous earnings. Grossly oversimplified, the formula to calculate entry pensions can be expressed as

$$P = B + ER,$$

where P = monthly old-age pension, B = universal base component and ER = individual earnings-related component. The latter is based on the assessment wage (AW), the – partially indexed – average of eligible monthly earnings since 1988.[22] ER increases degressively with the number of contributory years: for each of the first 10 contributory years, 33 per cent of AW is considered. However, it is only 2 per cent for the eleventh to twenty-fifth contributory years, 1 per cent for the twenty-sixth to thirty-second contributory years and 1.5 per cent from the thirty-third contributory year onwards. Hence, benefit accrual is declining as earnings and years of service increase. Beyond 32 years of service, 'there is almost nothing to be gained from continuing to work' (see Bagdy 1995: 42). The assessed pension of those newly retired who, after 20 contributory years, fail to meet a determined threshold is upgraded to the minimum pension, about 70 per cent of the minimum wage (see Simonovits 1999: 214).

Prior to 1993, current pensions had been growing considerably slower than wages and prices because of insufficient, largely *ad hoc* indexation, contributing to a compression of the pensioner income distribution towards low income (see Hancock and Pudney 1997).[23] This practice seems to have been motivated by fiscal considerations (see Hock 1998: 327; Simonovits 1999: 217). Thereafter, following a parliamentary decision in 1992, pensions have been adjusted twice a year, following the development of net average wages (see Bagdy 1995: 43). In 1997, the average monthly pension amounted to US$ 107 (see Marsh 1997: 2).

The VMB Funds

The early pension reforms in Hungary were not only devoted to modifications within the existing public PAYG scheme, but also included the creation of new old-age institutions. In order to promote supplementary provisions for old age on a voluntary basis, the Hungarian Parliament approved the introduction of IFF pension funds in November 1993. These financial institutions were set up as so-called 'voluntary mutual benefit' (VMB) funds, non-profit organisations owned by fund members themselves, i.e. the insured.[24] The preamble of the relevant bill asserts that 'the State budget is unable to cover the ever growing expenditures of the uniform compulsory social security system'.[25] Therefore, the 'principle of self-reliance' is stressed (Ministry of Finance 1994: 5). Furthermore, the newly introduced VMB funds were expected to provide long-term investment capital, thereby contributing decisively to the development of the Hungarian capital market (see Ministry of Finance 1994: 9).

VMB pension funds can be set up as open funds, company funds, trades union funds or professional funds, the first two being the most important types, with 43 and 32 per cent of members and 34 and 46 per cent of assets, respectively (1995). Participation in the system is voluntary, but an incentive is provided by a 50 per cent tax credit on contributions to the scheme (maximum HUF 200,000 p.a.). Employers' contributions are exempt from taxes and social security contributions, having gained particular weight in company and trades union funds. In 1997, about two-thirds of total contributions were paid by employers, whereas the share of individual contributions by fund members has been steadily decreasing (see Table 4.5). Hungarian VMB pension funds are being supervised by a specialised government agency, the Supervision Authority of Voluntary Mutual Benefit Funds (*Pénztarfelügyelet*, or PF), controlled by the Ministry of Finance.

Table 4.5   The VMB pension funds in Hungary, 1995–1997: general data

	1995-IV	1996-IV	1997-III
Number of funds	197	248	221*
Number of members	194,349	464,382	610,129
Members per fund	987	1,873	2,761
Members in % of labour force	4.7	11.5	15.3
Closing stock (HUF million)	6,808	23,337	42,194
Members' contributions as % of total contributions	43.2	29.3	25.2
Employers' contributions as % of total contributions	43.2	54.4	64.5
Operating costs	5.1	6.0	7.0

Note: * 1997-II

Sources: Pénztarfelügyelet (1996, 1997a, b); own calculations.

In his early analysis of Hungarian VMB pension funds, Vittas (1996: 9) stressed the striking degree of market fragmentation, persisting until today. In 1997, there were no less than 221 VMB pension funds. As the average monthly contribution amounted to only US$ 18, or 5 per cent of the average gross wage (see Ministry of Finance 1997: 9), it comes as no surprise that VMB pension funds had accumulated only HUF 42 billion in late 1997 (about US$ 250 million).[26] Participation rose from 4.7 per cent (1995) to 15.3 per cent (1997) of the labour force, but, at 0.6 million, membership in VMB funds falls considerably short of the 3 million fund members expected by experts (see Pénztarfelügyelet 1996: 17).

As far as portfolio composition is concerned, the vast majority of assets is still being placed in government bonds (1997: 67 per cent). Only 16 per cent of the total portfolio is invested in company shares, although VMB pension funds are authorised to place up to 60 per cent of assets in equity investments (see Table 4.6). Annual rates of return amounted to 3.0–5.5 per cent in real terms (see Vittas 1996). It should be noted that VMB funds were barred from investing in foreign securities, in spite of the 'present embryonic phase' of Hungary's capital market (World Bank 1995: 33). VMB funds are allowed to transfer their financial management and investment activities to a professional service provider, providing a window of opportunity for foreign banks and insurance companies, such as Nationale Nederlanden, Crédit Lyonnais, Raiffeisen and Sedgwick Nobel Lowndes.

Table 4.6   The VMB pension funds in Hungary, 1995–1997: portfolio

	1995-IV		1996-IV		1997-III	
	HUF million	*in % of closing stock*	*HUF million*	*in % of closing stock*	*HUF million*	*in % of closing stock*
Cash, bank accounts	946	13.89	2,011	8.62	1,013	2.40
Government bonds	4,945	72.64	15,967	68.42	28,065	66.51
Bank deposits and papers	625	9.17	1,186	5.08	291	0.69
Shares and bonds (listed)	11	0.17	1,643	7.04	6,753	16.00
Investment securities	0	0	39	0.17	630	1.49
Others	281	4.12	2,492	10.68	5,443	12.90

Source: Based on Pénztarfelügyelet (1997b); own calculations.

4.3   THE WAY TOWARDS SYSTEMIC PENSION REFORM

The Limits of the Early Reforms

The previous subchapter has made it clear that, in the early years of transition, Hungarian policymakers resorted to rather cautious reforms in the areas of organisation, financing, eligibility and benefits, without making any attempt to fundamentally restructure the existing old-age scheme. The introduction of VMB funds changed the public–private mix in Hungarian old-age provision, yet market fragmentation and low participation rates indicate the limited success of this new voluntary scheme.

Most authors agree that the early reforms of the existing Hungarian old-age scheme, that have been reviewed in the previous subchapter, were slow, piecemeal and not sweeping enough. The intended strengthening of the insurance principle, that was aimed at improved incentives to contribute to the pension scheme, and which would have required a substantial modification of the pension formula, as well as indexation rules, could not be implemented (see Simonovits 1997: 68). As explained by Götting (1998: 162), this was mainly due to fiscal reasons: a greater differentiation of benefit levels is a costly project, requiring extra financial means to improve the financial position of middle and high lifetime earners, if minimum benefits are already very low and cannot be decreased. In 1993 Hungarian policymakers received legal backing from the Constitutional Court for their current practice of *de facto* weakening of the contribution–benefit link by an inadequate indexation of the past earnings history (see Czúcz 1993: 747).

Regarding Hungarian pension policy in the early post-communist years, it has been concluded that the 'conflict between the need for fiscal restraint and pressures to improve or at least maintain current benefits has contributed to a degree of policy paralysis' (CCET 1995: 99). Although pension expenditures had started to fall in 1995 and 1996, both in absolute terms and in per cent of GDP, the Hungarian old-age scheme remained dependent on subsidies from the government budget.

At the same time, many pensioners suffered from inadequate benefit levels (see CCET 1995; Boller 1997), whereas employment opportunities for pensioners became increasingly unavailable in the context of transition-induced unemployment. The number of employed pensioners decreased from 432,000, or 16.9 per cent of pensioners, in 1990 to 129,000, or 4.2 per cent of pensioners, in 1996 (see Central Statistical Office 1997: 39). Household surveys conducted in the mid-1990s revealed that only 4.3 per cent of pensioners' household income consisted of wages, and that 35.7 per cent of pensioners lived below the poverty line (see Grootaert 1997).[27] 'The recent performance of the public pension insurance provoked many criticisms from all sides concerned: employers, employees, pensioners, different ministries, foreign investors, international organisations' (Csaba and Semjén 1997: 16).

Conflicting Blueprints for Comprehensive Reform

The first comprehensive pension reform proposal in post-communist Hungary dates back to 1991, when Parliamentary Resolution No. 60/1991 endorsed a three-tier approach, comprising a universal, flat-rate first tier, financed by the general budget, an earnings-related, contribution-financed second tier with a close contribution–benefit link and a voluntary, supplementary third tier. While the first two tiers were to be publicly managed, the third one would be administered by private entities (see Czúcz 1993: 749–50; CCET 1995: 127). This decree aimed at separating the provision of social welfare, to be assumed by the first tier, from social insurance functions, to be taken over by the second tier (see Antal, Réti and Toldi 1995: 199). However, apart from the introduction of the VMB funds that constituted the third tier, the three-pillar blueprint envisaged in 1991 was never turned into practical policy (see Augusztinovics and Martos 1996: 119). In the remainder of this subchapter, I will focus on the pension reform proposals launched from the mid-1990s onwards, on the respective political actors supporting them and on the resulting political process that preceded the passage of radical pension reform by the Hungarian Parliament in July 1997.

It was a government decree that reopened the case for comprehensive pension reform in December 1994, by setting up the Committee of the Reform of the Treasury, directed by the Finance Minister (see Ferge 1999: 235). The duty of preparing a comprehensive pension reform was delegated to one of its seven subcommittees, the Subcommittee on Social Welfare. In June 1995, this subcommittee presented its proposal – a thorough restructuring of the existing public PAYG scheme, while maintaining it as the only mandatory pension tier – to the Committee of the Reform of the Treasury (see Czúcz and Pintér 1998: 20–21). In spite of being received with approval by this committee, it was only a few weeks later that the latter, i.e. the Minister of Finance, surprisingly presented a fundamentally different pension reform plan to the Hungarian government. This new proposal suggested pension privatisation, thus amounting to a significant paradigm change in Hungarian old-age security.

This incident made it clear that the early consensus among Hungarian pension experts and policymakers about the reform path to be followed had faded by the mid-1990s (see Gál 1996; Simonovits 1997). The local followers of the new pension orthodoxy (see subchapter 2.4) – notably the Ministry of Finance – claimed that privatising old-age security would grant more freedom of choice to citizens and strengthen their individual responsibility. Also, a private old-age scheme would be safer than a public one, while having the additional advantage of enabling the insured to bequeath the accumulated savings to their relatives. The private system's transparency would reinforce contribution incentives. Furthermore, pension privatisation would provide favourable macroeconomic effects: a development of the Hungarian capital market, as well as an increase of saving and growth (see Ferge 1999: 236). Finally, it has been stressed that the existing public PAYG scheme is financially inviable and 'could explode' in the next decade (Rocha 1996: 14).

Contrary to this, the Hungarian advocates of Bismarckian–Beveridgean traditions (see subchapter 2.2) – the Subcommittee on Social Welfare, the Pension Fund's self-government and initially also the Ministry of Welfare – stressed that a pension system should not be designed to bring about macroeconomic desiderata, but to serve the aged. They pointed out that, through the provision of widow/ers' and orphans' benefits, the idea of inheritance was also present in the public PAYG scheme. Finally, transparency and equity could be achieved just as well within a fundamentally reformed public tier, while the existing voluntary VMB funds were deemed sufficient to promote savings (see Ferge 1999: 237).

Conspicuously, from the mid-1990s onwards, the Hungarian discourse reflected the international pension reform controversy outlined in subchapter 2.4, only shortly after the World Bank, with its well-known policy advice modelled on Latin American-style pension privatisation (see subchapter 2.3), had started its local involvement (see Ferge 1997c). Hence, in 1995 and 1996 there were two competing pension reform blueprints in Hungary, to be set out in the following (see Table 4.7 for an outline). The proposals did not only differ in paradigmatic terms, but also with regard to the attention they received: it was the Ministry of Finance's blueprint that was presented to the public as the 'single valid solution' (Ferge 1999: 237), even if it was heavily contested on many occasions. In comparison, the three counter-proposals, prepared by the followers of the Bismarckian–Beveridgean traditions, were prominent with Hungarian social security experts, but 'were never made properly public' (Ferge 1999: 237).

Advocates of Pension Privatisation

The Hungarian followers of the new pension orthodoxy have dismissed a mere reform within the public PAYG scheme, as proposed by the 'Bismarckian–Beveridgean faction' in Hungary. Instead, they proposed 'moving not to where Germany and Austria are and have been, but to where they will be, after considerable agony on their part, in another decade' (Deutsch 1996: 8). The pension reform blueprint advocated by the Ministry of

Finance can be described as a Latin American-style pension privatisation. A first version of this plan, presented by the then Minister of Finance, the neoliberal Lajos Bokros, proposed a full privatisation of Hungarian old-age security (see Ferge 1999: 236), following the Chilean precedent.[28] However, it turned out that Chile was ill-suited as an example, because Hungarians tended to associate the 'Chilean model' with the Pinochet dictatorship under which the famous pension reform had been conducted (e.g. Ferge 1999: 240–1). Moreover, in the eyes of Central Europeans, Latin America carried the stigma of being a less developed region (see Orenstein 1998a: 27). This might have been one of the reasons why both the Hungarian reformers and their World Bank advisors sought to distance themselves from the Chilean precedent and avoid all reference to Latin American reforms (e.g. Rocha 1996: 15). At the same time, the portion of public old-age provision to be privatised was lowered to 50 per cent of contributions, while it was stressed that the new system would 'retain an important role for the state and, at the same time, would develop more possibilities for the private sector' (Rocha 1996: 15).[29] Based on conceptual observations, the 1996 blueprint can be characterised as following more closely the mixed Argentine than the substitutive Chilean approach to old-age security reform (see Charlton, McKinnon and Konopielko 1998: 1423).

In its 1996 version, the Ministry of Finance's blueprint has been described as a three-pillar approach, with two mandatory tiers and one voluntary tier (see Rocha 1996). The first tier should consist of a downsized public PAYG scheme, financed by employers' contributions, while aiming at redistribution and poverty alleviation. To contain costs, eligibility conditions were to be tightened. The second tier would be formed by a system of mandatory private pension funds, financed by employees' contributions and supervised by the state. Voluntary retirement savings were to make up the third tier. Under the new system, employees would thus receive their retirement benefits from both the publicly operated PAYG scheme and the private pension fund tier. As to the speed of the transition to the new system, two possible options were proposed: one scenario would oblige only the new entrants to the labour market to enter the new scheme, while all other contributors would remain in the current system. In another, accelerated scenario, current contributors would be free to opt out of the public PAYG scheme. In the long run, a reduction of payroll taxes was envisaged.

Table 4.7   Conflicting pension reform proposals in Hungary, 1996[a]

Proponents	Ministry of Finance	Subcommittee on Welfare, Self-government of Pension Fund, Ministry of Welfare[b]
First tier		
Type	basic pension for contributors[c]	universal flat-rate minimum pension
Financing	PAYG; contributions to be paid only by employers	PAYG; tax-financed
Level	25% of average net wage	60–70% of subsistence minimum
Second tier		
Type	mandatory private, defined contribution	mandatory public, earnings-related
Financing	IFF; contributions to be paid only by employees	PAYG; contributions shared between employers and employees
Level	depending on investment returns and on entire earnings history	depending on entire earnings history ('German point system')

Notes: [a] As both proposals agree about a third, voluntary tier, it is not included in this summary table.
[b] Minor differences between these three proposals are left out of consideration.
[c] To be supplemented by means-tested, tax-financed social assistance.

Source: Based on Ferge (1997c: 10).

The Ministry of Finance's privatisation approach has been actively supported by the World Bank's Central European office in Budapest (see Rocha 1996; Palacios and Rocha 1997). In an early country study (World Bank 1992), its advice was limited to reforms within the existing public PAYG scheme.[30] The World Bank's campaign for pension privatisation in the region started at a regional seminar in late 1992, where most Hungarian experts rejected the plan as 'sheer lunacy' (Ferge 1999: 235). After the release of the Bank's well-known document 'Averting the Old Age Crisis' (World Bank 1994a), its pension reform recommendations to the Hungarian government became more explicit. This is reflected in the subsequent country study on Hungary, in which the World Bank argues for a 'systemic change, involving splitting the current single public scheme into two mandatory pillars – a flat citizen's pension and a ... fully funded second pillar' (World Bank 1995: 38–40).

After its successful attempts at agenda-shifting, the Bank's Budapest office became directly involved in the Hungarian pension reform around 1995, at the request of the Ministry of Finance (Ferge 1999: 236). 'Technical assistance from the World Bank became essential to the reform's success, because groups with alternate plans could not compete in terms of modelling capacity, and thus did not have the technical sophistication to counter the government's arguments' (Orenstein 1998a: 29). In addition, the Bank's support included inviting international pension experts to Hungary, such as Patricio Arrau from Chile and Rafael Rofman from Argentina, as well as channelling major financial support to the reform task force, including funds from the United States and other bilateral donors (see Nelson 1998: 10). The World Bank experts deliberately took no active role in public discussion, so as to avoid the perception that pension reform was dictated by the international financial institutions (see Orenstein 1998a: 34).

The 'Bismarckian–Beveridgean Faction'

In Hungary, pension reform proposals directed at reforming the public PAYG tier without resorting to pension privatisation have been presented by the Subcommittee on Social Welfare, the Pension Fund's self-government and – at least initially – the Ministry of Welfare (see Table 4.7). Although the three blueprints differ in some details (see Palacios and Rocha 1997: 17–18; Czibere 1998: 33–4), for greater convenience they will be treated here as a single counter-proposal. These reform plans are firmly embedded in the West European mainstream regarding old-age security, and seek to combine the Bismarckian insurance tradition with Beveridgean universalism (see Table 2.1). 'We suggest to give European type answers based on our own historical traditions to the social and economic challenge requiring the reform of the Hungarian Pension System' (Bod 1995a: 174). The 'Bismarckian– Beveridgean faction' rejects the new pension orthodoxy's pension privatisation proposal: 'The quotation of Latin American examples does not prove its assumed positive effect with regard to revival of the economy. At the same time its individual, social and budgetary consequences seem clearly negative' (Augusztinovics and Martos 1996: 157). Mandatory private pension funds were also seen as shifting considerable risks towards future pensioners. Contrary to this, voluntary IFF schemes, supplementing the public PAYG scheme, were welcomed.

Following the reform blueprint presented by the Subcommittee on Social Welfare in June 1995, while also taking up the three-tier model agreed upon in Parliamentary Resolution No. 60/1991, both the Ministry of Welfare and the Pension Fund's self-government started to elaborate their own pension reform plans in 1995 and 1996.[31] Reportedly, it was not easy to convince the majority of trade union representatives within the Pension Fund's self-government that sweeping changes within the existing public PAYG scheme were really necessary. Finally, trades unionists accepted the reform proposal elaborated by a group of experts from the self-government and the Hungarian Academy of Sciences (see Augusztinovics 1995; Martos 1995).

These blueprints, based on a macro-simulation model developed by Mária Augusztinovics (see Augusztinovics 1995), suggested a thorough reform of the existing public PAYG system aimed at separating the provision of assistance-type benefits, to be taken over by the first tier, from social insurance functions, to be assumed by the second tier. The first tier would provide universal flat-rate minimum pensions, financed by general taxation. The second tier would exhibit a strong contribution–benefit link by introducing a point system, following the German example (see subchapter 2.2). Benefit calculation would thus take the entire earnings history into account. The proposal includes the introduction of collective funding, in order to counteract the unfavourable demographic situation early in the 21st century. To this end, a temporary reserve is to be built up from the Pension Fund's surpluses, to be expected after the increase of the pension age. Extensive simulations (see Réti 1996a, b) were used to underpin these recommendations, concluding that 'it is possible to reform the current PAYG system' (Réti 1996b: 23; own translation). To sum up, the 'Bismarckian–Beveridgean faction' is convinced that 'the problems of the Hungarian Pension Reform can be solved without a forced paradigm shift' (Bod 1995a: 174).

The Ministry of Finance–Ministry of Welfare Agreement

As noted above, the Hungarian Ministries of Welfare and Finance favoured competing reform paths in 1995 and early 1996, effectively preventing either of the two blueprints from being implemented. Even so, the basic conflict between both portfolios was settled in April 1996, and Minister of Welfare György Szabó, and Bokros' successor, Minister of Finance Péter Medgyessy, presented a joint pension reform blueprint four weeks later (see Ministry of Welfare and Ministry of Finance 1996). Accounts vary as to how this agreement came about, pointing either to Prime Minister Gyula Horn as the driving force behind the narrowing down of differences within his cabinet, or to the fact that the Ministry of Finance had finally agreed to lower the portion of public old-age provision to be privatised from 50 to 30 per cent of contributions, amounting to a compromise between both portfolios.

The joint Ministry of Finance–Ministry of Welfare proposal (see Ministry of Welfare and Ministry of Finance 1996) strongly resembles the Ministry of Finance's earlier stance, although the relative share of the IFF tier has been further diminished. The reform plan aims at a mixed pension system with two mandatory tiers, a public PAYG tier (two-thirds) and a private IFF tier (one-third), seeking to integrate the advantages of both schemes into Hungarian old-age provision. Partial pension privatisation is justified by macroeconomic reasoning, being expected to diminish distortions of the labour market, to boost the development of the capital market, to increase savings and, finally, to achieve economic growth (see Ministry of Welfare and Ministry of Finance 1996: 9–10). In the words of Ádám Gere, former head of the government pension reform task force: 'If things continue as they are, the only thing sure is that the pension system will go bankrupt. It's a ticking time bomb' (quoted from Marsh 1997: 2).

The envisaged comprehensive pension reform would consist of two simultaneous parts (see Ministry of Finance 1997): on the one hand, reforms of the existing public PAYG tier would include a strengthening of the link between contributions and benefits in the pension formula and a tightening of eligibility, e.g. by eliminating credits for non-contributory years and by limiting access to disability pensions. On the other hand, a partially mandatory, privately-run IFF tier was to be created, designed along the lines of the already existing VMB pension funds. The envisaged comprehensive pension reform was to be made politically palatable by bundling up the unavoidable, yet politically sensitive reforms of the public PAYG tier with the introduction of individual pension fund accounts – a more visible move, relatively attractive for the younger part of the population (see Palacios and Rocha 1997: 19).

The new pension fund tier would be mandatory for all new entrants to the labour market, whereas current contributors would be given approximately one year to choose between both systems (see Czibere 1998: 33). When opting out of the current system and switching to the new one, one-third of total pension contributions would go to a private pension fund, whereas the remaining part, including the entire employers' contribution, would still go to the public PAYG scheme. To avoid part of the high transition costs of large-scale pension privatisation in the Hungarian context of fiscal constraints, there would be disincentives for current contributors to switch to the new system, i.e. only partial compensation for acquired pension claims. Originally, a mandatory cut-off age of 40 (later 47) years was envisaged, above which opting-out would not be allowed, since the remaining years of service were not expected to be sufficient for the accumulation of sizeable investment returns in the IFF tier. However, in the legislative process this age threshold was seen as discriminatory against the elderly contributors, and was thus dropped on constitutional grounds (see Palacios and Rocha 1997: 22). Even so, the fact that second-tier pension funds may pay out benefits only after 15 years of membership amounts to a strong incentive against the switching of those insured close to retirement age.

It should be noted that in spite of the inter-ministerial agreement reached in April 1996, there was still no political unanimity on the pension reform issue in Hungary: the Pension Fund's self-government and most social security experts stuck to their original pension reform proposal, continuing their protest against government plans for partial pension privatisation, e.g. by holding a pension reform conference jointly with the MSZOSZ in September 1996, denouncing the Latin American experiences as a 'dangerous exercise' (Autonóm Szakszervetek et al. 1996: 1) – yet apparently without much political impact.

Towards the Legislative Process

After the joint Ministry of Finance–Ministry of Welfare proposal (see Ministry of Welfare and Ministry of Finance 1996) had been accepted by the Hungarian government, the Committee of the Reform of the Treasury and all its subcommittees were dissolved. Instead, an inter-ministerial pension reform committee led by István Györffy, Commissioner of the Minister of Finance, was set up to work out the technical and legal details of the envisaged pension reform. It is interesting to note that in spite of the reconciliation of portfolios reached in April 1996, preparations for pension reform, though part of social policy, were still largely dominated by the Ministry of Finance. It seems, however, that there was a certain 'division of labour', with the Ministry of Welfare being responsible for elaborating the reform measures affecting the first tier, while the Ministry of Finance was preparing the introduction of the second tier. Another notable feature is the extraordinarily tight deadline under which the pension reform task force worked after the April 1996 reconciliation, preparing a draft law until May 1997, six months later than the original target date. With parliamentary elections scheduled for 1998, the government's objective was to win legislative approval for the envisaged pension reform well before that date (Nelson 1998: 9).

On 28 May 1997, a reform package comprising fundamental changes to the Hungarian old-age security system was finally submitted to the Hungarian parliament (see Ministry of Welfare and Ministry of Finance 1997), where the socialist-liberal government coalition could count on its strong majority of 72 per cent of overall seats. A total of five pension reform draft laws, replacing Act II/1975, were to regulate the general framework and financing of social insurance, the public pension scheme, the private funds, mandatory health insurance and the introduction of social assistance for the elderly. The following reform guidelines were spelt out: while inter-generational risk sharing was to remain a dominant trait of the Hungarian pension system, individual self-care would be introduced as an additional feature. From now on, redistributive elements were to be functionally separated from insurance elements, thereby strengthening the contribution–benefit link decisively. But pension supplement rates in the reformed PAYG scheme were to be maintained at the current 55–65 per cent of the individual's average lifetime income, and the individual's contribution burden would be held constant. Pension entitlements obtained in the past would not be affected by the reform, particularly concerning the paying out of current pensions (see Ministry of Welfare and Ministry of Finance 1997: 1–2).

Although there were over 400 proposals of amendments to the five pension reform draft laws, few of these concerned fundamental issues, and the MPs' interest in the pension reform issue appeared to have been rather limited (see Ferge 1999: 238–9). Reportedly, a number of MPs had business interests linked to the pension reform proposal, as they had been involved in setting up VMB funds (see Orenstein 1998a: 30). As early as 15 July 1997, after only six weeks of debate, the Hungarian parliament passed the five pension reform bills with a relatively slight margin.[32] The reform took effect from 1 January 1998, preceded by an extensive PR campaign, announcing that 'the old pension system retires' (for details see Ferge 1999: 239–40).

Other Forces Shaping Pension Reform

The main political actors considered in the above analysis – the Ministries of Finance and Welfare, the Pension Fund's self-government and the World Bank – did not meet with a political vacuum when trying to bring about comprehensive pension reform. Whereas other political groups turned out to be relatively unimportant in determining the basic paradigmatic reform outcome, the shift towards a mandatory private pension fund tier, their demands and protests, whether manifest or anticipated, did shape some of the details of Hungarian pension reform policy. Reformers finally decided to enter into a dialogue with potential opponents towards the end of the reform process, ready to make some concessions in order to win them over (see Palacios and Rocha 1997: 20).

The most important modifications were the elimination of the cut-off age to the partial opting out of the public PAYG scheme, and the reduction in the contribution rate to the private pension fund tier from 10 to 8 per cent of gross wage (6 and 7 per cent, respectively, in the first two years), thereby lessening the reduction of the public PAYG tier to about one-quarter.[33] Other concessions included postponing a change in indexation rules until 2001, while the introduction of the new benefit formula and tax regime was even postponed until 2013 (see Palacios and Rocha 1997: 20–1).[34] Furthermore, the envisaged reform of the disability scheme was delayed by one year, effectively excluding it from the overall reform package (see Ministry of Finance 1997: 10).

As early as May 1996, it had been resolved that '[r]egular talks shall be initiated with the National Health Insurance Self-Government and the National Pension Insurance Self-Government, and the interest associations and civil societ[y]' (Ministry of Welfare and Ministry of Finance 1996: 6). Yet, at first, 'reluctance of the government to inform and to involve the public' prevailed (Ferge 1999: 237). During late 1996 and early 1997, members of the pension reform task force finally held a series of meetings, e.g. with MSZOSZ and SZEF, the two largest trades unions, employers' representatives, the National Alliance of Pensioners, the Council of the Elderly, the Association of Large Families, the Pension Fund's self-government, the Social Policy Association and prominent academic opponents of the reform (see Orenstein 1998a: 34; Ferge 1999: 237).[35]

Among these additional pension reform actors the role of the Hungarian trades unions stands out. It should be noted that the Hungarian trade union movement is fragmented, exhibiting eight different federations (see Sell 1998a). Here, the main focus will be on MSZOSZ, the largest trade union. As noted above, trades union representatives formed a major part of the board members of the Pension Fund's self-government. Another institutionalised channel to influence government policy was the tripartite Interest Reconciliation Council (*Érdekegyeztető Tanács*, or ÉT), that comprised representatives of trades unions, employers and the government (see Kurtán 1994; Ladó 1997). Furthermore, the post-communist MSZOSZ was an important faction of the Hungarian Socialist Party that was governing Hungary – together with its liberal coalition partner, the Alliance of Free Democrats – from 1994–98, i.e. during the crucial period of pension reform.

It has been noted that the trades unions' initial position was to defend the *status quo*, opposing any comprehensive pension reform, even the 'mild' blueprint elaborated by experts around the Pension Fund's self-government. When persuaded to follow the Bismarckian–Beveridgean reform blueprint, they started to voice considerable opposition against the government's pension reform plans and, in one instance, even threatened to go on strike (see MSZOSZ 1997: 2; Orenstein 1998a: 35). At a conference on pension reform in February 1997, organised by Sándor Nagy, former head of MSZOSZ and the Pension Fund, as well as Socialist MP, a majority of experts argued against the envisaged reform path that was defended by Finance Minister

Medgyessy, the new Welfare Minister Mihály Kökény and the World Bank's Roberto Rocha (see Trend/Prognózis Rt. 1997; Ferge 1999: 238).

However, the trades unions' most important opportunity to modify the pension reform plans was still to come: in May 1997, shortly before being submitted to parliament, the draft law on pension reform was presented to the tripartite Interest Reconciliation Council (ÉT), that had repeatedly voiced disagreement with the government's reform plans and had backed the 'Bismarckian–Beveridgean faction' instead (see Orenstein 1998a: 33). As pointed out by Ladó (1997: 18–19), by this time the functions of this tripartite body had been reduced to pre-legislative consultation, with no formal veto powers attached to it. However, parliament had made ÉT's approval of the envisaged pension reform a precondition of its own stance (see Orenstein 1998a: 36), so the government was keen to obtain ÉT's consent, giving in to some transitory modifications of the draft, in exchange for a last-minute reversal of the trades unions' stance towards pension privatisation.[36]

As regards other interest groups that may have had an impact on the pension reform process in Hungary, private insurance and pension management firms are relevant stakeholders when it comes to pension privatisation. As noted above, VMB pension funds had been set up in the mid-1990s on a voluntary basis. These financial institutions were politically represented by both the Hungarian Federation of Mutual Funds and the Supervision Authority of Voluntary Mutual Benefit Funds. Their first reaction to the government's pension reform blueprint was ambivalent: on the one hand, the reform plans amounted to the creation of a new, attractive market segment that, due to its partially mandatory character, would be much larger than the already existing voluntary business. On the other hand, VMB funds feared that their clients would be less inclined to engage in voluntary retirement provision, once the IFF tier were created. In any case, prominent members of the Supervision Authority had been involved in the Ministry of Finance's pension reform efforts since mid-1995. The fact that the corporate constitution of the new, mandatory pension funds mirrors that of the existing VMB funds is largely seen as a political concession to the latter (see Orenstein 1998a: 26). By meeting a number of prerequisites, the already existing VMB funds may upgrade their voluntary activities to the newly introduced mandatory business (see Nelson 1998: 15).

Contrary to conventional wisdom (see chapter 3), pensioners' associations – the National Alliance of Pensioners and the Council of the Elderly – were not nearly as influential as one might have assumed, given the radical character of the reform and the significance of this constituency, that is estimated to amount to 40 per cent of all voters. Apparently, the Hungarian government succeeded in calming current pensioners by assuring them that they would not be affected by the envisaged reform. 'It is a very important requirement that through the implementation of ... the new pension system, the situation of the already retired persons does not worsen and ... the acquired rights are not hurt through the transition' (see Ministry of Welfare and Ministry of Finance 1996: 8).[37] Furthermore, it should be noted that pensioners have been represented rather indirectly by another interest group: post-communist trades unions, as the elderly form a sizeable part of their membership – hence the inconsistent position of the latter that reflects the interests of both beneficiaries and contributors.

Finally, it might be asked to what extent public opinion supported the pension reform blueprint presented by the Hungarian government. Some insights are provided by opinion polls conducted by TÁRKI in 1995–1996 at the request of the pension reform working group.[38] Over 60 per cent of those questioned thought that the state had an absolute obligation to provide a decent living for the elderly. Yet a mixed pension system was clearly favoured by a majority, being supported by 56.5 per cent of those questioned, while 21.4 per cent preferred a state scheme and 18.5 per cent a market-based solution (TÁRKI 1996: 52).[39] While the market-based solution was favoured more strongly by those aged 39 years and younger, approval of the state-run option was negatively correlated with the educational level of those questioned, reaching from 38.4 per cent for Hungarians with basic education to as little as 2.7 per cent for Hungarians with university education. Strikingly, the mixed system was preferred in all educational, occupational and age groups by a strong majority – with the sole exception of agricultural workers (TÁRKI 1996: 63).

4.4   THE NEW HUNGARIAN PENSION SYSTEM

General Description

Since 1 January 1998, Hungary's new pension system has been in force. It is of a mixed type, combining a still dominant, mandatory public PAYG scheme with a partially mandatory IFF tier. Strictly speaking, there are four tiers in the new Hungarian system (see Palacios and Rocha 1997: 41): apart from the mandatory PAYG and IFF tiers (tiers 1 and 2), there is a 'zero' tier consisting of a means-tested income guarantee for the elderly, replacing the pre-reform system of minimum and partial pensions, and a third tier of voluntary savings for old age, e.g. in VMB pension funds. Here, the focus is on the mandatory PAYG and IFF tiers, since they will provide the bulk of old-age security in Hungary, offering a purely public as well as a mixed pension option on a mandatory basis.[40]

Table 4.8   Hungarian pension contributions, pre- and post-reform

	pre-reform	1998	1999	from 2000
Employers, nominal (in % of gross wage)	24.5	24	23	22
Employees, nominal (in % of gross wage)	6	6+1[a]	7+1	8+1
Total, nominal (in % of gross wage)	30.5	31	31	31
Employers, standardised[b] (in % of stand. gross wage)	21.3	20.8	19.9	19.0
Employees, standardised (in % of stand. gross wage)	5.2	5.2+0.9	6.1+0.9	6.9+0.9
Total, standardised (in % of stand. gross wage)	26.5	26.9	26.9	26.8

Notes: [a] In nominal terms, 1% of contributions is directed to the public tier, regardless of the insured's decision whether or not to join a private pension fund.
[b] On standardisation see note 16 in this chapter.

Source: Based on Czibere (1998); own calculations.

The first, PAYG tier, to be financed by the entire employers' and a small part of the employees' contributions (see Table 4.8), is mandatory for everybody, at least as first tier. It is undergoing sweeping reform, that comprises *inter alia* the following measures: eligibility criteria are tightened, e.g. by reducing the number of non-contributory years of service. From 2001, annual pension adjustments will change from wage indexation to the Swiss formula, that considers half the change in the consumer price index, combining it with half the change in the average industrial wage. The retirement age will gradually be increased from 55 for women and 60 for men to 62 for both sexes by 2008.[41] From 2013, the pension formula will be fundamentally restructured by introducing uniform accrual rates, and by removing the degressive weighting of earnings, contributing decisively to streamlining benefit calculation in the public tier.[42]

The second, IFF tier consists of a newly created pension fund system, financed entirely by employees' contributions (see Table 4.8). The new mandatory pension funds are being set up parallel to the already existing voluntary VMB funds. Although the new funds are legally structured along the lines of the latter, separation of both systems is necessary because mandatory pension funds require stricter government supervision than voluntary ones. In particular, they will be subject to a minimum size (2,000 members), will have to constitute minimum internal reserves (0.5 per cent of contributions), will be obliged to contribute to a centralised Guarantee Fund (0.3 per cent of contributions) and will be required to submit quarterly reports to the Supervising Agency. Investment guidelines have been designed to avoid excessive risk exposure (see Ministry of Finance 1997: 8).[43]

Originally, only limited guarantees for second-tier accounts were envisaged. Due to public debates, this approach had to be modified, engendering two layers of protection (see Palacios and Rocha 1997: 25): first, after 15 years of participation in the new system, annuities may not be less than 25 per cent of the value of the individual's first pillar pension.[44] Second, there is a relative rate of return guarantee, backed by the resources of the Guarantee Fund: a minimum annual yield requirement will be specified in advance by the Supervising Agency, albeit on a discretionary basis rather than following transparent rules.

The Transition

All Hungarians entering the labour market after 30 June 1998 are obliged to join the new two-tier scheme, paying a quarter of the total pension contribution into the new private pension funds, while the remaining three-quarters will continue to go to the existing PAYG tier (mixed pension path). Individuals that already have an insurance history but are not yet retired are free to do the same – alternatively, they may stay in the old scheme with the whole of their contribution (purely public pension path). The insured have to decide between September 1997 and August 1999 whether or not they want to switch to the mixed pension path. Until December 2000, switching back to the purely public pension path will be possible. After that date, employees will be permanently affiliated either with the reformed PAYG scheme or with the new, mixed system.[45] However, fund-switching within the IFF pillar will be allowed twice a year, after a transitional period.

Hence, regardless of the insured's decision for or against joining the private pension pillar, his or her employer's contribution will go to the public PAYG pillar. Under the mixed pension path, employees will thus receive their retirement benefits from both the publicly operated PAYG scheme and the private pension fund tier. While obtaining a life annuity upon retirement from the chosen pension fund, from 2012 onwards they will receive a proportionally reduced part of the 'normal' public pension.[46] The annual accrual rate of those who decide to switch will then be 1.22 per cent, which compares unfavourably with the 1.65 per cent p.a. granted to those insured who remain in the old system.[47] By extending this benefit reduction to the entire insurance history, including the pre-1998 years of service (see Simonovits 1999: 219), the Hungarian government made an effort to choose the valuation of accrued rights in such a way that only employees below the age of 35–40 would find it attractive to switch (see Palacios and Rocha 1997: 24–6).[48] However, age is by no means the only factor affecting the attractiveness of the switch. A level-headed choice will also mean considering – or, rather, trying to anticipate – the relative income level and the course of the earnings history, e.g. the frequency of interruptions, notably by periods of unemployment and child raising (see Ministry of Welfare and Ministry of Finance 1997: 18).

The Hungarian reform design implies that the public old-age scheme will have to cover pension claims acquired under the pre-reform PAYG scheme, by paying some sort of compensatory pension that is topped up by post-reform pension claims. Hence, the public PAYG tier remains with all the pre-reform pension liabilities, as well as the claims acquired by post-reform contributors, while at the same time an ever-increasing part of its revenues is diverted towards the newly created mandatory IFF tier. The resulting transition costs depend crucially on the proportion of the insured switching to the mixed scheme. The Ministry of Finance estimates the annual budgetary burden in the post-reform years at some US\$ 360 million, or 0.8–1.3 per cent of GDP (see Deutsch 1997: 20; Palacios and Rocha 1997: 27).[49] This would be rather low compared with Latin American experiences. The government hopes that these costs will be partially offset by falling interest rates resulting from the massive increase in long-term savings that, in turn, are expected to boost Hungarian GDP by 1.0–1.5 per cent annually from the year 2000 (see Marsh 1997: 2). These official calculations conspicuously follow the new pension orthodoxy's assumption that there is a strong positive link between savings and growth (see subchapter 2.4).

First Experiences and Early Evaluations

It being only a year (at the time of writing) since the start of the Hungarian pension reform, it is now definitely too early for a comprehensive evaluation of its strengths and weaknesses. It is seen as 'leading the rush' (Rutkowski 1998: 16) towards pension privatisation in transition countries – which is not entirely accurate, as Kazakhstan pre-empted Hungary by a few weeks, legislating a more radical, Chilean-type reform in June 1997, that became effective on 1 January 1998 (see Castello Branco 1998: 34).[50] As regards the more immediate geographical region, its importance is, however, considerable (see Deutsch 1997: 20). 'Passage of the Hungarian reform by

Parliament has demonstrated the political and economic feasibility of this type of reform in Central Europe' (Palacios and Rocha 1997: 42).

By the end of 1998, 38 mandatory pension funds had been set up in Hungary, most of them by the 'pioneers' who had gained experience in voluntary VMB funds; and 1.4 million Hungarians had decided – or, as career starters, were obliged – to join one of these newly created providers of old-age security, whose investment portfolio consisted mainly of state securities (78 per cent in the third quarter of 1998). Before the start of the reform, the government had expected that 1.5–2 million of the 4 million Hungarians eligible to choose would opt for the new, mixed pension path (see Langenkamp 1997b: 8). Considering the current trend, these numbers may well be surpassed by the deadline for switching, August 1999, implying an upward revision of deficit projections for the public pension scheme (see Pintér 1999).

In spite of official announcements that the pension reform would solve the economic problems of the public pension scheme, the financial situation of the post-reform public tier is thus likely to deteriorate (see Ferge 1999: 242–3), thereby further undermining the trust of the insured. On the other hand, the high overall contribution burden, largely seen as providing disincentives to employment and contribution compliance, was not decreased by the reform but only shifted from employers to employees (see Table 4.8). Further criticism concerns the fact that the 1997 pension reform postponed the amendment of the still dominant public pillar until 2013, notably the restructuring of the pension formula (see Simonovits 1999: 211–12).

4.5   SUMMING UP:
PROBLEMS, ACTORS AND POLICY CHOICES

By 1989, the need for fundamental reforms in Hungarian old-age security was widely acknowledged, as the inherited PAYG system was seen as inequitable, inadequate and unsustainable. Its financial problems were further aggravated during economic transformation: the number of contributors to the pension scheme plummeted while the number of beneficiaries increased dramatically. Early reforms introduced some changes to the organisation, financing and eligibility of the Hungarian pension scheme, but were not sweeping enough to ensure its financial viability, while further distortions were added by inadequate indexation practices. Moreover, the resistance of trades unions succeeded in delaying important reform measures, notably the raising of the retirement age. By comparison, the introduction of voluntary VMB pension funds in 1994 – the first move towards a diversification of old-age provision – did not meet with political obstacles.

In spite of the largely unsuccessful attempts to bring about thorough reform within the existing Hungarian old-age scheme, the Ministry of Welfare and the vociferous self-government of the Pension Fund stuck to the Bismarckian–Beveridgean traditions. Meanwhile, the public PAYG system's dependence on budgetary subsidies granted another political actor an important stake in the pension reform issue: the Ministry of Finance, inclined towards the neoliberal mainstream. Hence, the 'benefit of crises' hypothesis can be specified for the Hungarian case in such a way that the financial difficulties of the public old-age scheme resulted in a significant change of the constellation of actors relevant in the pension reform arena, thereby strengthening the 'privatisation faction'. Agenda-shifting was further facilitated by the World Bank – a major external actor in the light of Hungary's high external debt burden – and its local campaign for Latin American-style reforms.

The stalemate between the Ministries of Welfare and Finance in the pension reform issue lasted almost two years, until the conflict was settled in spring 1996. Although the joint reform blueprint strongly resembled the Ministry of Finance's earlier stance, its mixed overall approach can be interpreted as satisfying both of the previously competing factions by a compromise. Yet it is interesting to note that an inter-ministerial pension reform committee led by a Commissioner to the Minister of Finance was set up to work out the technical and legal details of the envisaged pension reform, thereby bypassing the exclusive competences of the Ministry of Welfare for the area of old-age security.

In terms of underlying role models, the Hungarian reform blueprint follows the Argentine approach to old-age security reform. However, in spite of the obvious conceptual parallels, both the Hungarian reformers and their World Bank advisors sought to avoid all reference to Latin American reforms as soon as they found out about the inconvenient connotations among the Hungarian public. Apart from this tactical packaging, the reformers' strategy amounted to bundling up some unavoidable, yet politically sensitive reforms of the public PAYG tier with the more visible and, at the same time, relatively attractive introduction of individual pension fund accounts. This bundling up increased the complexity of the envisaged reform, while, at the same time, lowering the visibility of the concomitant retrenchment elements – an obfuscation strategy in Pierson's terms (1994). Interestingly, the scope and financing of transition costs – a major distributional issue when it comes to a shift from PAYG to IFF schemes – was successfully shielded from public debate.

In mid-July 1997, after only six weeks of debate, the government met its objective of winning legislative approval for the envisaged pension reform well before the next elections, scheduled for early 1998, thereby defying conventional wisdom that retrenchment as well as radical reforms are unlikely to be enacted in a pre-electoral period. The extraordinarily quick passage of the pension reform laws was not only due to the governing coalition's strong parliamentary majority, but also to the government's strategy of pre-legislative compromising with relevant opponents over the pension reform draft. In particular, negotiations with the tripartite Interest Reconciliation Council (ÉT) – a potential veto player – can be interpreted as a proxy for parliamentary negotiations on pension reform.[51] It should be noted, however, that Hungarian pension reformers were only willing to compromise on first-tier reforms, while their basic paradigm choice was not put up for discussion with secondary pension reform actors, such as trades unions.

Hungary's new pension system, in force since 1 January 1998, is of a mixed type, combining a still dominant, mandatory public PAYG scheme (three-quarters of contributions) with a partially mandatory IFF tier (one-quarter of contributions). Even if the lion's share of Hungarian old-age security will still be provided by the public PAYG tier, the reform amounts to a partial privatisation of the existing public scheme. Hence it constitutes a paradigmatic departure from local social insurance traditions, dating back to 1912. It can be concluded that the 1997 reform, while failing to solve all the problems of old-age provision in Hungary, has clearly succeeded in creating a privatisation precedent in Central–Eastern Europe.

NOTES

1. Among the European countries to introduce social insurance, Hungary ranks third after Germany and Austria (see Maltby 1994: 122).
2. The self-governing bodies were made up of elected representatives of the insured and their employers, in equal numbers (Bod 1995b: 175).
3. It should be noted that agriculture was the predominant form of employment in Hungary up to 1945 (see Maltby 1994: 122–3).
4. See Ministry of Finance (1982: 12–13) for organisational details. In 1984, the National Administration of Social Insurance, a government agency, took over all social insurance tasks from SZOT (see Maltby 1994: 133).
5. In 1970, the so-called 'progressive pension contribution' was introduced, implying that employees' contributions ranged from 3 to 10 per cent of wages (see Ministry of Finance 1982: 11; Simonovits 1997: 60).
6. Employees of state-owned farms had been granted coverage in the 1949 reform (see Augusztinovics 1993: 307–8).
7. Here, the coverage ratio measures the number of insured (in their own right and as family members) in per cent of the entire population. Please note that in Table 4.1 two different indicators of coverage are used.
8. Similarly Ferge (1992: 205), who seeks to explain the high acceptance of socialist social policy among Hungarians with the fact that 'the organic link with the [pre-socialist] past was not completely destroyed in this case'.
9. The system dependency ratio is the number of pensioners, divided by the number of contributors to the old-age scheme. When the number of contributors is not available, the number of officially employed is used as a substitute.

10. Hock (1998: 84) gives the following average annual inflation rates: 6.3 per cent (1976–1980), 6.7 per cent (1981–1985), 10.2 per cent (1986–1990).
11. The authors, Zsuzsa Ferge and János Péteri, recommended *inter alia* the strict implementation of the insurance principle, the return to an independent, self-governed pension scheme and the introduction of voluntary private pension schemes (see Ferge 1997c: 2).
12. See subchapter 7.1 for a more detailed analysis of the impact of transformation on the existing old-age security schemes in Central and Eastern Europe.
13. In spite of the significance of disability pensions to account for overall trends in the pension system, I will not examine this branch of pension insurance here, as the focus of the present study is on old-age pensions only.
14. The old-age dependency ratio is the number of those in pension age to the number of those in active age. It is important to note that the ratio depends crucially on the cut-off age, hence not only reflecting demographic trends but also the underlying statutory retirement age (see Augustinovics 1999: 11–12).
15. See Ladó (1995) and Sell (1998b) on the changing industrial relations in post-communist Hungary.
16. Standardised contribution rates have been calculated on the basis of standardised gross wages, including 50 per cent of the total social insurance contribution, to eliminate those cross-national differences in the calculation base that are due to a non-proportional distribution of the contribution burden between employee and employer, and to facilitate international comparisons (see Simonovits 1999). See Table 4.8 for nominal contribution rates.
17. Mária Augusztinovics recommended that in order to assess the effective financial situation of the Hungarian Pension Fund, non-pension expenditures covered by the Fund should be deducted from its nominal deficit, turning it into a surplus (personal communication of 21 February 1999). Unfortunately, such alternative calculations are not available for any of the three country cases under comparison; hence, the official figures are used. For an inquiry into the factors explaining the Hungarian pension budget see Gál (1999).
18. According to Pataki's interpretation (1993: 59), this transfer was intended as a compensation for the nationalisation of Social Security's assets in 1950.
19. Ferge (1999: 232) argues that these delaying tactics were applied to avoid strengthening the financial independence of the Pension Fund, especially after the 1993 self-government elections had ended up with a majority of MSZOSZ representatives.
20. Interestingly, in late 1996, after a decision had been taken to raise the retirement age, the percentage of those opposing a change in the retirement age had decreased to 54.3 per cent (TÁRKI 1996: 59).
21. The Pre-pension Programme and the Early Retirement Programme have been criticised, among other things, for duplicating already existing paths to early retirement and for being more generous than regular retirement provision (CCET 1995: 110).
22. Monthly average earnings above a certain ceiling are only partially considered. Until the 1997 pension reform, earnings brackets were not indexed, turning this degressive element in the Hungarian pension formula into one of the distorting factors within the current pension formula, as earnings brackets are not indexed (see Ministry of Finance 1992: 19; CCET 1995: 120).
23. See Hancock and Pudney (1997: 423) for details on the highly complex pension increases from 1987–1993.
24. VMB funds can also be designed as mutual aid funds or health care funds. However, 90 per cent of all VMB funds are pension funds.
25. Act No. XCVI/1993, amended by Act No. XV/1996.
26. See Table 2.2 for a comparison with the Chilean and Argentine pension funds' performance.
27. Poverty incidence is measured here as the percentage of people below two-thirds of mean expenditures. Pensioners compare favourably with the unemployed, temporary employees and child care receivers, but their poverty incidence is clearly above the national average of 25.3 per cent. Poverty among female pensioners is even higher (see Grootaert 1997). Förster

and Tóth (1997: 25) found that those elderly living alone – 24 per cent of pensioners – were greatly at risk of being impoverished.
28. Two years earlier, a Chilean-style privatisation of Hungarian old-age security had been proposed in a paper by Chung (1993).
29. The initial proposal to switch fully to an IFF scheme was also dropped on fiscal grounds, since the level of Hungary's implicit pension debt would have resulted in very high transition costs (see Orenstein 1998a: 26–27).
30. The proposed reforms included an increase in the effective retirement age, the tightening of disability benefits, a limitation of the pension level, benefit indexation and the elimination of the inconsistent tax treatment of contributions and benefits (see World Bank 1992).
31. As noted by Orenstein (1998a: 27), the Ministry of Welfare developed its pension reform plan with the help of German advisors.
32. Act No LXXX/1997 on the scope of citizens eligible to social insurance services and private pension as well as the financing of the above benefits; Act No LXXXI/1997 on social pension benefits; Act No LXXXII/1997 on the private pension and the private mutual pension funds; Act No LXXXIII/1997 on the benefits of mandatory health insurance; Act No. LXXXIV/1997 on the modification of Act No. III/1993 on social administration and social benefits.
33. These are nominal contribution rates. For standardised rates see Table 4.8.
34. The government draft proposed the introduction of 'Swiss indexation', i.e. indexation to wages and prices in equal shares, which would be less favourable for beneficiaries than the current wage indexation rules. The new indexation formula was opposed by trades unions, but represented a compromise between the Ministries of Welfare and Finance (see Orenstein 1998a: 35).
35. It would be beyond the scope of this study to relate each of the modifications to individual interest groups. A detailed account of the negotiations between pension reformers and civil society in Hungary is given in Orenstein (1998a).
36. According to Nelson (1998: 13), the government's most important concession was not directly related to the pension reform issue: it gave in to trades unions' demands to change the formula for selecting their representatives in the self-governing bodies of social insurance by delegating their board members, instead of holding fresh elections in 1997. Orenstein (1998a) does not relate this political deal to the Interest Reconciliation Council's approval of the pension reform draft.
37. However, the switch towards 'Swiss indexation' affects current and future old-age benefits alike. Furthermore, this promise may be doubted on fiscal grounds (see Ferge 1999: 243–4). See subchapter 7.2 for details of this argument.
38. An earlier survey dates back to May-June 1995, when no comprehensive pension reform blueprint had been presented yet. It found that, relative to a poll conducted in 1988, the share of those who considered an old-age pension a citizen's right had diminished, while a strengthening of the insurance principle had gained approval (TÁRKI 1995: 8–9).
39. Unfortunately, these institutional alternatives did not correspond to the pension reform blueprints discussed in Hungary at that time: the 'state option' implied an unreformed public scheme, whereas the 'market option' suggested that individual old-age provision be voluntary. Misleadingly, the so-called 'mixed option' resembled the *parallel* pension reform model (see subchapter 2.3), i.e. a choice between a mandatory public PAYG and a mandatory private IFF scheme (see TÁRKI 1996: 16). Some belated caveats have also been made by the authors of this wording (see Csontos, Kornai and Tóth 1997: 5–6).
40. This general description of the new Hungarian pension system is largely based on Ministry of Finance (1997), Palacios and Rocha (1997), Czibere (1998) and Simonovits (1999).
41. Strictly speaking, the raising of the retirement age had been passed in 1996, i.e. well before the 1997 pension reform, but most authors consider this measure to be part of the comprehensive pension reform package (e.g. Simonovits 1999). For an overview on the transitional rules for those retiring between 1998 and 2012 see Gerencsér (1997).
42. The accrual rate is the factor by which one additional year of service increases the assessment wage.

43. Assets are grouped in three categories according to risk. The riskiest assets must not come to more than 30 per cent of the total asset portfolio. Investment in foreign assets is prohibited in the first two years of operation, but the ceiling will be raised to 10 per cent in 2000 and to 30 per cent in 2001, considering Hungary's expected accession to the EU (see Ministry of Finance 1997: 8).

44. This guarantee amounts to 93 per cent of the pension obtained, should the insured have opted for the purely public pension path (see Palacios and Rocha 1997: 25).

45. An exception is provided in case of disability during the accumulation period: then, the insured will have the choice of either remaining in the new, mixed system or transferring his/her pension fund balances back to the public scheme and receiving full disability benefits (see Palacios and Rocha 1997: 24).

46. The individual VMB member can choose one out of four types of annuities: (1) lifelong annuity for a single person; (2) life annuity payable to the member *or* his/her inheritor until the expiry of a predetermined period; (3) life annuity paid to the member, followed by an inherited annuity for a fixed period; (4) multiple life annuity, payable to the member *and* his/her beneficiaries as long as at least one of them is alive (see Simonovits 1999: 220). Under certain conditions, a lump-sum payment may be chosen instead of an annuity.

47. The reduction is proportional to the share of the IFF premium to the total nominal contribution, hence resulting in an accrual rate of $23/31 \times 1.65 = 1.22$ (see Simonovits 1999: 219).

48. In addition, 'the Government's information campaign strongly advises older workers not to switch to the new scheme' (see Palacios and Rocha 1997: 22).

49. Palacios and Rocha (1997: 28) report that the Hungarian pension reformers, trying to spread transition costs across generations, decided to resort to debt-financing in the first years of the reform and to tax-financing in the following decade. See Palacios and Rocha (1997: 29–38) for a simulation of the fiscal impact of the Hungarian reform.

50. However, the Kazakh reform, that had been assisted by the World Bank (see World Bank 1998d), is highly controversial. Criticism mainly refers to the absence of a sound capital market in this Central-Asian republic.

51. 'In essence, the [Interest Reconciliation Council] was a more important forum for bargaining than parliament itself' (Orenstein 1998a: 36).

5. Pension Reform in Poland

5.1 THE LEGACY: RETIREMENT SCHEMES BEFORE 1989

In 1918, when the Polish state was re-established after more than a century of non-existence, the most distinctive feature of its pension system was a diversity of regimes, shaped by the late German, Austrian and Russian rulers. In the former German areas, blue- and white-collar workers were covered by separate pension systems, introduced in 1889 by Chancellor Bismarck. In the previous Austrian regions, an old-age scheme for salaried employees had been established in 1906. Contrary to this, there was no old-age insurance in the late Russian territories (see Świątkowski 1993: 193–4).

Hence, in the interwar period, efforts were made to unify the existing retirement schemes and to extend coverage, while at the same time protecting acquired rights. In 1927, a unified pension insurance for white-collar workers was established, granting earnings-related benefits. The retirement age was 60 for women and 65 for men. A unified pension system for blue-collar workers was set up in 1933. Strictly speaking, this scheme paid out invalidity pensions, as a separate old-age scheme did not exist. However, at the age of 65 both sexes qualified for this kind of benefit (see Żukowski 1994: 156). Benefits were based on a two-part formula, consisting of a flat-rate part and an earnings-related component, being lower than in the white-collar scheme.

Neither the blue- nor the white-collar pension insurance was set up as a self-governed scheme, following the earlier, failed attempt to set up a self-managed health insurance. Both old-age schemes were fully funded, financed by employees' and employers' contributions and administered by the Social Insurance Institute (*Zakład Ubezpieczeń Społecznych*, or ZUS), set up in 1933. However, miners, railwaymen, public sector employees and other groups were protected by separate pension schemes, some of them non-contributory, whereas farm-workers – amounting to one-third of the total labour force – were not covered at all. The task of building up a unified, universal old-age scheme had not been completed when the 1939 German and Soviet invasions put an end to the regained independence of Poland. In 1940,

the Nazi occupants deprived Poles from all social security benefits (see
Świątkowski 1993: 194–8; Żukowski 1994, 1996).[1]

When Polish old-age insurance was rebuilt after World War II, the new
communist rulers switched to PAYG financing, as the reserves of the previous
pension funds had been lost during the war (see Czepulis-Rutkowska 1999:
144). Other early measures comprised the abolition of employees'
contributions (1945) and the financial integration of the existing social
insurance funds into the state budget (1949). Moreover, efforts were made to
extend and unify the coverage of the public pension scheme: farm-workers,
who had remained without old-age protection in the interwar period, as well
as some groups previously covered by non-contributory schemes – civil
servants and public employees – were included into the universal scheme
between 1950 and 1954. On the other hand, soldiers, militiamen, policemen
and prison guards were granted non-contributory retirement benefits by the
state, remaining outside the social insurance system (see Florek 1993: 43–4).

The 1954 'Act on Common Retirement Pensions' removed the remaining
differences between the retirement schemes for white- and blue-collar
workers. However, it turned out that the old system of differentiation
concerning eligibility and benefits had been replaced by a new one. All
occupations were classified into two work categories, reflecting their strategic
importance for the development of the socialist economy. The first category,
for those doing heavy, unhealthy or otherwise special work, such as miners,
school teachers, university professors, journalists, firemen and customs
officers, was granted higher old-age benefits, and benefited from a lower
retirement age (see Florek 1986: 399). First-category workers could retire at
the age of 60 (men) and 55 (women), compared with age 65 and 60,
respectively, for second-category occupations. The required employment
period was 25 years (men) and 20 years (women). Pensions, financed
exclusively by employers' contributions, were partly earnings-related and
calculated according to a degressive benefit formula.[2] At first, benefit levels
depended on individual earnings in the last twelve months of employment.
From 1956, the best two consecutive years out of the last ten (later twelve)
years were considered.

The Social Insurance Institute, ZUS, a state institution subordinate to the
Minister of Labour, Wages and Social Affairs that had been established in the
interwar period, remained in charge of all social security schemes, including
the pension system, with the exception of the period from 1955 to 1960.[3]
ZUS's supervising boards were composed of trades unions' representatives
(three-fifths) and representatives of state administration and organisations
(two-fifths). As regards ZUS's finances, the Pension Fund was separated from
the state budget in 1968, whereas the entire Social Insurance Fund (*Fundusz*

Ubezpieczeń Społecznych, or FUS) followed only in 1986 (see Żukowski 1997: 138).

A second wave of coverage expansion started in the 1960s: members of agricultural co-operatives (1962), craftsmen (1965), artisans (1972), writers and artists (1973), individual farmers (1977) and, finally, members of the clergy (1989) were granted their own subschemes within the public scheme. These subschemes largely followed ZUS's eligibility and benefit rules (see Ministry of Labour 1983: 22–8; Florek 1993: 43; Świątkowski 1993: 202–3).

Table 5.1   Insured, pensioners and pensions in Poland, 1950–1980

Indicators	1950	1960	1970	1980
Number of insured at ZUS (in thousands)	5,155	7,524	11,069	14,029
Number of insured at ZUS (in % of the economically active population)	50.6	60.7	72.9	80.9
Pensioners in % of population in pension age	n.a	39.2	44.8	83.4
Replacement ratio* (current pensions)	17.6	39.7	51.2	46.3
Replacement ratio (newly granted pensions)	n.a.	n.a.	89.2	86.1

Note: * average pension in % of average wage

Sources: Ministry of Labour (1983); Główny Urząd Statystyczny (1997); own calculations.

During the post-war decades, current retirement benefits were adjusted in an *ad hoc* fashion but not systematically indexed. Hence, they lagged behind newly granted pensions (see Table 5.1), a problem known as '*stary portfel emerytalny*' ('old pension portfolio'): the longer a pension was drawn, the lower its purchasing power (see Żukowski 1997: 138). From the late 1960s, various efforts were made to increase pension levels (see Ministry of Labour 1983: 15–17), albeit with limited success. It was only after pressure was exerted by the newly emerging *Solidarność* movement and the subsequent period of martial law that the indexation of current benefits was enacted (see Flakierski 1991: 97–8).[4] In 1982, annual increases of pensions in line with the average wage increases of the previous year were scheduled. FUS's financial problems, however, delayed the implementation of this indexation mechanism until 1986 and, due to its backward-looking character and the built-in time lag, it proved insufficient to protect pensioners against the extremely high inflation rates from 1988 onwards (see Żukowski 1994: 162).[5] The problem of benefit adequacy was well-known to policymakers, and Polish scholars had been presenting proposals for dynamic benefit adjustment. But the financial difficulties of ZUS during the economic crisis of the 1980s led to a continuation of the low-benefit policy (see Sowada 1996: 6–7).

It can be concluded that the communist rulers perpetuated some of the Bismarckian elements of the pre-war period, while introducing many Beveridgean features (see Żukowski 1994: 169). Furthermore, they succeeded in substantially extending access to retirement benefits: coverage is reported to have been expanded from 25 per cent of the employed in the interwar period to 99 per cent in 1989 (see Florek 1993: 46). Nevertheless, the '*stary portfel*' problem remained unresolved until the end of the communist era, resulting not only in a serious distortion of relative benefit levels, but also in insufficient retirement incomes (see Żukowski 1996: 103). Hence, it comes as no surprise that, during the 1970s and 1980s, about 40 per cent of the Polish population at pension age continued their gainful employment, the most important source of income for three quarters of them (Czajka 1985: 2–3).[6]

5.2   OLD-AGE SECURITY IN TRANSFORMATION: INITIAL MEASURES

Transformation and Old-Age Security

Economic crisis and high inflation had been afflicting Poland well before 1989, leaving its mark on the public retirement scheme (see Kondratowicz and Okolski 1993; Lavigne 1995).[7] The financial strain on Polish pension finances was further aggravated by economic transformation. Whereas the number of employed Poles fell by 14.4 per cent between 1989 and 1996, the number of pensioners rose by 34.8 per cent over the same period (see Table 5.2). Among the latter, the number of old-age pensioners jumped by 46.3 per cent, while the ranks of disability pensioners increased by 22.1 per cent. This suggests that the existing pension system was used to a considerable extent as a substitute for unemployment benefits, providing permanent instead of temporary social benefits to those affected by the restructuring of state-owned enterprises (see Perraudin and Pujol 1994; Heinrich 1996).

Table 5.2 Population, employed and pensioners: Poland, 1989–1996

	1989	1990	1991	1992	1993	1994	1995	1996
Population (millions)	38.0	38.1	38.2	38.4	38.5	38.5	38.6	38.6
20–59 years old (thousands)	20,022	20,035	20,080	20,160	20,274	20,412	20,566	20,745
60+ years old (thousands)	5,604	5,728	5,820	5,914	5,981	6,051	6,129	6,203
Employed (thousands)	17,558	16,280	15,326	14,676	14,330	14,475	14,735	15,021
Pensioners (thousands)	6,827	7,104	7,944	8,495	8,730	8,910	9,085	9,200
Old-age pensioners (thousands)	2,264	2,353	2,775	2,982	3,081	3,155	3,230	3,313
Disability pensioners (thousands)	2,152	2,187	2,318	2,435	2,497	2,567	2,629	2,627

Source: Based on Schrooten, Smeeding and Wagner (1999).

As the number of contributors to the pension scheme fell while the number of beneficiaries was on the rise, the system dependency ratio increased from a moderate 38.9 (1989) to 61.2 per cent in 1996. The resulting financial crisis of the Polish pension scheme is reflected in a dramatically rising ratio of pension expenditures to GDP: between 1989 and 1996, public pension expenditures to GDP more than doubled, increasing from 6.6 to 14.5 per cent (see Table 5.3). Table 5.4 indicates that the Polish Social Security Fund (FUS) was in permanent need of subsidies from the state budget, amounting to as much as 4.3 per cent of GDP in 1992. Demographic trends did not have a major impact on Polish pension finances, as the old-age dependency ratio has increased only slightly since the late 1980s (see Table 5.3).

Table 5.3   The Polish pension system, 1989–1996: selected indicators

Indicators	1989	1990	1991	1992	1993	1994	1995	1996
Old-age dependency ratio[a]	28.0	28.6	29.0	29.3	29.5	29.6	29.8	29.9
System dependency ratio[b]	38.9	43.6	51.8	57.9	60.9	61.6	60.7	61.2
Replacement ratio[c]	53.3	65.0	76.1	72.5	72.8	74.8	74.5	72.5
Pension expenditures in % of GDP	6.6	8.1	12.6	14.6	14.6	15.4	14.6	14.5

Notes: [a] 60+ years old in % of 20–59 years old
           [b] pensioners in % of contributors
           [c] average pension in % of average wage

Source: Based on Schrooten, Smeeding and Wagner (1999).

The following sections will review the early measures taken by the post-1989 governments to change the existing Polish pension scheme in terms of its organisation, financing, eligibility and benefits. Until late 1998, the public retirement system remained the only provider of old-age security, as there were neither voluntary nor mandatory private pension funds in Poland.[8] Although the State Insurance Company PZU had started offering individual retirement plans since the early 1970s, they fell into disuse when suffering massive depreciation during the high inflation of the 1980s and 1990s (see Topińska 1995: 65). So far, private insurance companies have only hesitantly stepped in (see Benio and Mladenova 1997: 140).

Organisation

The Polish old-age insurance scheme continues to be administered by the Social Insurance Institute, ZUS, an institution established in the interwar period. It is part of public administration, operating under the supervision of the Ministry of Labour and Social Policy. Since 1996, the Board has been composed of representatives of the insured and pensioners (one-half), employers (one-quarter) and the Ministry of Labour and Social Policy (one-quarter).[9] Since, however, the powers of this Board are limited, there is no real self-governance in ZUS (see Żukowski 1996: 106; Götting 1998: 163). ZUS does not only grant old-age, disability and survivors' pensions, but also other types of social benefits, such as sickness, delivery, maternity and funeral benefits (see Zakład Ubezpieczeń Społecznych 1997a).

Alongside ZUS, there are two other public pension schemes in Poland, one covering individual farmers and the other one the so-called 'uniformed services'.[10] Since 1991, farmers' pensions have been managed by a separate, highly subsidised scheme, KRUS (*Kasa Rolniczego Ubezpieczenia Społecznego*, or Farmers' Social Insurance Fund).[11] KRUS operates under the supervision of the Ministry of Agriculture, and the benefit and eligibility rules differ considerably from the ones in the ZUS scheme (see Boller 1997: 152–4; Golinowska, Czepulis-Rutkowska and Szczur 1997). Originally, farmers were supposed to pay one-third of total contributions, but the budgetary subsidy soon rose to 90 per cent of KRUS's revenues. In 1996, budgetary subsidies to KRUS amounted to 2.0 per cent of GDP and were thus even higher than subsidies to ZUS, totalling 1.8 per cent (see Schrooten, Smeeding and Wagner 1999: 283). Still, this expensive scheme proved to be immune to all reform attempts, as the Polish Peasant Party, PSL, had a strong position within government in 1993–1997 (see Golinowska 1999: 188).

The third scheme, covering policemen, soldiers and prison guards, is financed directly from the state budget. The uniformed groups receive their pensions from the respective ministries, without any previous contribution payments. On average, these non-insurance benefits are considerably higher than ZUS pensions (see Czepulis-Rutkowska 1999: 146–8).

Among these three schemes, ZUS is the largest provider of retirement pensions, with 65.4 per cent of the total, while KRUS pays out 31.3 per cent of all old-age benefits and the scheme for the uniformed services accounts for 3.3 per cent (see Cichon 1995: A3-154). In the remainder of this chapter, I will only refer to the old-age scheme administered by ZUS.

Financing

The mandatory public pension scheme administered by ZUS is based on PAYG financing. Revenues derive from contributions and state budget transfers. Contributions to the Polish Social Security Fund, FUS, amount to 36.7 per cent of standardised gross wage and are still to be paid by employers alone.[12] ZUS keeps no individual contributions records, except for the self-employed. Due to the financial problems of many firms and/or the lack of efficient sanctions, compliance is reported to have been low: in 1993, outstanding contributions amounted to 16.6 per cent of total annual contributions, or 1.5 per cent of GDP (see Maret and Schwartz 1994: 71). It should be noted that, in the context of two-digit inflation, late payment inflicted substantial financial losses on FUS. Compliance of state enterprises has been particularly low – they owed well over 70 per cent of unpaid contributions between 1991 and 1996 (see Golinowska and Żukowski 1998: 22).

The effective financial balance of the Polish pension system is hard to assess, as contributions are not earmarked for the retirement scheme, and 13.4 per cent of total FUS expenditures are made up by non-pension benefits (1996). But Table 5.4 indicates that, between 1992 and 1995, budgetary subsidies were higher than the amount needed to cover FUS's non-pension expenditures. In other words, a contribution rate as high as 36.7 per cent of standardised gross wage was not enough to cover pension expenditures in Poland. Consequently, from 1989 budgetary subsidies had to be paid to FUS, fluctuating between 1.1 and 4.3 per cent of GDP, while total pension expenditures reached 14–15 per cent of GDP (see Table 5.3). This dramatic increase in pension expenditures can be explained by a wave of early retirees and by a substantial increase in the real value of benefits, to be set forth in the next section.

Table 5.4   The Polish Social Security Fund, 1989–1996 (in per cent of GDP)

	1989	1990	1991	1992	1993	1994	1995	1996
Revenues of which:	8.0	9.9	13.8	16.1	16.0	16.2	14.7	14.5
– contributions	6.9	8.4	11.1	11.8	11.8	12.3	12.6	12.7
– budget	1.1	1.5	2.7	4.3	4.2	3.9	2.1	1.8
Expenditures[a] of which:	8.6	9.1	14.2	15.8	15.8	16.1	14.4	14.2
– pensions	5.8	6.9	10.9	12.8	12.7	13.2	12.4	12.3
– others	2.8	2.2	3.3	3.0	3.1	2.9	2.0	1.9
'Quasi-balance'[b]	−1.7	−0.7	−0.6	1.3	1.1	1.0	0.1	−0.1

Notes: [a] Please note that pension expenditure data differ from the ones given in Table 5.3. This discrepancy is not explained by the authors.
[b] budgetary subsidies to FUS minus FUS's non-pension expenditures

Source: Based on Schrooten, Smeeding and Wagner (1999); own calculations.

Eligibility and Benefits

As noted in the section on organisation, the Polish pension system is still far from being uniform. In the area of eligibility, there is further heterogeneity, as many of the old branch privileges remain in force, granting earlier retirement and higher benefits. To become eligible for a regular old-age pension, the insured must have reached age 65 (men) and 60 (women); respectively.

Furthermore, men require 25 and women 20 qualifying years, including eligible non-contributory periods, such as periods of university studies and care for children and frail persons. Non-contributory periods must not exceed one-third of contributory periods.

There are many windows for early retirement in Poland, none of which imply a reduction of old-age benefits. For instance, women with 30 years of employment can retire at 55.[13] Moreover, between 1991 and 1996, men with 40 and women with 35 qualifying years were entitled to retire notwithstanding their age, if they had been made redundant. Some privileged professions, such as those of miners, teachers and railwaymen, also enable early retirement. The scope of early retirement in Poland is highlighted by the fact that, in 1996, 39.5 per cent of all male and 28 per cent of all female recipients of an old-age pension had not yet reached the retirement age (see Zakład Ubezpieczeń Społecznych 1997b: 13).[14] The effective retirement age for both men and women is six years lower than the statutory age (see Mazur 1997: 219). Estimates suggest that over 40 per cent of old-age pensioners remain employed, while at the same time drawing full benefits, which is legally possible unless both sources of income exceed 120 per cent of the average wage (see Wiktorow 1996: 64). However, this practice conflicts with the original intention to use the pension scheme as an instrument of the labour market (see Lodahl and Schrooten 1998: 274–5). The cost of early retirement is estimated at 12 percentage points of the total nominal contribution rate of 45 per cent (see Góra and Rutkowski 1998: 19).

A new old-age benefit formula was introduced in 1990/1991, containing a universal lump-sum component and an individualised earnings-related element (see Götting 1998: 164–5). To resolve the '*stary portfel*' problem, all current pensions were reassessed on the basis of the new formula (see Żukowski 1994: 165). The new formula can be expressed as

$$P = B + (0.013 \cdot C + 0.007 \cdot N) \, AB,$$

where P = monthly old-age pension, B = universal base component, amounting to 24 per cent of the national average wage, C = number of contributory years and N = number of eligible non-contributory years. For every year of contribution payments, 1.3 per cent of the assessment base are credited, while each non-contributory year adds 0.7 per cent. The personal assessment basis, AB, is calculated according to the following formula (1998):

$$AB = [(AW_1/N_1 + \dots + AW_9/N_9) \cdot 1/9] \, N,$$

where AW = individual monthly average wage and N = national average wage. In 1998, the best consecutive 9 years out of the last 18 years prior to retirement were the relevant earnings for AW. Since 1992, when it was 3 out of 12 years, this period has been gradually extended, to reach 10 out of 20 years in 2000. The personal assessment basis AB must not exceed 2.5 times the national average wage. It should be noted that there is no such ceiling on contribution payments (see Topińska 1995: 62; Czepulis-Rutkowska 1999: 148–50).

In the pre-1989 years, benefit erosion had been considered the most pressing problem of the Polish pension scheme. Hence, when automatic indexation of old-age benefits to wage increases was introduced in 1990, it was welcomed as substantial progress.[15] Meanwhile, benefit indexation is seen as one of the most important factors accounting for the dramatic surge in pension expenditures (see Table 5.4), and in 1997, a switch from wage- to price-based indexation was enacted.[16]

As pointed out by Leven (1996), most Poles perceive old-age pensioners as having been more impoverished by transition than the rest of society, although available data do not support this notion (see Schwartz 1994: 86; Grootaert 1995).[17] The replacement rate has been raised from its rather low level in 1989 to well over 70 per cent of the average wage since 1991 (see Table 5.3). But even if, on average, pensioners have done better than the rest of Polish society, widely divergent benefit levels still prevail (see Leven 1996: 125–7; Zakład Ubezpieczeń Społecznych 1997b: 24). In early 1998, the average old-age pension paid out by ZUS amounted to US\$ 240 (see Czepulis-Rutkowska 1999: 148).

5.3   THE WAY TOWARDS SYSTEMIC PENSION REFORM

The Limits of the Early Reforms

The previous subchapter has made it clear that the post-1989 changes in organisation, eligibility and benefits did not succeed in making the Polish pension system financially viable. The trade-off between fiscal restraint and benefit adequacy faced by policymakers in transition economies was resolved in favour of the latter. While the '*stary portfel*' problem had been tackled, the replacement rate was substantially increased and automatic benefit indexation shielded Polish pensioners from old-age poverty, the retirement scheme was dependent on sizeable state subsidies and suffered from high contribution rates, a heavy burden on labour costs (see Perraudin and Pujol 1994: 670). The current Polish old-age scheme has also been criticised on fairness grounds, due to the strong redistributive element in the pension formula and the unequal benefit and eligibility rules for different professions.

Hence, social policy experts coincided in their analysis that the Polish pension system was in dire need of further reform. Yet, apart from a minimum consensus that it had to be made uniform, contributory and more transparent (see Mazur 1997: 220), there was considerable disagreement regarding the basic paradigmatic course to be followed when heading towards comprehensive reform. Moreover, policymakers had experienced strong resistance from the 'grey lobby' – notably pensioners' associations and trades unions (see below) – when trying to introduce relatively modest reforms in the early 1990s, such as a change in the pension formula, the modification of indexation rules and the abolition of branch privileges (see Sosenko 1995: 16–24). In many cases, successful appeals to the Constitutional Tribunal accompanied the public protests against the curtailment of pension benefits (see Żukowski 1996: 109; Götting 1998: 165; Hausner 1998: 14). Thus it comes as no surprise that many observers took a pessimistic view of the chances to reform old-age security in Poland: 'Redesigning the pension scheme is considered a political death wish in a country with a growing sentimentality for the good old days of guaranteed social benefits' (Rey 1996: 18).

Conflicting Blueprints for Comprehensive Reform

Since the early 1990s, a number of drafts for a comprehensive reform of the Polish pension system have been elaborated. While, in 1991, Chilean-style pension privatisation had been proposed by two social security experts (see Topiński and Wiśniewski 1991), the subsequent reform blueprints elaborated by the Ministry of Labour aimed at a thorough reform of ZUS, without introducing a mandatory IFF tier. Soon, a long-standing, polarised debate was unleashed about the pension reform strategy to be followed (see Golinowska, Czepulis-Rutkowska and Szczur 1997; Golinowska 1999), that reflected the international pension controversy reviewed in subchapter 2.4.

On the one side, the Ministry of Finance and some social security experts, mainly economists, advocated Latin American-style pension privatisation (see subchapter 2.3), arguing that a fundamental regime change was inevitable. In their view, a private IFF pension scheme represented the only appropriate alternative to the financially inviable public old-age security system. They were joined by the NSZZ *Solidarność* trade union.[18] The privatisation of Polish old-age security was also supported by the World Bank, a major external actor in pension reform with its internationally well-known stance. A shift to funding was claimed to have four major advantages: extra savings would be channelled into productive investment, thereby contributing to economic growth. In the longer term, the retirement system would be safeguarded against population ageing. Political pressure to increase benefit levels would be avoided, as an IFF scheme allows for higher pensions only if the capital stock increases. Finally, by setting up pension funds, new institutional investors are created that would assist privatisation (see Topiński and Wiśniewski 1991; World Bank 1993: 81).

On the other side, following the traditional Bismarckian–Beveridgean pension paradigm, there was the Ministry of Labour and another group of social security experts, mainly professors of social insurance law, who held that there was a great potential in the present social insurance system and considered a thorough reform of ZUS – including price indexation of benefits and an increase in the effective pension age – to be sufficient. A radical regime change in old-age security was seen not only as superfluous but also as detrimental by this faction, as it contradicted the legal doctrine of social insurance and threatened to destroy social solidarity (see Hausner 1998: 16–17; Nelson 1998: 16). Furthermore, the advocates of pension privatisation were criticised for prioritising economic objectives, such as the development of the capital market, over the social objectives of an old-age security system (see e.g. Kalina-Prasznic 1997; Jończyk 1997).

After having outlined the basic paradigmatic controversy, I will now briefly review the most important proposals put forward to reform the Polish pension system, before analysing the political dynamics that finally resulted in bringing about systemic reform in Poland.[19]

Advocates of Pension Privatisation

The very first proposal for comprehensive pension reform in post-1989 Poland was presented in 1991 by two social security experts, Wojciech Topiński and Marian Wiśniewski. Interestingly, Topiński was ZUS president in 1990/91 and had visited Chile, acquainting himself with pension privatisation. Topiński and Wiśniewski still departed considerably from the Latin American precedents by designing a *sui generis* mixed system, comprising two tiers: a PAYG tier, mandatory for all, insuring the part of the individual's salary below a threshold of 120 per cent of average earnings (see Topiński and Wiśniewski 1991). Additionally, individuals should be required to pay contributions on earnings above this threshold into a private IFF scheme. In spite of the foregone contributions for wages above 120 per cent of the average salary, current old-age and disability pensions would still have to be paid out by ZUS. Debt-financing of the resulting transition costs was suggested by the authors (see Tymowska and Wiśniewski 1993: 227–9).[20]

*Table 5.5   Early proposals for systemic pension reform in Poland**

Proponents	Topiński and Wiśniewski (1991)	Ministry of Finance Mazur (1995)	NSZZ Solidarność (1995)
First tier			
Type	public, mandatory, earnings-related	public, mandatory, flat-rate	public, mandatory; flat-rate + earnings-related component
Financing	PAYG	PAYG; 1/4 of total contributions	PAYG; taxes and contributions
Level	current ZUS formula	20% of average earnings	n.a.
Second tier			
Type	private, mandatory for those with salary above 120% of average earnings	private, ultimately mandatory for all	private, ultimately mandatory for all
Financing	IFF; 1/2 of total contributions	IFF; 3/4 of total contributions	IFF; 1/3 of total contributions
Level	defined contribution	defined contribution	defined contribution; can be modified in collective agreements

Note: * Please note that, due to space limitations, some privatisation proposals have not been not included in this analysis, notably Przedstawicielstwo (1996) and Golinowska (1997).

Source: Based on Golinowska (1999); own modifications.

In the early 1990s, the pension privatisation proposal was considered to be a too radical departure from the *status quo* in Polish old-age security. It was only in early 1994 that Topiński and Wiśniewski gathered a larger, like-minded audience at a conference mainly attended by social security experts with an economic background (see IPiSS and Institute for East West Studies 1995; Topiński and Wiśniewski 1995). However, another group of social security experts expressed strong opposition to a mandatory private old-age scheme, particularly professors of law, whose notion of old-age insurance excluded private providers. Moreover, the transition costs of a shift to funding, estimated at an additional 5 per cent of GDP for over a dozen years, were regarded as prohibitive (see Golinowska 1999: 180–1).

When presented to a Polish audience in 1994, the World Bank's newly designed pension reform concept encountered similar reservations (see Golinowska 1999: 180–1). The Bank's recommendations to reform Polish old-age security had included pension privatisation even before its universal strategy was promoted on a world-wide scale (see World Bank 1993, 1994b). In its 1994 country study, the Bank proposed a multi-tier system, consisting of two public tiers – a basic flat-rate social assistance tier and an income-related defined benefit tier – and a private IFF tier. All three tiers should be mandatory (see World Bank 1994b: 36–8).

In spite of its overall critical reception and the high fiscal costs associated with such a move, pension privatisation appealed to the Polish Ministry of Finance. Shortly after assuming office in April 1994, Minister Grzegorz Kołodko announced the so-called 'Strategy for Poland', an important policy document that included a transition to a funded pension scheme (see Kołodko 1996: 63). The main rationale behind this move, from the Ministry of Finance's point of view, was to limit the budgetary subsidies to the public pension system – certainly a long-term fiscal goal in the light of the considerable transition costs arising in the short and medium run (see Żukowski 1996: 121). The Ministry of Finance's thrust was, in turn, supported by the World Bank (see Barbone 1997: 34).

When the Ministry of Labour refused to operationalise the proposed move to funding (see below), the Ministry of Finance commissioned its advisor Marek Mazur to elaborate a blueprint for pension privatisation, clearly inspired by World Bank (1994a).[21] Mazur, acquainted with the Southern precedents after a study trip to Latin America, designed a parallel old-age system (see subchapter 2.3), in which the insured would be given a choice between a reformed ZUS and a newly created system of private IFF pension funds. The reform of ZUS proposed by Mazur sought to down-size this public tier by weakening the contribution–benefit link and fixing the base component at 20 per cent of the average wage. Furthermore, he suggested the introduction of an employees' contribution and the equalisation of the retirement age for men and women (see Mazur 1996). Mazur's blueprint was never formally submitted to government, but succeeded in having a considerable paradigmatic impact (see Orenstein 1998a: 45). The privatisation proposal was supported by the financial sector, mainly insurance companies and banks, the natural constituency of a mandatory IFF tier (see Nelson 1998: 15; Golinowska 1999: 181).

Interestingly, in 1995, a trade union joined the ranks of the advocates of pension privatisation. NSZZ *Solidarność*'s proposal (see Lewicka et al. 1996) suggests the conversion of ZUS into a public law institution with mandatory participation, accompanied by a second private IFF tier which is to be mandatory, except in the case of supplementary contribution under collective labour contracts ('contracting out').

The blueprints put forward by advocates of pension privatisation clearly reflect the paradigmatic influence of the Latin American precedents.[22] Apart from the reception of the Chilean experience by Topiński and Wiśniewski on the one hand, and Mazur on the other, a major channel for the transmission of the Southern experiences has been World Bank advice. In order to provide first hand information on Latin American pension reforms, the World Bank and USAID sponsored trips to Argentina and Chile for Polish social security experts, journalists, trades unionists and MPs. Moreover, individual Latin American reformers passed on their experiences to Polish policymakers, in person or via their writing (see e.g. Schulthess and Demarco 1995; Zabala 1995). A prominent example for the latter is the Polish edition of José Piñera's description of – what he calls – the 'Chilean pension reform battle' (Piñera 1996), with a preface by a Polish economist entitled 'Let's learn from the Chileans!' (Wilczyński 1996; own translation).[23]

The 'Bismarckian–Beveridgean Faction'

As noted above, there was by no means a consensus regarding the need to privatise the Polish old-age scheme. Following the traditional Bismarckian–Beveridgean pension paradigms, the Ministry of Labour and Social Policy and most professors of social insurance law have long opposed such a radical move. The pension reform blueprints put forward by this faction will briefly be reviewed below (see Table 5.6).

In 1993, the Ministry of Labour presented a pension reform draft, the so-called 'White Paper' (see Ministry of Labour 1993). The main co-ordinator of this project was the then vice-minister of Labour and Social Policy, Irena Wóycicka. The White Paper aimed chiefly at a reform of ZUS, and suggested a two-tier public PAYG system, consisting of a universal, flat-rate tier and an earnings-related component. In addition, a voluntary private IFF tier was to be created. Other reforms proposed in the White Paper included the introduction of an employees' contribution, a ceiling on contribution payments, an increase in the retirement age of women and the strengthening of the contribution–benefit link. At that time, the conviction that pension reform was necessary at all was not particularly widespread (see Góra and Rutkowski 1998: 5). Hence, the Ministry of Labour's reform blueprint, starting with the observation that the 'Polish social insurance system is in crisis' (Ministry of Labour 1993: 2), met with a controversial response. The White Paper, published in May 1993, was never put into practice, since early parliamentary elections, held in September 1993, resulted in a change of government (see Żukowski 1996: 121).

In his 'Strategy for Poland', Kołodko, the new Minister of Finance and Deputy Prime Minister within the post-communist government of SLD (*Sojusz Lewicy Demokratycznej*, or Left Democratic Alliance) and PSL (*Polskie Stronnictwo Ludowe*, or Polish Peasant Party) suggested, amongst other things, to move towards pension privatisation (see above).[24] In spite of its controversial reception, this strategy had been passed by the Sejm in late 1994 and, subsequently, was to be implemented by the respective ministries. Hence, the Ministry of Labour was responsible for developing a draft for the partial privatisation of old-age security. However, this portfolio, headed by Leszek Miller, was adamantly opposed to a shift to funding (see Nelson 1998: 9). Consequently, the reform blueprint presented by the Ministry in April 1995 stuck to the previously followed Bismarckian–Beveridgean course (see Ministry of Labour 1995a).

Like the 1993 draft, the new reform concept proposed a two-tier public PAYG system, to be supplemented by a voluntary IFF scheme. The draft suggested extending the universal part of the public pension system at the expense of the insurance-related part by introducing a tax-financed, flat-rate 'civic pension', amounting to 30 per cent of the national average wage (see Żukowski 1996: 122–3). This concept, that had been accepted as a government draft in May 1995, met with strong criticism (see IPiSS 1995; RSSG 1995; Borowczyk 1996). Opinion polls revealed that the proposed universal, flat-rate state pension conflicted with the prevailing notion of justice, as an earnings-related approach was more popular with the majority of the Polish population (see Golinowska 1999: 181). After extensive consultation with social partners and pensioners' representatives, the original proposal was modified in December 1995, leaving aside all redistributive elements and establishing a strong contribution–benefit link (see Ministry of Labour 1995b).

Towards a Consensus in Pension Reform

The above review has made it clear that, in 1996, there were three major pension reform proposals in Poland, the first by the Ministry of Labour and Social Policy, the second by the Ministry of Finance and the third by NSZZ *Solidarność*. All of these reform drafts were designed as multi-tier arrangements, comprising a PAYG and an IFF tier, but the roles assigned to both tiers differed considerably between the first draft on the one hand, and the second and third drafts on the other (see Tables 5.5 and 5.6).

Table 5.6   *A comparison of the Polish Ministry of Labour's reform*
              proposals

Proponents	Ministry of Labour (1993)*	Ministry of Labour (May 1995)*	Office of Gov't Plenipotentiary (1996)
First tier			
Type	public, mandatory, flat-rate	public, flat-rate, tax-financed, universal	public, mandatory, earnings-related
Financing	PAYG; contribution split between employers and employees	PAYG	PAYG; contribution split between employers and employees
Level	n.a.	30% of national average wage	notional defined contribution
Second tier			
Type	public, mandatory, earnings-related	public, mandatory, earnings-related	private; ultimately mandatory for all
Financing	PAYG; contribution split between employers and employees	PAYG; contribution split between employers and employees	IFF; financed only by employees' contributions
Level	n.a.	n.a.	defined contribution

Note: * Additionally, these proposals include a voluntary IFF tier.

Source: Based on Golinowska (1999); own modifications.

For a year and a half, there was a stalemate between the portfolios of Labour and Finance – both manned by SLD ministers – on the pension reform issue (see Rey 1996: 18).[25] It was ended by a paradigmatic shift in the Ministry of Labour's stance, moving considerably closer to the Ministry of Finance's earlier pension reform blueprint, even though the Ministry of Labour's reform draft had already been accepted as the official government proposal in May 1995. The shift in the Ministry of Labour's position followed a cabinet reshuffle in February 1996 in which Leszek Miller was shifted from the Ministry of Labour to another portfolio, being replaced by Andrzej Bączkowski, an independent with a *Solidarność* background within the SLD-PSL cabinet. The replacement of Miller by Bączkowski has been interpreted as a defeat of the Ministry of Labour in another pension-related conflict with the Ministry of Finance (see Orenstein 1996: 19; Götting 1998: 165–6): between 1993 and 1995, there had been considerable dispute between both portfolios about the indexation formula for old-age benefits pensions.[26]

After having been appointed government plenipotentiary for pension reform in August 1996, Bączkowski set up a special task force for old-age reform, the so-called 'Office of the Government Plenipotentiary for Social Security Reform'.[27] This Office was attached to the Ministry of Labour and headed by a World Bank economist on leave, Michał Rutkowski, firmly committed to the Bank's blueprint for pension privatisation. Subsequently, the Polish reform team was actively supported by the World Bank, which provided international networking as well as technical and financial support (see IPiSS 1997; A.F.T. 1998a; Kavalsky 1998; Nelson 1998).[28]

In October 1996, under the heading 'Pension 2000' a rough outline of the pension reform plans prepared by the Office of the Government Plenipotentiary was published (see A.F.T. 1996; Biuro 1996; Koral 1996b). The proposal was deliberately presented as a synthesis of the three major pension reform proposals mentioned above, put forward by the Ministry of Labour, the Ministry of Finance and NSZZ *Solidarność*. A closer look reveals, however, that the Office's draft contains few if any elements of the first blueprint (see Table 5.6).[29]

Bączkowski's team proposed to supplement a reformed, down-sized ZUS with a newly created mandatory tier of private IFF pension funds. While it would be mandatory for young people to join the latter, those between age 30 and 50 would be able to choose between a purely public and a mixed pension option. Concerning the reforms envisaged in the existing public PAYG scheme, the Office announced the abolishment of all social components, e.g. the universal lump-sum component within the pension formula and the recognition of non-contributory periods. Branch privileges would only be granted on condition that higher contributions be paid. Benefit levels would be strictly related to the average life expectancy at retirement and to previous contribution payments of the individual, requiring the establishment of historical, individualised contributions records at ZUS, so-called 'notional accounts', from 1 January 1998. There would be a minimum pension age (62), allowing the insured to retire later with a considerably higher pension. Owing to the reform, current pensioners and people close to retirement would neither benefit nor lose, as today's benefit and eligibility rules would continue to apply to them, and they would have no access to the second, IFF tier. With its mixed overall approach, the Polish reform draft was clearly inspired by the

Argentine reform precedent, while also exhibiting elements of the recent Latvian and Swedish reform in the first tier – the pension formula and the notional defined contribution accounts (see subchapters 2.2 and 2.3). Hence, the Polish design choices reflect both the co-operation with World Bank experts and with a Swedish advisory team (see Office 1997: i).

When in November 1996 Bączkowski died unexpectedly at the age of 41, the work of the Office of the Government Plenipotentiary towards systemic pension reform had only just begun. As Bączkowski had turned into the most important individual actor in Polish pension reform, it was feared that without him the Office, whose collaborators were closer to the liberal UW (*Unia Wolności*, or Freedom Union) than to the then governing SLD-PSL parties, might lack the necessary political backing (see Koral 1996a; Piskorski 1997). But although the new Minister of Labour, Tadeusz Zieliński, opposed radical pension reform, the envisaged reform path was continued, partly reflecting a cross-party gentlemen's agreement about the need for systemic pension reform (see Golinowska 1999: 182). Moreover, Jerzy Hausner, a former advisor to the Minister of Finance who was nominated Government Plenipotentiary for social security reform in February 1997, succeeded in getting the Office attached to the Prime Minister, thereby removing it institutionally from the Ministry of Labour and gaining room for manœuvre, so as to carry on with the pension reform project (see Hausner 1998: 20; Nelson 1998: 9). He was firmly backed by Kołodko's successor, Marek Belka, the new Minister of Finance, who stressed the need to move speedily ahead with pension reform (see Bobinski 1997).

With its new extra-ministerial leeway and the political backing of the Ministry of Finance, the Prime Minister and the President, the Office of the Government Plenipotentiary intensified its preparations for systemic pension reform. In February 1997, a hundred-page report provided detailed information on the Office's reform plans, coining the catchy slogan 'Security through Diversity' for the envisaged multi-tierism (see Biuro 1997).[30] Moreover, a uniform logo, graphically representing the dawning of a new era in old-age security, was used on every document and at all public events concerning the envisaged pension reform, exemplifying the professional PR management of the reform process.

Legislating Radical Reform in Poland

Minister Bączkowski's original aim was to get the pension reform laws passed before the upcoming parliamentary elections that were due in September 1997 (see Koral 1996b), but time proved to be too short to effectively pass the whole of the reform package within a few months. This implied postponing the envisaged reform start from 1 January 1998 to early

1999. Furthermore, the original package deal of bundling up the politically difficult reforms of ZUS with the fairly popular introduction of private pension funds was abandoned.[31] Instead, the SLD-PSL coalition resorted to unbundling and deliberate sequencing: while the laws on the private pension fund tiers were enacted in summer 1997, the more intricate part – ZUS reforms – was left to the incoming UW-AWS government. In the context of the election campaign, this new strategy was also chosen by the SLD-PSL government, to present itself with a nearly completed pension reform, even though only the easiest part of this task had been accomplished (see Żukowski 1999: 170).[32] In any case, it is interesting to note that the former Polish government found it politically attractive to start a radical pension reform in a pre-electoral situation.

In June and August 1997, three pension reform laws were passed that concern the second and third tier, as well as the financing of the costs of the partial privatisation of Polish old-age security: the 'Act on Using Means from Privatisation of State Assets for Social Insurance Reform' of 25 June 1997, intended to partially cover the arising transition costs, the 'Act on Employee Pension Programmes' of 22 August 1997, introducing occupational schemes as possible third-tier institutions, and the 'Act on Organisation and Financing of Pension Funds' of 28 August 1997, concerning the functioning of the yet to be created second tier (see Łoboda and Szałkiewicz-Zaradzka 1998; Żukowski 1999: 168–9). The two remaining draft laws on first-tier reforms were expected to be politically sensitive, as they included issues such as raising the retirement age, lowering the minimum pension, slowing down indexation and abolishing occupational privileges, currently granted to one in every four Poles (see Markiewicz 1998: 25).

Unexpectedly, the reform did not lose momentum after the change of government in autumn 1997. In spite of the politically difficult task left to them by their predecessors, the new UW-AWS government decided to continue the reform started by their political opponents, the previous SLD-PSL coalition (see AWS and UW 1997: 12–13) – a rare exception in the Polish context: 'In the past, a new political constellation had often started to work on the [pension] reform from scratch' (Żukowski 1999: 169). The continuation of the reform course can be explained by the above-mentioned cross-party consensus about the need for systemic pension reform (see Rymsza 1998: 3). Moreover, the new coalition could well be expected to carry on with the reform, given its political closeness to the pension reform team: Bączkowski, the first plenipotentiary for social security reform, was an early member of *Solidarność*, and the Office staff had an UW background. In late 1997, Ewa Lewicka, NSZZ *Solidarność*'s senior pension expert, was appointed Vice-Minister of Labour, as well as Government Plenipotentiary for Social Security Reform (see Żukowski 1999: 160). In the pension reform issue, she has a higher profile than the new Minister of Labour, Longin Komołowski.

In May 1998, the two remaining draft laws were submitted to the Sejm: the 'Act on the Social Insurance System', the so-called *'ustawa matka'* ('mother law'), stipulating the allocation of old-age security functions between ZUS and the newly created second tier, and the 'Act on Pensions from the Social Insurance Fund', containing the unpopular ZUS reforms. An all-party parliamentary committee was set up to prepare the passage of both laws, but started its work only in July (see Rymsza 1998).

As expected, considerable debate surrounded the efforts to reform the existing public tier, ZUS, resulting in modifications of the original reform drafts (see Rymsza 1998: 5–6). Attempts to equalise the retirement age for men and women until the year 2035 had to be withdrawn from the draft law, mainly due to resistance from trades unions (see A.F.T. 1998a). The reformers' intention to abolish the pensioners' right to go on working while drawing a pension was criticised on legal grounds (see Jędrasik-Jankowska 1998). Hence, the draft law was modified, allowing those who have reached the pension age to draw a pension and earn a salary at the same time, without any ceiling, whereas those retiring early will be subject to roughly the same limits as today. An alternative proposal was to forbid early retirees the current 'double-dipping' altogether (see A.F.T. 1998c; Góra and Rutkowski 1998: 20). Furthermore, the idea of abolishing the non-contributory benefits granted to the so-called 'uniformed services' was only partially put into practice, introducing mandatory contributions only for those who were to start their service after 1 January 1999 (see Koral 1998). The reform was also criticised on fiscal grounds: the SLD opposition in parliament warned that the envisaged pension reform would lead to a 'financial catastrophe' (see Olczyk and Pilczyński 1998).

After an unusually short legislative process, the 'mother law' was enacted on 13 October 1998, following an urgent request of Stanisław Alot, the president of ZUS, who had pointed to the extensive preparations necessary to enable a reform start on schedule, including a full computerisation of ZUS. Finally, the last remaining law was passed by the Sejm on 26 November 1998. Due to the late passage of these laws, the overall launch of the Polish pension reform had to be partially postponed: whereas ZUS reforms were scheduled to start from 1 January 1999, private pension funds would commence operations only on 1 April 1999.

Other Forces Shaping Pension Reform

When they tried to bring about comprehensive pension reform, the main political actors considered in the above analysis – the Ministries of Finance and Welfare, as well as the World Bank – by no means acted within a political vacuum. It is suggested here that the constellation of these main actors determined the basic paradigmatic outcome of Polish pension reform –

the shift towards a mandatory private pension fund tier – while the demands and protests of other groups did shape some of the details of Polish pension reform policy. The above analysis has shown that Polish policymakers were particularly willing to compromise on first pillar reforms, in order to gain the approval of potential opponents of the envisaged systemic reform.

The pension reform team was well aware of the need to engender social support for the radical change of old-age security (see Hausner 1997: 9; Office 1997: 179). As noted above, Polish policymakers had experienced strong resistance from the 'grey lobby' – notably pensioners' representatives and trades unions – in the early 1990s, when they tried to introduce relatively modest reforms, such as a change in the pension formula, the modification of indexation rules and the abolition of branch privileges. Hence, consultations with social partners and with pensioners' organisations formed part of the reformers' agenda. The formal forum for discussion with the former was the *Komisja Trójstronna*, or Tripartite Commission (see Nawacki 1995); yet a smaller and less formal group was set up to screen the pension reform process (see Nelson 1998: 12).[33]

Having a large number of pensioners among their members, the Polish trades unions have traditionally appeared as relevant political actors in the pension reform arena. In the early 1990s, both the post-communist OPZZ, which is part of SLD, and NSZZ *Solidarność*, a strong faction within AWS, have fiercely opposed even modest attempts to reform Polish old-age security. Hence, it is interesting to note that nowadays both unions seem to agree with the Polish government's radical reform plans (see Gadomski and Adamczewska 1997; Golinowska 1999: 186).

Within OPZZ, there is even a special institution for pensioners, called 'Council of Labour Veterans', with strong links to the pensioners' party KPEiR (see below). Having been critical towards systemic pension reform for a long time, OPZZ finally accepted this type of reform in principle, but emphasised certain conditions (see OPZZ 1997). 'OPZZ's conditional support often translated into effective opposition at the legislative stage' (Orenstein 1998a: 54). Recently, OPZZ has set out to participate in the mandatory pension fund business, jointly with the National Chamber of Industry and Commerce: both social partners are the shareholders of the newly created pension fund '*KPTE Razem*' (see Więcław 1998b). This highlights the fact that partial pension privatisation, unlike retrenchment within the public PAYG scheme, entails the possibility of handing out potentially attractive stakes to opponents, rendering it politically easier than conventional retrenchment policies, even though it marks a substantial change in the underlying social contract.

NSZZ *Solidarność* even participated in the conceptual debate on systemic pension reform in Poland. Its pension reform proposal of 1995, supporting a partial shift to funding, gained considerable importance as a potential alternative to the conflicting drafts presented by the Labour and Finance portfolios. The high profile of NSZZ *Solidarność* concerning the pension reform issue is highlighted by the fact that the trade union's senior pension expert, Ewa Lewicka, was appointed government plenipotentiary for social security reform by the new AWS-UW government (see Żukowski 1999: 160).

Pensioners are another potential pressure group when it comes to the reform of old-age security, amounting to 40 per cent of Polish voters (see Golinowska and Żukowski 1998: 29). Interestingly, the reaction of pensioners' representatives was much stronger when the government tried to carry through reforms within the public PAYG scheme than in the case of partial privatisation of public old-age security. In Poland, a specialised Pensioners' Party, the KPEiR (*Krajowa Partia Emerytów i Rencistów*, or National Party of Invalidity and Old-Age Pensioners), was established in May 1994 and joined the left-wing SLD (see Śpiewak 1997). To protect the social interest of their constituency, the KPEiR frequently appealed to the Constitutional Tribunal and the Civil Rights Ombudsman, whenever attempts were made to amend eligibility and benefit calculation. In July 1997, shortly before the parliamentary elections, in which the KPEiR set out to take part independently, arousing considerable attention, a second pensioners' party, called KPEiR-RP, was set up, supported by AWS. Nelson (1998: 11) points out that, strikingly, neither pensioners' party attacked systemic pension reform during the 1997 election campaign. Pension reformers had effectively sought to calm this constituency, indicating that the elderly would not be affected by the envisaged changes (see Golinowska 1999: 177). Finally, the competition between KPEiR and KPEiR-RP contributed to the eventual failure of both newly set-up parties to win seats in the Sejm (see Bikont 1997).

Somehow defying conventional wisdom, ZUS, the institution currently managing the lion's share of the pension system, did not offer active opposition to radical pension reform, even though its own role in providing old-age security will be transformed significantly (see Orenstein 1998a: 47). On the one hand, the low profile of ZUS in the pension reform debate can partly be explained by a lack of institutional autonomy. On the other hand, ambivalent positions appear to exist within ZUS, reaching from reservations against the envisaged reform (see Golinowska 1999: 187) to supporters of pension privatisation. It should be recalled that the first proposal to partially privatise Polish old-age security had been co-authored by the then president of ZUS, Wojciech Topiński.

Finally, recent opinion polls may provide some insights into the level of public support of the latest pension reform efforts. In an opinion poll conducted in April 1997, 84.9 per cent of those questioned held that current

pensions did not allow pensioners to make a reasonably good living.[34] Only
9.7 per cent considered the existing pension system as good or rather good,
whereas 44.4 per cent thought that it was decidedly bad and needed radical
changes.[35] Finally, when given the choice between a public, a private and a
mixed pension scheme, only 23.3 per cent of those questioned supported the
mixed option, while 28.0 per cent preferred ZUS and 36.5 per cent favoured
private old-age provision (see Office 1997: 180–3). However, in an opinion
poll conducted in mid-1998, when information on the envisaged pension
reform was already more widespread, only 20 per cent of those between age
30 and 49 favoured the purely public pension path. Contrary to this, 60 per
cent of those aged 30 to 39 announced their decision to switch to the mixed
pension option, while 39 per cent of those aged 40 to 49 followed suit.[36] This
poll also revealed that one-third of those questioned had high hopes of the
reform, while yet another third was afraid of it (see Fandrejewska 1998a).

5.4   THE NEW POLISH PENSION SYSTEM

General Description

Poland's new pension system gradually came into force in 1999. Whereas
first-tier reforms were scheduled to start from 1 January 1999, the newly created
second tier would be fully operative from 1 April 1999. The new scheme is of a
mixed type, combining a still dominant, mandatory public PAYG scheme,
that is being downsized and made more transparent, with a partially
mandatory IFF tier. Strictly speaking, there are four tiers in the new Polish
system: apart from the mandatory PAYG and IFF tiers (tiers 1 and 2), there is
a 'zero' tier consisting of a minimum pension for the elderly, and a third tier
of voluntary savings for old age.[37] Here, the focus is on the mandatory PAYG
and IFF tiers, since they will provide the bulk of old-age security in Poland,
offering a purely public as well as a mixed pension option on a mandatory
basis.[38] While also exhibiting elements of the recent Latvian and Swedish
reform in the first tier, with its mixed overall approach the Polish reform is
clearly inspired by the Argentine reform precedent (see Wóycicka 1998: 26).
However, in spite of the obvious conceptual parallels, the Polish reformers
sought to distance themselves from the Latin American reforms, in order to
enhance its acceptance among the Polish public (see Góra and Rutkowski
1998: 2; Rutkowski 1998).[39]

    The first, PAYG tier, to be financed by the entire employers' and more
than half of the employees' contributions (see Table 5.7), is mandatory for
everybody, at least as first tier. This tier is constituted of the old ZUS scheme,
that is undergoing fundamental restructuring, perceived as 'revolutionary'

(Office 1997: ii; Markiewicz 1998: 24). The new first tier will be based on the principle of 'notional defined contributions' (NDC; see subchapter 2.1), mimicking an IFF scheme, while remaining PAYG financed. This implies the introduction of a completely new pension formula, that can be simplified as

$$P = C/E,$$

where P = old-age pension, C = virtual retirement capital of the insured, made up of the accumulated lifetime social insurance contributions, indexed according to wage growth, and E = average life-expectancy at the time of retirement.[40]

As noted above, ZUS did not keep any individual contributions records. Hence, to allow for the creation of NDC accounts, a so-called 'starting capital' will have to be assessed for every insured who has begun an employment before the start of the reform and was born after 31 December 1948. A hypothetical retirement value will be calculated for every insured, on the basis of the old pension formula adjusted for age, reflecting his/her acquired rights until the end of 1998 (for details see Office 1997: 38–40; Góra and Rutkowski 1998). Post-reform contribution payments will be added subsequently to the individual starting capital.[41] Annual statements of NDC accounts will enable the insured to check the hypothetical amount of their retirement pension.[42] It should be noted, however, that it will take ZUS until early 2004 to calculate millions of hypothetical retirement values, given the incomplete information on pre-1999 insurance careers (see Fandrejewska 1998b).

Other first-tier reforms concern eligibility issues. Contrary to original reform plans, the current retirement ages – 60 for women and 65 for men – will remain unchanged. But from now on, later retirement will increase old-age benefits by an annual 9–10 per cent. The general rule is that there will be no accrued rights other than those derived from contributions paid by the individual: 'Additional rights will be created only if an additional contribution [is] paid, by employees, employers or the government ... This will make the trade-offs in granting special privileges clearer' (Góra and Rutkowski 1998: 19–20). Hence, non-contributory years will no longer be eligible for insurance years. However, the envisaged abolition of branch privileges, albeit mitigated by transitory rules, has not succeeded. So far, only general rules have been settled for an act on branch privileges, that has not been passed yet. Especially the issue of branch-specific early retirement rules meets with strong opposition from the trades unions (see Solska 1999; Żukowski 1999: 167).

The reform changes the legal status of ZUS, which will cease to be a central government institution, turning into a legal personality. Hence, ZUS will be able to create its own salary system, raising its employees' hopes for better compensation. Furthermore, the competences of ZUS's Supervisory Board will be increased (see Żukowski 1999: 166). In the future, the provision against the four different risk-types covered by ZUS – old-age, disability, sickness and accident insurance – will be administered in separate programmes. Furthermore, a Demographic Reserve Fund will be set up, fed by possible first-tier surpluses, privatisation revenues and, temporarily, 1 per cent of pension contributions (see Góra and Rutkowski 1998: 12).[43]

The second, IFF tier consists of a newly created pension fund system, financed entirely by employees' contributions (see Table 5.7). Pension funds are being created and managed by private pension companies, i.e. joint stock companies with a minimum capital of ECU 4 million. Pension assets will have to be separated, both legally and physically, from the respective pension company, being kept in an independent depository, not interlaced with either the pension company or the pension fund. There are several other safety regulations, e.g. a minimum return threshold and strict investment rules.[44] Pension funds will be supervised by the Pension Funds' Supervisory Board (*Urząd Nadzoru nad Funduszami Emerytalnymi*, or UNFE).

Second-tier beneficiaries will be further protected by the indexation of their prospective pensions, at least to consumer prices and at most to average wages.[45] Annuities offered in the second tier may not vary according to sex, health or region. A minimum benefit guarantee will be granted to those who choose the mixed pension path: if their old-age pension from both ZUS and the pension fund of their choice is lower than the minimum pension, the remaining difference will be paid from the state budget, provided the insured meets age and service requirements (see Góra and Rutkowski 1998: 11, 14).

The first eight licences for mandatory pension funds were granted in October/November 1998, even before all pension reform laws had been enacted. Another ten licences are expected to be conferred later on. Among the shareholders of the newly created Polish pension funds are Polish banks and insurance companies, but also British, Swiss, Dutch and US investors, such as Commercial Union, Winterthur, Nationale Nederlanden, Citibank and Pioneer, as well as the EBRD (see E.L. 1998; Rzeczpospolita 1998).

The third, voluntary tier will consist of additional private insurance and savings schemes, including life insurance and occupational pension schemes. The latter may be created by a company with a minimum of 5 employees, provided at least 50 per cent of its employees will have the possibility of joining the programme. The mandatory pension contribution will be reduced by 7 per cent if the corresponding amount is paid to an employee pension plan, to enable employers to contribute to third-tier plans without any additional cost (see Czechowska 1998; Góra and Rutkowski 1998: 10, 17–19).

All Poles under 30 are obliged to join the new two-tier scheme, paying one-fifth of the total pension contribution to a private pension fund of their choice, while the remaining four-fifths will continue to flow to ZUS (mixed pension path). Individuals who already have an insurance history, and are between 30 and 50 years of age, are free to do the same – alternatively, they may stay in the old scheme with the whole of their contribution (purely public pension path). This age group is granted one year to decide whether or not they want to switch to the mixed pension path. People over 50 and pensioners are required to remain in the old system, since 'there are neither sufficient funds nor technical capabilities to introduce a system containing funded social insurance for all persons, especially those close to retirement age' (Office 1997: 27). Hence, it will not be until 2010 that the first cohorts retire under the new system.

Table 5.7   Polish pension contributions, pre- and post-reform

	Pre-reform	Post-reform	
Destination of paid contributions	ZUS	ZUS	private funds
Employers, nominal (in % of gross wage)	45	24	0
Employees, nominal (in % of gross wage)	0	12	9
Total, nominal (in % of gross wage)	45	45	
Employers, standardised* (in % of stand. gross wage)	36.7	19.6	0
Employees, standardised (in % of stand. gross wage)	0	9.8	7.3
Total, standardised (in % of stand. gross wage)	36.7	36.7	

Note: * On standardisation see Chapter 4.

Source: Based on Żukowski (1999).

Regardless of the individual's decision for or against joining the private pension fund pillar, the entire employers' contribution and at least 57 per cent of the insured's own contribution will continue to go to ZUS. Under the mixed pension path, employees will thus receive their retirement benefits from both mandatory tiers. During a (long) transitional period, the respective size of both parts of future retirement benefits will depend crucially on the pension entitlements acquired under the pre-reform scheme. In the final system, however, applying to those newly entering the labour market without any pre-reform claims, all insured will participate in the mixed system. It should be noted that then the relative share of *ex ante* entitlements accrued in the private and public tiers, respectively, will not be 20 to 80, but 37.5 to 62.5, as only part of the total ZUS contributions are being credited to the NDC accounts, thereby further diminishing the role of the public scheme in overall old-age provision.[46] The reformers' declared long-term aim is a 50–50 share of both pillars (see Góra and Rutkowski 1998: 25).

Financing the Transition

Like every partial or full shift from PAYG to FF financing, the Polish pension reform implies considerable transition costs. ZUS still has all pre-reform pension liabilities and the claims acquired by post-reform contributors, while at the same time an ever-increasing part of its revenues is diverted towards the newly created mandatory IFF tier. The scope of the resulting fiscal burden depends crucially on the share of the insured switching to the mixed scheme. Reportedly, for people over 45 it will not pay off to choose the mixed pension path (see Więcław 1998a). Somewhat cautiously, Polish pension reformers assume that half of those aged 30 to 50 will decide to switch to the mixed pension path, apart from those below age 30, who are obliged to do so. Additional costs stem from the restructuring of ZUS, e.g. the introduction of a ceiling on contributions, and from the opting-out option towards the newly introduced third-tier schemes (see Góra and Rutkowski 1998: 22).[47]

Interestingly, there are no official estimates of the total transition costs resulting from the Polish pension reform, although it had been claimed that one of the goals of the reform was 'to ensure a financially self-sufficient pension system' (Office 1997: 27).[48] The expected reform-related fiscal burden is available only for four selected years, rising from 1.48 per cent of GDP (2000) to 2.22 per cent in 2017, when the aftermath of pension privatisation will by no means be over (see Office 1997: 19–20). Polish policymakers intend to finance part of the expected transition costs by means of a rationalisation of ZUS and by the use of privatisation proceeds. In addition, the reformers expect that 'much of the revenue diverted to funded pensions will return to the state treasury through increased demand for bonds' (Góra and Rutkowski 1998: 22). The aim is to avoid, to the greatest possible extent, that the high costs of a transition to funding increase the budget deficit (see Office 1997: 80–5).

Part of the transition costs may be financed by rationalising the public pension scheme ZUS, e.g. via a higher effective retirement age, the introduction of price indexation, and the extension of the calculation base period.[49] Since these measures will only gradually become effective in financial terms, there is a need for an additional source of financing during the first five to seven years of the reform. Although it is acknowledged that they will by no means suffice (see Office 1997: 19–20), proceeds from the privatisation of state property shall be used to fill part of the gap. The creation of a specific fund for earmarked privatisation revenues was, however, not deemed necessary: if privatisation proceeds accrued before the reform were used to decrease public debt, this would help to finance the reform just the same (see Office 1997: 82–4).

It should be noted that the Polish pension reform team supported only a specific linkage between privatisation and pension reform, that is, using privatisation proceeds – directly or indirectly, via a reduction of public debt – to cover the ZUS deficit. Only if privatisation does not proceed quickly enough to provide the necessary revenues in a given fiscal year, privatisation bonds, later to be converted into shares in privatised enterprises, are considered a useful instrument (see Office 1997: 82–4). However, the Office of the Government Plenipotentiary opposed a distribution of shares in state-owned enterprises to the newly created private pension funds, a demand raised by the *Solidarność* camp, under the label of '*uwłaszczenie*', or 'propertisation'. According to *Solidarność*'s programme, state-owned property is the result of the work and ideas of all generations of Polish citizens, who, therefore, are the legitimate heirs of these assets and should receive 'enfranchisement vouchers' (see Chwila 1997). In the 1997 election campaign, 'propertisation' was among the promises of AWS: the new private pension funds were to be awarded controlling stakes in the remaining state-owned enterprises (see Bowdler 1997/98), hence precluding the use of privatisation revenues to cover the reform-related ZUS deficit. These mutually exclusive ideas about the use of privatisation proceeds for pension reform created considerable tension between the Office of the Government Plenipotentiary and part of the new government, even though the 'Act on Using Means from Privatisation of State Assets for Social Insurance Reform' of 25 June 1997 had already been passed. Currently, the Polish government is facing difficult choices between allowing citizens to tangibly profit from privatisation ('propertisation') and a fiscally sustainable transition to a funded pension system.[50]

5.5   SUMMING UP:
PROBLEMS, ACTORS AND POLICY CHOICES

While economic crisis and high inflation had been afflicting Poland's pension system – ZUS – since the 1980s, the financial strain on Polish pension finances was greatly aggravated by economic transformation, when ZUS was used to a considerable extent as a substitute for unemployment benefits. The post-1989 changes in organisation, eligibility and benefits tackled the long-standing problem of benefit adequacy, but did not succeed in making the Polish pension system financially viable, in spite of its high contribution rate. Moreover, social security experts criticised the existing pension system on fairness grounds. However, policymakers had experienced strong resistance from the 'grey lobby' – notably pensioners' associations and trades unions – when trying to introduce relatively modest reform measures.

The large number of pension reform drafts put forward since the early 1990s indicates the degree of disagreement about the reform path to be followed. While the Ministry of Labour and professors of social insurance law held that a thorough reform of ZUS was sufficient and politically viable, the Ministry of Finance and social security experts with an economic background advocated Latin American-style pension privatisation. The Finance portfolio's involvement in the pension reform issue, a genuine matter of social policy, was triggered by the fact that ZUS was financially dependent on sizeable budgetary subsidies. Hence, in line with the 'benefit of crises' hypothesis, it is argued here that the financial difficulties of ZUS changed the relevant constellation of actors in such a way that the 'privatisation faction' was reinforced decisively.

For a year and a half, pension reform was deadlocked by the conflict between the portfolios of Labour and Finance, until in early 1996 the substitution of the Minister of Labour succeeded in moving this portfolio considerably closer to the Ministry of Finance's position. To circumvent existing opposition to this partial privatisation of Polish old-age security, a special task force for old-age reform was set up, the so-called 'Office of the Government Plenipotentiary for Social Security Reform'. The Office was headed by a World Bank economist on leave, firmly committed to the Bank's blueprint for pension privatisation, granting the Bank a pivotal channel to support the local reform efforts, apart from its overall leverage in the Polish context of high external debt.

The inter-ministerial compromise, published in October 1996, amounted to combining a reformed, down-sized ZUS with a newly created, mandatory tier of private IFF pension funds. While exhibiting major elements of the recent Latvian and Swedish reform among the envisaged first-tier reforms, with its mixed overall approach the Polish reform is clearly inspired by the Argentine reform precedent. Like their Hungarian counterparts, however, the Polish reformers resorted to tactical packaging, distancing themselves from the conspicuous Latin American models and stressing the originality of local reform efforts. In another tactical move, Polish pension reformers refrained from disclosing the scope and financing of transition costs – i.e. the 'redistributional calculus' (World Bank 1997: 146) of the shift to funding.

In terms of reform strategy, the initial idea was to get all pension reform laws passed before the parliamentary elections, due in September 1997, thereby defying conventional wisdom on political business cycles. As time proved to be too short, the original package deal of bundling up the politically difficult reforms of ZUS with the fairly popular introduction of private pension funds was abandoned. Instead, Polish policymakers resorted to unbundling and deliberate sequencing: the laws on the private pension fund tiers were enacted before the elections, whereas the more intricate part – ZUS reforms – was left to the incoming government. It is difficult to evaluate the effect of unbundling in the Polish case: while this move increased the visibility of the retrenchment elements, making them more difficult to enact, the preceding passage of the second-tier laws may be interpreted as having created a path dependence in the sense that the subsequent enactment of the more difficult laws was facilitated.

Throughout the legislative process, the pension reform team, well aware of the need to engender social support for the radical change of old-age security, negotiated with potential opponents of the envisaged reform, notably trades unions and pensioners' organisations. While the basic paradigm choice was not put up for discussion with these secondary actors, Polish pension reformers agreed to some modifications of the envisaged first-pillar reforms that were finally enacted in late 1998.

Whereas ZUS reforms were scheduled to start from 1 January 1999, private pension funds would commence operations only on 1 April 1999. Poland's new pension system will be of a mixed type, combining a still dominant, public PAYG scheme (four-fifths of contributions) with a newly set-up private pension fund tier (one-fifths of contributions). The old ZUS scheme will undergo fundamental restructuring, the most important change being a shift towards the NDC principle. The partial privatisation of Polish old-age security amounts to a significant departure from local social insurance traditions, dating back to the end of the last century.

'Let us hope that several years of preparatory work by pension experts ... will result in an old-age system that our children – may they have a long career and a high income – consider to be good. And our grandchildren are going to change it anyway' (Hagemejer 1998; own translation).

NOTES

1. There is no information available on social security regulations in the territories occupied by the Soviet Union (see Świątkowski 1993: 198).
2. Compulsory social insurance contributions from employers, that had been raised several times until reaching a nominal 43 per cent in the late 1980s, were fixed as a proportion of total payroll costs (see Okrasa 1987: 22–3). In 1968 employees' contributions had been reintroduced, but they were abolished four years later (see Żukowski 1996: 104).
3. Between 1955 and 1960, ZUS had been dissolved, and the trades unions were entrusted with the administration of short-term benefits. The rationale behind this administrative change was the following: according to communist ideology, the state was about to wither away, and its functions were to be taken over by the organised working class, but old-age pensions and disability benefits remained exempt from this move, being run by public administration (see Świątkowski 1993: 200).
4. In the early 1980s, the *Solidarność* movement, the first independent trade union to be admitted in communist Eastern Europe, demanded, *inter alia*, that 'pensions should increase systematically and be linked to changes in the lowest wages. The government should raise pensions to the level of the social minimum and gradually equalise the old portfolio of pensions with the new one' (Flakierski 1991: 98).
5. Annual inflation amounted to 61 per cent in 1988, to 244 per cent in 1989 and to 586 per cent in 1990 (see Żukowski 1994: 162).
6. Old-age and other pensions were not reduced when the beneficiary was employed part-time, provided the salary did not exceed the minimum wage. In areas suffering from labour shortage, the admissible earnings threshold was higher (see Ministry of Labour 1983: 15).
7. In Poland, economic crisis broke out in 1979, shaking the country during the 1980s. In an annual average, net material product fell by 0.8 per cent in 1981–1985 and by 0.5 per cent in 1986–1990 (see Lavigne 1995: 58).
8. The first six licences for mandatory pension funds were granted on 27 October 1998 (see Rzeczpospolita 1998). See subchapter 5.4 for the details of the systemic pension reform to be implemented in Poland.
9. Previously, the Supervisory Board was made up of elected representatives of trades unions (five-ninths), self-employed (two-ninths), pensioners (one-ninth) and government representatives (one-ninth); see Strunk et al. (1994: 251).
10. Moreover, ZUS's special subsystems for members of agricultural co-operatives, craftsmen, artisans, writers, artists and the clergy continue to exist, but add up to less than 10 per cent of ZUS's total insured (see Cichon 1995: A3-153).
11. As noted above, old-age security for individual farmers had been introduced in 1977 (see Ministry of Labour 1983: 19–22). The significance of this scheme is highlighted by the fact that in 1996, as many as 28 per cent of the employed worked in the agricultural sector (see Główny Urząd Statystyczny 1997: 111).
12. The nominal contribution rate was as high as 45 per cent. See Chapter 4 for details on the standardisation of contribution rates.
13. See Żukowski (1996: 108) and Golinowska, Czepulis-Rutkowska and Szczur (1997: 10–11) for an enumeration of other windows for early retirement.
14. Żukowski (1996: 114) reports that in the early 1990s, as many as 86.3 per cent of men and 77.8 per cent of women retired early.
15. Pensions were raised when expected wage increases in the next quarter exceeded 10 per cent (5 per cent until March 1992). Only minimum pensions were revaluated at 100 per cent of the national average wage. For all other pensions, this rate was only 91 per cent from 1993 onwards, being increased to 93 per cent from mid-1994 (see Topińska 1995: 62).
16. Now, pension adjustments are at least making up for the increase in the pensioners' consumer basket, but the government can enact higher rises (see Czepulis-Rutkowska 1999: 151).
17. See OECD (1996: 88) on the subjective evaluation by pensioners' households of their material well-being, compared with other groups. Pensioners' own perception of their

material situation has improved since 1993, but continues to be much worse than that of most other groups.

18. It should be noted that nowadays, *Solidarność* is both a trade union and a political party. For the sake of clarity, I will use 'NSZZ *Solidarność*' when referring to the former, and to AWS (*Akcja Wyborcza Solidarność*, or Solidarity Electoral Action) when referring to the latter, even though the trade union forms part of the party.

19. While, in the present analysis, the conflicting parties are denoted as the 'Bismarckian–Beveridgean faction' vs. the 'advocates of pension privatisation', it is interesting to note that radical reformers themselves have labelled these contending groups as the 'rationalisers' vs. the 'reformers' (Góra and Rutkowski 1998: 5). For some semantic observations regarding the term 'pension reform' see subchapter 3.1.

20. For an in-depth analysis of the Topiński–Wiśniewski proposal in the light of the Chilean experience see Diamond (1994). See Maret and Schwartz (1994: 79–81) and Apolte and Chomiuk (1995) for a discussion of Chilean-type proposals for Poland.

21. Reportedly, Mazur's proposal even contains lengthy, literally translated passages from the well-known World Bank document 'Averting the Old Age Crisis' (World Bank 1994a).

22. On the relevance of the Latin American experience for general economic policy in Poland see Berríos (1995).

23. The Chilean José Piñera was Minister of Labour and Social Security from 1978 to 1980, initiating the radical pension reform in his country.

24. Both the 'Strategy for Poland' and a second major document, 'Package 2000', launched in March 1996 (see Kołodko 1996), met with considerable resistance within the governing SLD, notably from the trades union faction – OPZZ (*Ogólnopolskie Porozumienie Związków Zawodowych*, or All Poland Trades Unions Alliance) – within the party (see Ziemer 1996: 40).

25. While Minister of Labour Leszek Miller represented centre-left factions within the SLD, Grzegorz Kołodko, the Minister of Finance, was an 'outside' economic expert with market-oriented views (see Orenstein 1998a: 45).

26. The Ministry of Finance advocated a slow-down in indexation on fiscal grounds, whereas the Ministry of Labour aimed at improving the financial position of pensioners (see Götting 1998: 165–6).

27. This special task force was set up to commit the government to radical reform, to simplify inter-departmental co-ordination and to make the pension reform independent of the Ministry of Labour (see Orenstein 1998a: 46).

28. On the overall role of the World Bank in Poland see Nowakowski (1996).

29. Later, the pension reformers disclosed their strategy (Góra and Rutkowski 1998: 8): 'Bączkowski ... began work[ing] on a completely new reform program. However, for political reasons, it was presented merely as an update and an expansion of the previous proposal.'

30. Security of old-age pensions was presented as the main aim of the reform, while diversity of the retirement income – through the various tiers of the pension system – was seen as the means to achieve this aim (see Żukowski 1999: 160).

31. See Góra and Rutkowski (1998: 6) on this package deal: 'Social-insurance reform should, if possible, not simply be associated with cuts and stringency, but with new opportunities for a generation with many working years before it. New horizons will show not only clouds of change, but also rays of new opportunity, which would make the reform more politically acceptable.'

32. An alternative interpretation is that the passing of at least part of the pension reform laws was intended to create a path dependence that facilitated the subsequent legislating of the more difficult laws.

33. Following a government decree of 15 February 1994, the Tripartite Commission was created, in order to serve as a forum for dialogue on economic and social affairs between government, trades unions and employers' associations (see Nawacki 1995: 53).

34. It should be noted that in an earlier opinion poll, conducted in January 1997, 40 per cent of those questioned did not expect the envisaged reform to guarantee them a safer pension (see A.F.T. 1997).

35. The total percentage of those who considered the current pension scheme as 'rather bad' or 'decidedly bad' amounts to as much as 64.9 (see Office 1997: 180).
36. The percentage of indecisive persons was as high as 41 among those aged 40 to 49, whereas it reached only 20 among those aged 30 to 39 (Fandrejewska 1998a).
37. This minimum pension guarantee will be financed from general taxation. The eligibility criteria for a minimum pension, amounting to 28 per cent of the average wage, will be 25 insurance years and 65 years of age (see Żukowski 1999: 162).
38. This general description of the new Polish pension system is largely based on A.F.T. (1998b), Fandrejewska (1998b), Góra and Rutkowski (1998), Koral (1998), Markiewicz (1998), Olczyk and Pilczyński (1998) and Żukowski (1999).
39. Rutkowski's (1998) leitmotif that the 'new generation' of pension reforms in Poland and Hungary is different from the existing Latin American blueprints has been questioned by Müller (1998c: 29).
40. Here, the statistical average of male and female life-expectancy is considered to avoid gender-specific discrimination. For details see Office (1997: 32).
41. When the purely public pension path is chosen, the amount credited will come to 19.5 per cent of standardised gross wage, whereas it will be 12.2 per cent in the case of the mixed pension path. The remaining 17.1 per cent of gross wage will be used to finance disability and survivors' pensions, as well as sickness and work injury provisions; see Góra and Rutkowski (1998: 9–10).
42. To avoid misunderstandings regarding the NDC accounts, Polish newspapers have been trying to clarify the issue: 'In contrast to classic bank accounts, it will not be possible to withdraw the deposits at will, and the accumulated money will not be heritable. In practice, ZUS accounts will document the amount of contributions a person has paid' (Fandrejewska 1998b; own translation). Góra and Rutkowski (1998: 11) have been more straightforward: 'There is no money in the account'.
43. On the exact distribution of the total contribution rate on the different risk types see Góra and Rutkowski (1998: 10). It should be noted that the reformers' aim to reduce the contribution burden has not been met.
44. Each pension fund will be required to achieve a minimum rate of return, amounting to half of the average for all the funds. If the rate of return of a given fund is lower, the pension company will be obliged to cover the difference from its own reserve fund. In case of an insolvency, the pension company managing the respective fund will be closed, and the difference to the minimum rate of return will be covered by the Guarantee Fund, established from the means of all funds. If this is not enough, the state budget will pay the difference (see Żukowski 1999: 168).
45. See Davis (1998: 18) for the required annuity design to allow for an indexation of funded pension benefits.
46. The share of total contributions channelled to the public tier is $(19.6 + 9.8)/36.7 = 80.1$, while $7.3/36.7 = 19.9$ go to the private tier (see Table 5.7). However, only part of the contributions to ZUS create entitlements (see note 41 above).
47. This newly introduced ceiling – 250 per cent of average earnings – is estimated to cost an annual 0.35 per cent of GDP (see Office 1997: 19–20).
48. According to Wóycicka (1998: 26), Ewa Lewicka, the Government Plenipotentiary, estimated the total transition costs at US$ 6 billion, while Leszek Balcerowicz, the Minister of Finance, assumed a considerably higher fiscal burden – US$ 16 billion (about 5.4 and 14.6 per cent of GDP respectively). Both estimates seem to be much too low, considering the annual costs given above.
49. For a detailed analysis of the financial effects of PAYG pillar rationalisation see Office (1997: 115–44).
50. For a full discussion of the potential links between systemic pension reform and privatisation in Poland and their political economy implications see Gesell, Müller and Süß (1998).

6. Pension Reform in the Czech Republic

6.1 THE LEGACY:
RETIREMENT SCHEMES BEFORE 1989

As early as 1771, a public pension scheme was set up in Bohemia and Moravia, then part of the Austro-Hungarian empire. Coverage was limited to civil servants. It took almost a century until any other professional group was granted old-age security: introduced in 1854, the miners' pension scheme was based on Mutual Benefit Funds (see Ministère Fédéral du Travail 1980: 4). The first Bismarckian-style social insurance laws were passed in 1887/88, introducing accident and health insurance for manual workers, while pension insurance followed only decades later with the Salaried Employees' Pension Act of 1906. Thus, the new Czechoslovak Republic, founded in 1918, inherited a low-level old-age scheme that covered only a small part of the population of Bohemia and Moravia (see Götting 1995: 352). Furthermore, the fragmentation of Czechoslovak old-age security was increased by the fact that different pension schemes existed in Slovakia and Carpatho-Ukraine, which had formed part of Hungary until 1918 (see Strunk et al. 1994: 268).

It was not until 1924 that the Manual Workers' Social Insurance Act granted old-age insurance to all those employed who had not been covered so far, including agricultural workers.[1] The self-governed scheme created by this law was fully funded, being financed in equal parts through employers' and employees' contributions, supplemented by a state subsidy.[2] Pension benefits consisted of a flat-rate basis and an earnings-related part, being granted from age 65. Besides the separate schemes for civil servants, miners, employees and workers, a fifth old-age scheme was set up in 1929, paying out means-tested, tax-financed social assistance pensions (see De Deken 1994: 14).[3] These five pension schemes survived with relatively small changes until the end of World War II, in spite of the significant territorial modifications which Czechoslovakia had to endure after the Munich Agreement (1938), not to mention the overall political changes brought about by the German occupation of Bohemia and Moravia (1939–45).[4]

As the reserves of the pre-war pension schemes had been depleted by both the German occupants and wartime inflation, the new communist rulers switched to PAYG financing in 1948, when the National Insurance Act introduced a unified system of social insurance by standardising eligibility rules for blue- and white-collar workers (see De Deken 1994: 56–65).[5] The newly created Central Social Insurance Institute was governed by elected representatives of the insured, and integrated into the state budget. During a transitory period of four years, it was financed in equal parts from employers' and employees' contributions, until the latter were converted into a wage tax in 1952, formally abolishing the insured's contributions (see De Deken 1994: 81–2).[6]

Table 6.1   The Czechoslovak pension system, 1960–1980: selected indicators

Indicators	1960	1965	1970	1975	1980
System dependency ratio[a]	20.2	24.8	31.4	33.4	34.8
Population in pension age in % of the total population	17.3[b]	18.7	20.0	19.3	18.8
Pension outlays in % of national income[c]	7.1	9.0	8.2	7.7	9.0
Average pension in % of average net wage	59.6	57.5	53.9	49.3	53.9
Newly set pension in % of average net wage	70.3	60.2	61.2	56.5	64.2

Notes: [a] pensioners in per cent of economically active population
[b] 1961
[c] material net product in current prices

Source: Based on Adam (1983).

In 1951, the administration of the Central Social Insurance Institute was transferred to the Central Council of Trades Unions, following the Soviet example. Meanwhile, the 1948 reform had been criticised by Stalinist social security experts for its 'excessive egalitarianism' (De Deken 1994: 74). Consequently, the 1956 Social Security Act introduced some important departures from universalism (see De Deken 1994: 89–98).[7] All occupations were classified into three work categories, according to the difficulty of the activities to be performed and to the strategic importance of the respective sector within the centrally planned economy, with a bias towards manual work in heavy industry. Employees in categories I and II were granted higher benefit levels and earlier retirement (for an overview see Adam 1983: 279; De Deken 1995: 276).[8] The flat-rate component of the pension formula was abolished; instead, benefit calculation was fully based on years of service, the level of earnings and the work category. Moreover, the 1956 Social Security Act lowered the retirement age to 60 for men and to 55 for women. In an amendment enacted in 1964, the retirement age of women was linked to the number of children raised, varying between age 57 for the childless and age 53, in the case of five or more children. Furthermore, the vesting period was increased from 20 to 25 years for both sexes (see De Deken 1994: 118–19).

In the following 25 years, the Czechoslovak pension system remained exempt from further fundamental changes while gradually maturing. The gap between the replacement ratio of average and newly set pensions (see Table 6.1) indicates that current pensions suffered from insufficient adjustment, in spite of numerous *ad hoc* increases. 'Pensioners do not have the same clout as employees ... therefore government attention is mainly directed to economically active persons' (Adam 1983: 289). Due to the lack of systematic indexation of retirement benefits to wages and/or prices, the economic situation of pensioners gradually deteriorated, forcing many retirees to continue their gainful employment (see Halásek 1995: 139; Boller 1997: 385–6).[9] During the last years of the communist era, this problem was recognised by the Czechoslovak government. Another major reform of the pension system was prepared, that would have included a system of automatic valorisation (see De Deken 1994: 129), but the systemic change and the break-up of Czechoslovakia effectively prevented these modifications from being implemented.[10]

6.2   OLD-AGE SECURITY IN TRANSFORMATION

Transformation and the Czech Pension System

Compared to its counterparts in Hungary and Poland, the Czech retirement system did not suffer much from economic transformation (see Table 6.4). Any attempt at interpreting the Czech pension system's remarkable financial stability has to take the country's relatively unimpaired labour market into account.[11] The number of employed experienced only a 6.6 per cent reduction between 1989 and 1996: from 1989 to 1993, it fell by 10.3 per cent, while recovering by 4.0 per cent between 1993 and 1996. At the same time (1989–1996), the overall number of pensioners rose by a mere 3.8 per cent. The ranks of old-age pensioners increased by 5.4 per cent, while the number of disability pensioners grew by 11.5 per cent (see Table 6.2).[12] These figures indicate that the Czech pension system was used as a substitute for welfare and unemployment benefits to a lesser extent than retirement schemes in other Central European countries, maintaining a more adequate relation between temporary and permanent social benefits (see Heinrich 1996).

Table 6.2   Population, employed and pensioners: Czech Republic, 1989–1996

	1989	1990	1991	1992	1993	1994	1995	1996
Population (millions)	10.4	10.4	10.3	10.3	10.3	10.3	10.3	10.3
20–59 years old (thousands)	5,456	5,430	5,453	5,496	5,557	5,638	5,719	5,798
60+ years old (thousands)	1,829	1,837	1,845	1,855	1,858	1,859	1,857	1,857
Employed (thousands)	5,403	5,351	5,059	4,927	4,848	4,885	5,012	5,044
Pensioners (thousands)	2,939	2,952	2,997	3,033	3,052	3,051	3,057	3,052
Old-age pensioners (thousands)	1,713	1,737	1,777	1,804	1,815	1,811	1,811	1,806
Disability pensioners (thousands)	477	483	494	505	518	527	537	532

Source: Based on Schrooten, Smeeding and Wagner (1999).

As both the decrease in contributors and the increase in beneficiaries turned out to be relatively small, the system dependency ratio rose only slightly: from 54.4 (1989) to 60.5 per cent (1996). At the same time, the demographic situation showed a slight improvement, a result of pro-natalist policies pursued in the early 1970s (see Lodahl 1997: 766). Table 6.4 shows that, until 1996, the Czech pension system did not require any budgetary subsidies, as contributions sufficed to cover expenditures. The notable fall of the replacement ratio from 1992 onwards contributed to stabilising the financial situation of the Czech pension system. Nevertheless, pension expenditures were on the rise between 1989 and 1996 (see Table 6.3).

Table 6.3   The Czech pension system, 1989–1996: selected indicators

Indicators	1989	1990	1991	1992	1993	1994	1995	1996
Old-age dependency ratio[a]	33.5	33.8	33.8	33.7	33.4	33.0	32.5	32.0
System dependency ratio[b]	54.4	55.2	59.2	61.6	63.0	62.5	61.0	60.5
Replacement ratio[c]	63.8	65.2	70.4	67.7	60.5	57.2	56.6	56.0
Pension expenditures in % of GDP	8.3	8.0	8.9	8.1	8.4	8.5	9.1	9.0

Notes: [a] 60+ years old in per cent of 20–59 years old
[b] pensioners in per cent of contributors
[c] average pension in per cent of average net wage

Source: Based on Schrooten, Smeeding and Wagner (1999).

In the following sections, I will review the changes within the Czech old-age security scheme in the post-1989 era, particularly in the areas of organisation, financing, eligibility and benefits. I will then focus on the introduction of supplementary private pension funds in 1994. Contrary to similar sections in the case-studies on Hungary and Poland, where the reforms within the existing PAYG systems were characterised as first-phase reforms, no systemic change has been envisaged to date in the Czech Republic. Hence, the measures described in the following shaped the ultimate public–private mix chosen by the Czech pension reformers.

Organisation

To increase the transparency of the Czech system of social protection, it was divided into three complementary areas: social insurance, social support and social assistance (see Višek and Klimentová 1996: 5–11).[13] In 1993, the area of social insurance, while entrusted to the Czech Social Security Administration (*Česká Správa Sociálního Zabezpečení*, or ČSSZ) since 1990, was split up into separate schemes for old-age security, health insurance and employment (see Halásek 1995: 139). The pension scheme continues to be administered by ČSSZ, a state body subordinate to the Ministry of Labour and Social Affairs (see Kudlová, Skývová and Pechar 1995: 15; Ministry of Labour 1996a: 13–14). While, in 1993, the introduction of a tripartite administration of ČSSZ had been envisaged, following pre-war traditions (see Potůček 1994), Prime Minister Václav Klaus finally dismissed the creation of such corporatist structures that could have limited the government's leeway in social policy (see Král 1995: 179; Götting 1998: 170).

Financing

The mandatory public pension scheme is still based on the PAYG principle. In connection with a comprehensive tax reform that came into effect on 1 January 1993, separate contributions were introduced for pension, health and unemployment schemes. This move included the re-establishment of employees' contributions, that had been abolished in 1952 (see Halásek 1995: 139). In 1996, standardised contribution rates were lowered from 24.3 (employees 6.0 per cent; employers 17.9 per cent) to 23 per cent of standardised gross wage (5.8 and 17.3 per cent, respectively).[14]

Table 6.4   The Czech Pension Fund, 1993–1996 (in per cent of GDP)

	1993	1994	1995	1996
Pension contributions	9.1	9.8	10.0	9.5
Pension expenditures	8.4	8.5	9.1	9.0
Balance	0.5	1.1	0.7	0.3

Source: Based on Schrooten, Smeeding and Wagner (1999).

Interestingly, pension contributions were more than sufficient to cover expenditures (see Table 6.4). Instead of requiring budgetary subsidies, like its Hungarian and Polish counterparts, the Czech pension system supplemented the state budget with its surplus (see Götting 1995: 372). This practice was made possible by the financial integration of ČSSZ into the budget, arousing considerable debate. The separation was mainly demanded by the representatives of contributors, i.e. employers' associations and the trade union federation (see Král 1995: 178–9). From 1 January 1996, annual pension surpluses were finally earmarked for future deficits, by introducing a special account within the state budget (see Skývová 1996: 3).

Eligibility and Benefits

With the extension of old-age protection to the self-employed in 1990, the coverage of the Czechoslovak pension system had been further expanded. In early 1993, the old-age scheme was also made more uniform, as all former branch privileges – the work categories I, II and III – had been abolished. The political feasibility of this move was facilitated by recognising all pension rights previously acquired under these categories (see Ministry of Labour 1996a: 5).[15] The abolition of the work categories reinforced the insurance principle, as benefits became more closely related to previous earnings and the number of contributory years (see Král 1995: 175).

In 1995, the retirement age was 60 for men and 53–57 for women.[16] It will be gradually increased until reaching 62 for men and 57–61 for women in 2007, which is still low by international standards. Early retirement is possible but entails a reduction of the earnings-related element within the pension formula.[17] It is also possible to retire later; in this case the retirement benefit will be increased permanently. To become eligible for an old-age pension, 25 qualifying years are required, including substitute periods.[18]

The benefit formula comprises a basic part, amounting to CZK 1,060 in October 1996, and an earnings-related element.[19] It can be simplified as

$$P = B + Y \cdot 0.015 \cdot A,$$

where P = monthly old-age pension, B = universal base component, Y = number of qualifying years and A = average of individual monthly earnings during the last 12 years before retirement (1998). This period is to be extended by one year p.a., until reaching 30 years in 2016. However, only the first CZK 5,000 of monthly income are credited fully; additionally, 30 per cent of earnings from CZK 5,000 up to CZK 10,000 and 10 per cent of earnings exceeding CZK 10,000 are considered. For every year of service, 1.5 per cent of the assessment base are credited (see Ministry of Labour 1996b: 9–10).

The 1991 Pension Act indexed minimum pensions to the cost-of-living index, whereas higher pensions were raised only on an *ad hoc* basis (see Götting 1995: 371).[20] Pensions are adjusted when the growth of the overall retail price index exceeds 5 per cent. Table 6.3 shows that pensions have been lagging behind wages since 1993. In 1998, the average monthly pension amounted to US$ 153 (see Mortkowitz 1998).

The New Private Pension Funds

In the early 1990s, the Czechoslovak government had decided to supplement the mandatory public pension system by a voluntary private scheme (see Štangová 1993: 734). The Ministry of Labour and Social Affairs first suggested introducing company pension schemes, a proposal supported by the trades union federation and employees' associations (see Hiršl, Rusnok and Fassmann 1995: 34). However, Prime Minister Václav Klaus preferred an individualistic approach to supplementary old-age provision and got his own way (see Götting 1998: 169).[21] In February 1994, the Czech parliament approved Act No. 42/1994 Coll. on the establishment of supplementary pension funds. The first funds started operation in September 1994, set up by banks, insurance companies and other enterprises, some of them still state-owned (see Hřích and Larischová 1998: 73). Foreign investors include German, Austrian and Dutch companies, such as Allianz-Hypo, Creditanstalt, Winterthur and Nationale Nederlanden (see Elliott 1995: 74).

Table 6.5   Private pension funds in the Czech Republic: general data

	1995	1997
Number of funds	42	44
Number of members (millions)	1.3	1.6
Members per fund	30,571	36,682
Members in % of labour force	30	33
Assets (US$ million)	150	675
Members' contributions as % of total contributions	75	75
State contributions as % of total contributions	25	25

Sources: Vittas (1996); Jelínek and Schneider (1999).

The Czech pension funds are IFF joint stock companies, providing defined-contribution plans for individual citizens (see Vittas and Michelitsch 1995; Ministry of Labour 1996b; Vittas 1996). To encourage the Czechs to join the scheme, the government provides a subsidy for participants, which amounts to 25 per cent of all contribution payments (see Table 6.5). The maximum state incentive to be added to individual contributions is CZK 120, or US$ 4.[22] Employers are not required to pay additional contributions on behalf of their staff. If they choose to do so, their contribution payments may only be taken from after-tax profits, rendering this practice highly unattractive.

At present, there are 44 private pension funds in operation, a number generally recognised as being too large for a potential pool of participants estimated at 2–3 million (see Jelínek and Schneider 1999: 263).[23] At the end of 1997, Czech pension funds had accumulated about US$ 675 million. They had been joined by a total of 1.6 million participants, 65 per cent of whom were concentrated in the six largest funds (see Jelínek and Schneider 1999: 263). With 33 per cent of the labour force participating in the voluntary pension funds, the newly set-up scheme has gained a relatively wide acceptance.[24] However, only 25 per cent of participants of the voluntary pension fund scheme are below age 40. This is a rather unfavourable age structure for a financial instrument that, for its success, relies heavily on long-term investments (see Ministry of Labour 1996a: 33). Moreover, the average monthly contribution remained low: CZK 305, or US$ 11. Only 0.1 per cent of all clients contributed more than CZK 1,000 per month (see Jelínek and Schneider 1999: 264).

Table 6.6   *Private pension funds in the Czech Republic: portfolio composition (in per cent of the total portfolio)*

	1995	1996
Government bonds	3	0
Bank bonds	12	41
Firm bonds	33	31
Shares	17	8
Deposits	30	19
Other (real estate)	5	1
Total	100	100

Source: Based on Jelínek and Schneider (1999).

Whereas information on overall investment returns is unavailable, individual funds have reported real rates of return of −4.0 to 3.5 per cent p.a. in 1997 (see Kabilka 1998). The available information on aggregate portfolio composition suggests a substantial change of investment strategy between 1995 and 1996. Strikingly, the share of government bonds remained as low as 3 and 0 per cent, respectively, and investment in shares has been slack with 17 and 8 per cent (see Table 6.6). No specialised agency has been set up to supervise the supplementary pension funds in the Czech Republic – this task is performed by the Ministry of Finance, which has not suceeded in bringing about much transparency regarding the financial performance of the funds.

6.3   PENSION POLITICS IN THE KLAUS ERA

The Czech Approach to Pension Policy

The Czechoslovak version of the much-discussed 'three-pillar approach' was elaborated in 1990, and consists of a compulsory, earnings-related state pension, a voluntary complementary scheme, and individual saving for old-age (see Klimentová 1994: 21). According to mainstream conventions (see subchapter 2.4), this boils down to a two-pillar approach.[25] With the current design of old-age security in the Czech Republic, the Ministry of Labour and Social Affairs claims to have encountered a 'suitable combination' of PAYG and IFF financing of pensions (Ministry of Labour 1996b: 8), trying to avoid problems inherent in both systems. By setting up a voluntary IFF tier instead of a mandatory one, as demanded by the new pension orthodoxy, the Czech government has chosen a slow-track option to enable the emerging local financial market to cope with the influx of pension capital.[26] Concerning the public PAYG system, the Ministry of Labour and Social Affairs is well aware of the need to adapt its technical variables from time to time: to avoid deficits in the pension system after the year 2001, higher contributions, an increased retirement age, tightened eligibility criteria and/or a partial collective funding have to be considered (see Ministry of Labour 1996b).[27]

There is a clear separation of competences: while the Ministry of Labour and Social Affairs is directing the mandatory public scheme, the Ministry of Finance is responsible for the supplementary private pension funds. No major conflict of interests between both ministries has emerged so far. This may well be due to the fact that current surpluses in the public scheme have long accrued to the general budget, a practice facilitated by the lack of an autonomous pension administration. As the Czech pension scheme was financially viable without subsidies from the general budget, the Ministry of Finance had no stake in the pension reform issue. The World Bank is a notable absentee in the Czech case.[28]

The 1995 Pension Reform

The unanimity within Czech government does not imply that there is a similar consensus within Czech society about the government's pension policy. Heated debates preceded the passing of the 1995 Pension Insurance Act, a comprehensive pension reform package intended to re-codify all existing retirement laws (see Götting 1998: 169–70).[29] The most controversial element of this draft was the gradual increase of the retirement age, that was to reach 62 years for men and 57–61 years for women in 2007. Moreover, it comprised a reform of the pension formula to strengthen the insurance principle, e.g. instead of the best 5 out of the last 10 years, the average earnings of the last 30 years would gradually be taken into account (see Schneider 1996a: 26). Pensions would be adjusted when the cumulative price increase exceeded 5 per cent. Furthermore, access to disability pensions was restricted. During a transition period of ten years, benefit calculation would still be based on the old rules if they proved to be more beneficial to the retiree (see Višek and Klimentová 1996: 8).

The strongest opposition to the government's reform proposal was expressed by the Czech and Moravian Chamber of Trades Unions (ČMKOS), that protested against the raising of the pension age, and demanded a separation of the pension insurance from the state budget.[30] A petition against the reform proposal, signed by 630,000 people, was handed over to parliament.[31] In December 1994, the trade union federation called a symbolic one-hour protest strike. In March 1995, the ČMKOS organised a huge anti-government rally with over 60,000 attendants, the biggest since 1989. Moreover, the tripartite Council of Economic and Social Agreement was suspended in 1994/95 for six months because of the pension reform issue. One of the concessions that the Klaus government finally made concerned the pension formula (see Götting 1998: 170): instead of it becoming fully earnings-related, a flat-rate component was introduced alongside the individualised part. Although the Christian-Democratic coalition partner, the KDU-ČSL (*Křest'anská a demokratická unie – Československá strana lidová*), remained opposed to the reform draft and finally boycotted the voting, the government draft was passed with a narrow majority in June 1995, and the Pension Insurance Act No. 155/1996 Coll. came into force on 1 January 1996.

The 'Klaus Paradox'

The Czech pension policy analysed in this study has been shaped under the government of Václav Klaus, the long-serving Czech Prime Minister (1992–1997) and former Minister of Finance (1990–1992). Some scholars have been quick to label the social policy approach during the Klaus era – particularly in the pension arena – as neoliberal (see e.g. Rys 1995: 203). Contrary to this assessment, the previous subchapter has made it clear that the Klaus government did *not* follow the new pension orthodoxy's neoliberal blueprint (see subchapter 2.4), but remained well within the bounds of the Bismarckian–Beveridgean traditions, unlike its post-communist counterparts in Hungary and Poland. In the following, I will focus on what might be called the 'Klaus paradox', part of which will only be disentangled in the comparative analysis of subchapter 7.3.

Without a doubt, Klaus is a 'self-proclaimed Thatcherite' (Orenstein 1996: 16). His rhetoric has indeed been ultra-liberal, as his well-known call for a 'market economy without an adjective' has made unequivocally clear: 'Adjectives like "social" or "environmental" are merely efforts to ... introduce market-alien elements. We need an untainted market economy, and we need it now' (Klaus 1991: 8). However, a clear distinction must be made between Klaus's discourse and the practical policy implemented by his government (see Kabele and Potůček 1995: 24).[32] As pointed out by Stark and Bruszt (1998: 168), 'Klaus's actual practice was most marked by an ability to make unorthodox departures from his orthodox ideology. Not economic dogmatism but political realism was the key to Klausian pragmatism'.[33]

In the area of social policy, Klaus's policy reflects some compromises with his Christian-Democrat coalition partner, KDU-ČSL, an advocate of rather traditional social welfare policy (see Turnovec 1996: 5).[34] A different explanation is ventured by Večerník (1996: 191): 'The social democratic tradition of prewar Czechoslovakia and the proximity of "Social Europe" has prevented unrestrained capitalism from returning'. Somehow corroborating this assessment, Turnovec (1996: 17) demonstrated on the basis of a median voter analysis that 'radical changes in present design of social welfare in the Czech Republic ... [are] politically infeasible'.[35]

To shed light on the *sui generis* combination of radical economic reform and cautious social policy during the Klaus era, it may be helpful to distinguish between two phases of post-1989 social policy. In both periods, Czech(oslovak) policymakers sought to cushion the social costs of economic transformation, a crucial element being continued consumer subsidies, notably of rents, heating, electricity and transport (see Orenstein 1995b: 181), alongside the so-called 'employment miracle' (Dangerfield 1997: 451).[36]

The first phase of social policy development lasted until mid-1992 and has been characterised as 'social democratic' (Orenstein 1996: 16; Večerník 1996: 196). It was shaped by the then Minister of Labour and Social Affairs, Petr Miller (see Miller et al. 1992), while Klaus's influence was confined to the Ministry of Finance. The first post-1989 Czechoslovak government elaborated a social policy blueprint, the 'Scenario for Social Reform' (see Tomeš 1994a: 142–7). It was adopted by parliament in September 1990, together with the fundamental 'Scenario for Economic Reform', boiling down to a political compromise, while also underlining the interdependence of social and economic reform (see Tomeš 1991: 198; Orenstein 1998b: 48). This early blueprint established the principles of social guarantee, of social solidarity and of citizens' participation (see Štangová 1993: 733).[37] Among the first steps to translate these principles into practical policy was Law 463/1991 on the living minimum. During this social democratic phase, the

'Council of Economic and Social Accord' (*Rada hospodářskej a sociálnej dohody*, or RHSD) was created, the first tripartite institution to be set up in Central–Eastern Europe. With seven representatives each, the trades union federation, the employers' associations and the government are represented on an equal basis.[38] All important social policy proposals have to be discussed in the RHSD before being submitted to parliament. Furthermore, until 1994, so-called 'General Agreements' were signed on an annual basis to define the general policy agenda (see Král 1995: 178). The RHSD proved to be instrumental in securing the low-wage/low-unemployment strategy followed in the Czech Republic (see Stark and Bruszt 1998: 185).

The second phase of social policy development, ushered in by Klaus taking over the Czech premiership, has been labelled as 'social-liberal', as it combined social democratic and neoliberal elements. Elements of the residual model – such as means-testing and targeting (see Heady and Smith 1995; Coulter et al. 1997) – were introduced, yet without bringing about a fully-fledged paradigm shift towards a 'Thatcherite' social policy. Klaus opposed yet continued the consultative policymaking exemplified by the creation of the RHSD, while trying to downgrade its significance (see Dangerfield 1997: 452).[39] As consensual agreements had no legal status, the participation of ČMKOS and employers' associations was limited in practice. The Klaus government was not prepared to compromise on core elements of its social policy, as the conflict preceding the 1995 Pension Insurance Act made unmistakably clear (see Orenstein 1995a: 347–8).

In the area of pension reform, the need to make a distinction between Klaus's discourse and the actual policy measures carried through is particularly relevant: 'One of his greatest political skills has been to talk like a Friedmanite or Thatcherite liberal and yet act like a social democrat when necessary' (Orenstein 1998b: 53). The frequent assessment that the Czech old-age security reform has followed a neoliberal course (see e.g. Orenstein 1996: 18; Götting 1998: 170; Mácha 1999b: 248) is based on the government's repeated announcement that the relative weight of the mandatory public tier would, in the long term, be reduced to as little as 35 per cent of the average wage, in order to increase the scope for voluntary private pension funds (see Klimentová 1994: 24; Götting 1998: 171). This much-proclaimed intention, boiling down to a 'slow but steady contracting out of the welfare state' (Dangerfield 1997: 452), was, however, not translated into practical policy before the end of the Klaus era. Instead, a public–private mix based on West European pension traditions emerged, combining Beveridgean and Bismarckian elements. Hence, with the benefit of hindsight and with a view to the Hungarian and Polish pension reforms, the label 'neoliberal' is clearly inapplicable to Czech retirement policy.[40]

6.4   THE RECENT PENSION REFORM DEBATE

Since 1997, the Czech discourse on old-age security has started to reflect the international pension reform controversy (see subchapter 2.4). While in the debate preceding the 1995 Pension Insurance Act the basic conflict was about how to reform the existing public scheme from within, in recent months advocates of full or partial pension privatisation have made themselves heard. Consequently, public discussion has started to focus on the advantages and disadvantages of a public PAYG vs. an IFF scheme.

It has been noted that the main transmitter of the new pension orthodoxy – the World Bank – was absent in the Czech case. What accounts, then, for the recent shift in the Czech pension reform debate? It has been suggested that young Czech economists with strong connections to the international orthodoxy – 'market komsomols' in local jargon – have joined forces with the stakeholders from the financial community and the small liberal party ODA to place pension privatisation on the local agenda.[41] Moreover, the recent pension reform experiences of other countries in the region, notably Hungary and Poland, have not gone unnoticed in the Czech Republic (see Klimentová 1997a). However, the conspicuous efforts at agenda shifting did not succeed in having an impact on the overall pension strategy pursued by the Czech government. In the following, I will attempt to identify the participants in the Czech pension discussion, briefly presenting their respective stances.

Advocates of Pension Privatisation

Transition from the current PAYG to an IFF scheme is being demanded by liberal Czech economists (see e.g. Schneider 1996a, b; Jelínek and Schneider 1997a, b), joined by representatives of banks and investment funds. In their opinion, the advantages of a private IFF system are both micro- and macroeconomic: the privatisation of Czech old-age security would strengthen individual responsibility for old-age provision and would reduce moral hazard. Furthermore, by increasing the amount of investment capital, economic recovery would be supported. A similar approach has been adopted by the Czech National Bank (ČNB) and by the existing voluntary pension funds, represented by the Association of Pension Funds, an important group of stakeholders, newly created by the present two-pillar approach to pension reform.

These advocates of pension privatisation are backed by demography experts from Charles University Prague and Masaryk University Brno, who have warned that the ageing of the Czech population will be more substantial and faster than the existing forecasts show. Most of them propose a transition from the current PAYG to an IFF scheme, as well as a further increase of the retirement age to 65 for both sexes in 2015 (see Mácha 1999b: 253–4).

The 'Bismarckian–Beveridgean Faction'

ČMKOS, the Czech trades union federation, used to be a fierce critic of the Klaus government's approach to old-age security. This became particularly manifest during the conflicts surrounding the 1995 Pension Insurance Act (see above). Meanwhile, a shift in the ČMKOS's position can be observed: while the trade union federation's early stance was more oriented towards the maintenance of the *status quo*, it has recently turned into one of the main adversaries of the newly emerged pension privatisation faction, claiming that the existing options to reform the public PAYG scheme have not yet been exhausted in the Czech Republic. While favouring the expansion of the existing voluntary pension fund tier, they oppose the introduction of a mandatory IFF tier. In their view, such an old-age scheme would destroy social solidarity. Its introduction would imply high transition costs, resulting in a double burden on the current working-age generation (see Rusnok 1997). Moreover, they stress that a mandatory IFF scheme is unable to protect pension benefits against inflation, and tends to high marketing and administration costs. The trade union federation's position is shared by representatives of pensioners' organisations – the Association of Trades Unionist Pensioners, forming part of ČMKOS, and the independent Union of Pensioners – whose main aim is to improve or at least maintain the living standard of old-age pensioners (see Mácha 1999b: 254).

But even if ČMKOS experts have now turned into staunch defenders of the government's two-pillar approach, they remain critical of some details of the latter: in the trades union federation's view, reform is needed to ensure a replacement rate of at least 50 per cent, and to create voluntary pension schemes on an occupational basis, fostered by substantial tax allowances for employers (see Rusnok 1997). Interestingly, even an increase of the retirement age, strongly opposed in 1995, is no longer ruled out by the ČMKOS, now that the overall perception of reform alternatives has shifted.

Political Parties

The liberal Civic Democratic Alliance (*Občanská demokratická aliance*, or ODA) represents the strongest and most unequivocal advocate of partial pension privatisation among Czech political parties (see Král and Mácha 1998: 19). The conservative Civic Democratic Party (*Občanská demokratická strana*, or ODS), the party of former Prime Minister Václav Klaus, is divided on the pension issue. The Christian-Democrat KDU-ČSL objects to any change in the current level of social solidarity and emphasised the maintenance of the current replacement ratio during the 1998 election campaign (see Mácha 1999b). Hence, it might be less of a surprise that under the Klaus government, which relied on a coalition government of ODA, ODS and KDU-ČSL, no radical pension reform was enacted, especially in consideration of the relative strength of these three parties.[42]

The Czech Social Democratic Party (*Česká Strana Sociální Demokracie*, or ČSSD) – that has been ruling the Czech Republic since July 1998 – strictly opposes any radical change in the existing PAYG system, as a shift to mandatory private pension funds would destroy inter-generational solidarity (see Hřích and Larischová 1998: 74). However, some reforms of the *status quo* are deemed necessary, such as the establishment of a separate pension insurance fund, fed both from current contributions and surplus capitalisation. The party had demanded the restitution of the former, lower retirement age until long after the 1995 Pension Insurance Act (see Král and Mácha 1998: 19). A return to the old retirement age and a raising of the real value of old-age pensions has been demanded by the Communist Party of Bohemia and Moravia (*Komunistická strana Čech a Moravy*, or KSČM).

A party called 'Pensioners for a Secure Life' (*Důchodci za Životní Jistoty*, or DŽJ) did not manage to enter Czech parliament following the 1992 and 1996 elections (see Turnovec 1995, 1996). With its membership of 55,000, this left wing, single-issue party had gained prominence during the 1998 election campaign and was even considered a possible coalition partner by the ČSSD (see Mortkowitz 1998), but then fell short of the 5 per cent threshold again. Effectively 'a pressure group rather than a party' (Crawford 1998), DŽJ had tried to reap the benefits of pensioners' discontent over low old-age benefits, demanding to raise the replacement rate to 60–70 per cent of gross wage (see Kohler 1998).

Public Opinion

It may be asked whether Czech public opinion tends to favour a change in the current retirement scheme or rather a maintenance of the *status quo*. There are no surveys reflecting the intra-temporal dynamics of public attitudes on the pension reform issue, yet some insights are provided by an opinion poll conducted by the RILSA/STEM consortium in early 1998 (see Haberlová 1998). By then, a substantial awareness of the need for some kind of pension reform had been created, as a mere 5.3 per cent of those questioned believed that the existing old-age security system could remain unchanged. At the same time, only 13.7 per cent favoured systemic change, while the remaining 81 per cent held that small or substantial reforms of the current system would do. When asked to assess four specific reform scenarios (no changes, reforms within the present system, partial and full pension privatisation), the best evaluation was obtained by the pension reform path actually pursued in the Czech Republic – maintaining the existing state-controlled retirement scheme, while conducting certain parametric reforms. Almost two-thirds of those questioned regarded this reform scenario as acceptable.[43] Full or partial pension privatisation was only supported by one-third, and 60.9 per cent of those questioned explicitly opposed the introduction of mandatory, supplementary saving with a private pension fund, i.e. the mixed reform path followed in Hungary and Poland. As to the relation between a person's preference for one of the specific reform scenarios and his/her age, education and economic status, the RILSA/STEM researchers found it to be rather weak. In comparison, the impact of general political and social value orientations is quite strong (see Haberlová 1998: 18).

A Change of Course in Pension Policy?

Despite the recent demands to introduce a mandatory IFF tier, pension privatisation models such as the Chilean or Argentine ones were not pursued during the liberal Klaus era. In contrast to the Hungarian and Polish cases, the only portfolio involved in the Czech pension reform efforts is the Ministry of Labour and Social Affairs. Due to the subordinate institutional shape of the Czech Social Security Administration (ČSSZ), there were no conceptual inputs from this body to the pension reform discussion – a marked difference to the Hungarian case. As the public pension scheme does not depend on budgetary subsidies, the Ministry of Finance, another potential intra-governmental actor, has no stake in the issue.

Pension experts at the Ministry of Labour are well-informed about the international pension reform debate and the recent privatisation precedents in Central–Eastern Europe and in Latin America (see Klimentová 1997a, b).[44] Czech policymakers are not closing their eyes to the advantages of an IFF system, but emphasise the resulting fiscal costs, as well as potential risks (see Klimentová 1997c): the severe economic and financial crisis that seized the Czech Republic in 1997 revealed that the bases of the local capital market are still shaky.[45]

Hence, after simulating the overall impact and costs related to a partial privatisation of the Czech pension scheme in 1997, as against the alternative, a thorough reform of the existing PAYG scheme, the Ministry of Labour's experts concluded that there was still sufficient leeway within the existing public PAYG system to face the challenges of the next decades (see Mácha 1999b: 254).[46] At the same time, they are aware of the political resistance that such reforms are expected to face (see Klimentová 1997c; Polívka 1997).[47] The social democratic ČSSD minority government that took over in mid-1998 has not yet decided on the concrete pension reform path to be followed (see Sedlar 1998: 2). Given its previous stance on the pension issue (see Král and Mácha 1998: 22) it is even less likely to abandon the Bismarckian–Beveridgean course than the Klaus government used to be.

6.5   SUMMING UP:
PROBLEMS, ACTORS AND POLICY CHOICES

Contrary to the Hungarian and Polish cases, the Czech retirement system did not suffer much from economic transformation. As both the number of the unemployed and the ranks of pensioners increased only slightly, the Czech pension system exhibited a surplus that helped to relieve the financial strains of the general government budget. The changes that the Czech old-age security scheme underwent in the post-1989 era were not limited to the areas of organisation, financing and eligibility: the introduction of voluntary private pension funds in 1994 changed the public–private mix in the provision of old-age security. Overall, the Czech reforms remained well within the bounds of the West European pension traditions (see subchapter 2.2), combining Beveridgean and Bismarckian elements in the public pillar, while granting private pension providers only a supplementary role.

This paradigm choice beyond the dominant international mainstream might appear surprising, given the neoliberal discourse of the long-standing Czech Prime Minister, Václav Klaus, seemingly a good match for the new pension orthodoxy. However, a closer look reveals that Klaus frequently departed from his 'market economy without an adjective' rhetoric when it came to practical politics. In the case of pension reform, the 'Klaus paradox' is further disentangled when the constellation of relevant political actors is considered: the only portfolio involved in the Czech pension reform efforts was the Ministry of Labour and Social Affairs, traditionally inclined towards the Bismarckian–Beveridgean paradigms. As the public pension scheme was financially viable without subsidies from the general budget, the Ministry of Finance, a potential intra-governmental actor with rather a neoliberal orientation, had no stake in the pension reform issue. But the most notable absentee in the Czech case is probably the World Bank, an important catalyst in other pension reform arenas. The Bank's lack of leverage in the Czech Republic coincides with a low level of external debt, compared with the Hungarian and Polish cases.[48]

Still, even without the involvement of this financial institution, some degree of agenda-shifting has taken place in the past two years, reflecting a change in the local perception of available pension reform alternatives: while in the heated debate preceding the 1995 Pension Insurance Act, the basic conflict was about how to reform the existing public scheme from within, in recent times public discussion has started to focus on the advantages and disadvantages of a public PAYG vs. an IFF scheme, thereby mirroring the international pension reform controversy. However, until the end of the Klaus era, the political leverage of the newly emerged advocates of a mandatory IFF scheme was clearly insufficient to induce a revision of the Bismarckian–Beveridgean course in Czech pension policy, that takes up the local social insurance traditions dating back to the beginning of this century.

NOTES

1. However, a large part of the Czechoslovak rural population remained without old-age insurance, as farmers were granted social security only in 1945 – during the last weeks of the Nazi 'Protectorate of Bohemia and Moravia' (see De Deken 1994: 23–4).
2. The Central Social Insurance Institute that administered this pension scheme was governed by a committee made up of representatives of the insured and the employers, and of a number of social security experts appointed by the government (see De Deken 1994: 8).
3. For a comparison of eligibility, financing and organisation of these five pension schemes see De Deken (1995: 232).
4. See De Deken (1994: 19–24) for an analysis of the changes in the Czechoslovak old-age security system from 1938 to 1945.
5. Special arrangements for miners and civil servants were maintained, the latter only until 1950. These privileges comprised mainly a lower retirement age and higher benefits. As a consequence of the 1956 reform, the miners' privileges were extended to other occupational groups of strategic importance (see De Deken 1994: 60–1, 90).
6. In the same year, old-age protection was granted to members of the newly created agricultural co-operatives. It was not until 1976 that this scheme was integrated into the unified pension system (see De Deken 1994: 86–9, 127).
7. According to official discourse, the Czechoslovak pension system still rested on the 'principles of unity and universality' (Ministère Fédéral du Travail 1980: 11; own translation).
8. The highest category, I, comprised, e.g., miners, army officers, policemen and pilots (see Večerník 1996: 213). According to De Deken (1994: 91), the number of people covered by categories I and II reached 8–9 per cent of the labour force in 1983.
9. After the 1956 Social Security Act, pensioners were allowed to work while receiving their retirement benefit (see De Deken 1994: 94–5).
10. The Czech and Slovak Republics separated on 1 January 1993. While having focused on the whole of Czechoslovakia in this subchapter, I will in the following only consider developments in the Czech Republic. It should be noted that separate policymaking in the two republics started well before 1993 (see Štangová 1993: 734).
11. Low unemployment in the Czech Republic is mainly due to the fact that the restructuring of the enterprise sector has been delayed (see Adam 1996: 166–7). Furthermore, the Czech Republic benefited from extensive foreign tourism and, after the 'velvet divorce', remained largely without structurally disadvantageous branches, situated in Slovakia (see Cichon and Hagemejer 1995: 81). Heinrich (1996: 23–4) stresses the impact of overall economic policy, notably wage moderation, on the Czech labour market.
12. It should be noted that a third category of pensions – benefits for widows, widowers and orphans – decreased by 4.7 per cent between 1989 and 1996.
13. While social insurance comprises health, pension, accident and unemployment schemes, social support mainly comprises family allowances. Social assistance aims at guaranteeing basic needs to those threatened by material and social indigence (see Král 1995: 175–7).

14. Nominal contribution rates were 27.7 (employees 6.8 per cent; employers 20.4 per cent) before and 26 per cent of gross wage (6.5 and 19.5 per cent; resp.) after 1995. See Chapter 4 for details on the standardisation of contribution rates.
15. As early as 1990, the so-called 'personal pension' for political merits had been abolished (see Tomeš 1994a: 137).
16. The retirement age of Czech women is still dependent on the number of children raised.
17. There are two basic ways to early retirement. For both, 25 insurance years are required. To retire two years earlier, the applicant must have been in the register of an unemployment office for at least 180 days. Benefits are reduced by 1 per cent for every 90 days of pension taken prior to retirement age. When reaching retirement age, the reduction is lifted. When retiring three years early (four from 2001 and five from 2007), the reduction is lower, but permanent: 0.6 per cent of the calculation base for every 90 days (see Ministry of Labour 1996a: 9).
18. These non-contributory periods include secondary schooling or university studies, military service, unemployment, child-raising and care for persons close to the insured (see Ministry of Labour 1996a: 7–8).
19. CZK 28 = US$ 1. To avoid distortions, this amount, as well as the earnings thresholds mentioned below, are to be adjusted regularly. However, this adjustment is discretionary, as the Czech government refrained from fixing any indexation rules.
20. See Ministry of Labour (1996a: 6) for an overview of pension adjustments from 1990 until 1995.
21. For a general discussion of occupational versus personal funded pensions see Davis (1998: 10–12).
22. This ceiling applies to contributions of CZK 500 and over. See Boller (1997: 394) and Jelínek and Schneider (1999: 261) for the state subsidy paid when contribution amounts are lower.
23. By the end of 1998, the number of private pension funds had decreased to 26, while the number of participants had increased to 1.7 million (Mácha 1999a).
24. However, Czech scholars are rather critical of the voluntary pension funds, as a much higher acceptance of the scheme had been expected (see Rusnok 1997; Jelínek and Schneider 1999).
25. Meanwhile, the Ministry of Labour and Social Affairs has adopted these conventions, describing the Czech pension system as a 'two-pillar approach' (see e.g. Klimentová 1997a: 3).
26. For a general discussion of mandatory versus voluntary provision of funded pensions see Davis (1998: 5–7).
27. For some tentative calculations regarding trends in the Czech pension system from 1996 to 2020 see Ministry of Labour (1996b).
28. The World Bank's absence from the Czech pension reform arena can be explained by the country's low level of external debt (see Table 7.6). Moreover, Václav Klaus's general reluctance concerning the involvement of foreign advisors, as expressed in Blejer and Coricelli (1995: 63), has to be taken into account.
29. Please note that the modifications resulting from the 1995 Pension Insurance Act have already been included in the account on organisation, financing and eligibility given in subchapter 6.2. Here, the main focus is on the political controversies surrounding the 1995 reform.
30. The unitary Czechoslovak Confederation of Trades Unions (later *Českomoravská komora odborových svazů*, or ČMKOS) emerged from a grass-roots take-over of the old regime's trades union federation in early 1990 (see Stark and Bruszt 1998: 184). For further demands of the ČMKOS campaign against the 1995 pension reform draft see ČMKOS (1994a, b).
31. Rys (1995: 205) reports that the largest government party denounced this action as an attack on parliamentary democracy, calling for measures to protect the working population from trades unions.
32. For other examples of 'talking the talk, but not walking the walk' in the Czech case see Jacoby (1998: 23–30).

33. Stark and Bruszt (1998: 169–70) argue that, in the Czech case, the executive's limited institutional room for manœuvre resulted in a moderated policy course.
34. Because of his party's narrow majority in parliament, Klaus was in no position to ignore his junior coalition partners (see Stark and Bruszt 1998: 182).
35. A similar conclusion is reached by Mareš, Musil and Rabušic (1994: 87): 'In the Czech cultural milieu, it would seem likely that movement towards a residual welfare state could be enforced only with great difficulties'.
36. In the midst of the severe economic crisis, gradual rent and energy deregulation started in July 1997 (see McClune 1997).
37. 'The major aim could be defined as a transition from a paternalistic, ideologically based political culture towards a democratic and civic society with earmarked expenditures and programmes related to effective action, both private and public, in a pluralistic social environment ... This requires a complete restructuring of social institutions and practices' (Tomeš 1994a: 139).
38. When setting up the RHSD in October 1990, 'the Czech government needed to find suitable employers' associations to participate. Since a single representative business association did not exist, the government felt that one had to be created' (Desai and Orenstein 1996: 29).
39. In 1995, the RHSD was renamed 'Council for the Dialogue of Social Partners'. The Klaus government, opposed to all kinds of corporatism (see Rys 1995: 205), would have preferred to transform the RHSD into a bipartite collective bargaining organisation, where the government would have played only an arbitrating role (see Desai and Orenstein 1996: 35).
40. Another argument used by Götting (1998: 171) and others to corroborate the hypothesis that Klaus's pension policy deserves the label 'neoliberal' is his disapproval of corporatist self-governing structures. Even though self-governing can be interpreted as forming an integral part of the Bismarckian concept, it should be noted that it is absent in the Beveridgean tradition, the other main current within the traditional West European welfare paradigm (see subchapter 2.2).
41. The Prague-based *Liberální Institut*, a liberal think tank, set out to 'influence the discussion outcome towards a radical switch from the current pay-as-you-go model to a funded pension scheme with individual pension accounts for all citizens, which would be invested with the private pension funds' (see Jelínek and Schneider 1997a), thereby co-operating with two World Bank pension experts and a representative of the local financial community ('Patria Finance').
42. In the 1996 (1992) elections, ODS gained 34 (38) per cent of parliamentary seats, KDU-ČSL obtained 9 (7.5) per cent, and ODA was the smallest coalition partner with 6.5 (7) per cent (see Turnovec 1995: 5, 1996: 6).
43. Interestingly, those questioned significantly preferred to increase the contribution rate, even to as much as 35 per cent of gross wage (67 per cent), rather than to introduce stricter rules or a higher retirement age (23 per cent); see Haberlová 1998: 23.
44. See an article by Jana Klimentová, a senior pension reform expert at the Czech Ministry of Labour and Social Affairs, significantly entitled: 'Pension reform – the recommendations differ' (Klimentová and Polívka 1997; own translation).
45. Moreover, after the much-criticised partial privatisation of Czech health care (see Adam 1998), the government may well have been inclined to proceed more cautiously in the pension reform arena.
46. The proposed pension scheme would have consisted of three mandatory tiers, each of which was to provide 15 per cent of gross wage: (1) a flat-rate, tax-financed public scheme; (2) an earnings-related public scheme; (3) a private IFF scheme. In all, the authors of this proposal claimed that today's replacement rate – 45 per cent of gross wage – would be maintained. See Rusnok (1997) for the ČMKOS's critique of this proposal.
47. A recent example is the reaction of the Czech Association of Industry to a proposal to raise pension contributions. The Association's President, Štěpán Popovič, warned that such a move would make lay-offs unavoidable, leading the Czechs 'straight to hell' (quoted from Mlada Fronta Dnes 1998: 12; own translation).

48. An alternative, but less convincing explanation for the Klaus' government's refusal to choose pension privatisation would recall that strong governments do not always embark on radical reform, as concentrated authority is tantamount to concentrated responsibility, providing little chance of blame avoidance (see Pierson 1996).

7.   Central–Eastern European Pension Reforms in a Comparative Perspective

7.1   FROM A COMMON LEGACY TO BIFURCATING REFORM PATHS

When designing blueprints for old-age security in Central–Eastern Europe, the post-1989 pension reformers did not start from scratch. Rather, a more difficult task had to be tackled – the rebuilding of the already existing institutional framework, that exhibited largely similar traits in the region (see Götting 1994: 5). This common legacy – both from the interwar period and the decades of socialist rule – will be outlined below. I will then compare the post-socialist problem settings and initial measures, before turning to the divergent paradigm choices in Poland and Hungary on the one hand, and the Czech Republic on the other.

Old-Age Security Prior to 1989

In Hungary, Poland and Czechoslovakia, mandatory public pension insurance preceded the socialist era, dating back to the turn of the century. These Bismarckian-type pension schemes were mostly self-governed, and consisted of separate schemes for blue- and white-collar workers, financed by employers' and employees' contributions.[1] Other typical features of the interwar pension schemes in Central–Eastern Europe included their incomplete coverage, notably of the rural labour force, and the existence of privileged groups with non-contributory schemes. It is interesting to note that in all three countries, these schemes were originally fully funded but lost their reserves during World War II, resulting in a post-war shift to PAYG financing.

During the decades of socialist rule, the existing pension schemes were unified and, as a rule, integrated into the state budget, cross-subsidising other expenditure items.[2] Employees' contributions were largely abolished,

149

rendering employers' contributions the only source of financing.[3] The administration of the old-age scheme was taken over by trades unions in the 1950s, following the Soviet example.[4] A major achievement of the post-war years was the gradual expansion of coverage, becoming universal by the 1960s or 1970s. Furthermore, the retirement age was lowered to 60 for men and 55 for women.[5]

Although the existing contribution–benefit link was weak and there was little benefit differentiation, pension privileges granted for occupations of strategic importance within the centrally planned economy marked an important departure from universalism.[6] Moreover, the insufficient adjustment of current pensions to inflation implied that newly granted pensions were considerably higher than average pensions, giving rise to problems of inter-cohort fairness and of benefit adequacy, known as the '*stary portfel*' issue in Poland. Hence, many pensioners continued their gainful employment to top up their low old-age benefits.[7]

Transformation and Old-Age Security

Economic transformation affected the existing PAYG systems in Central–Eastern Europe in a number of ways (see Brabant 1998: 329–30). Price liberalisation and the curtailment of subsidies on basic goods and services, for example, required a shift from indirect to direct transfers, resulting in rising expenditures for old-age security. The restructuring of state-owned enterprises had an effect on both the revenue and the expenditure side of public pension schemes. The privatisation, downgrading and closing-down of enterprises was accompanied by a mounting number of disability pensions and by early retirement policies. Designed to avoid large-scale unemployment, this policy led to an increased number of pensioners and a falling number of contributors to the schemes (see Table 7.1).

As a result, the system dependency ratio of the existing old-age security schemes rose from 38.9 (1989) to 61.2 per cent (1996) in Poland, from 51.4 (1989) to 83.9 per cent (1996) in Hungary and from 54.4 (1989) to 60.5 per cent (1996) in the Czech Republic. Since the respective old-age dependency ratios remained largely unchanged over the same period (see Tables 4.3, 5.3 and 6.3), it can be concluded that the threat to the financial viability of the existing pension schemes in the region did not stem from population ageing but was transformation-induced.[8] Whereas all three countries considered in this study exhibited mounting levels of pension expenditure to GDP, only Poland surpassed the West European average.[9]

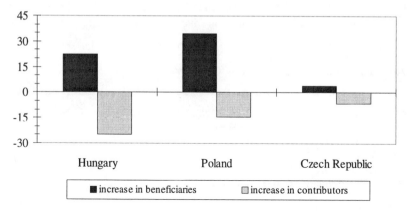

Source: Based on Schrooten, Smeeding and Wagner (1999); own calculations.

*Figure 7.1   Increase in beneficiaries and contributors 1989–1996
(in per cent of 1989 data)*

While the Hungarian and Polish old-age schemes became dependent on budgetary subsidies (see Table 7.1), the post-1989 pension crisis did not extend to the Czech Republic. The local PAYG system continued to exhibit a surplus, while charging lower contribution rates than the Hungarian and Polish schemes (see Table 7.2). The remarkable financial stability of the Czech pension system is largely due to the country's relatively unimpaired labour market (see Table 7.6), implying that both the increase in beneficiaries and the decrease in contributors to the PAYG scheme were far less pronounced in the Czech Republic than in Hungary and Poland: between 1989 and 1996, the number of employed Poles and Hungarians dropped by 14.4 and 25.0 per cent, respectively, whereas the number of employed Czechs fell by only 6.6 per cent. In the same period, the increase in pensioners amounted to a mere 3.8 per cent in the Czech Republic, while it sky-rocketed in Poland and Hungary (34.8 and 22.4 per cent, respectively).

Early Pension Reform Measures

In the first half of the 1990s, a consensus emerged in all three countries that the old-age security systems inherited from the socialist past were in need of reform, both to secure their financial sustainability and to adapt some of the previous design features to the new economic order (see Schmähl 1995; Heinrich et al. 1996). Local social security experts disagreed whether the link between contributions and benefits should be strengthened, following the Bismarckian tradition, or whether a move towards a Beveridgean-style flat-rate scheme would be more appropriate (see Table 2.1).[10] Another highly controversial issue concerned the introduction of a mandatory IFF tier (see below).

Table 7.1   Hungarian, Polish and Czech pension systems: indicators, 1996

Indicators	Hungary	Poland	Czech Republic
Old-age dependency ratio (OADR)[a]	35.6	29.9	32.0
System dependency ratio[b]	83.9	61.2	60.5
Replacement ratio[c]	56.7	72.5	56.0
Average monthly pension (1998, in US$)[d]	107	240	153
Increase in beneficiaries, 1989–1996 (in % of 1989 data)	22.4	34.8	3.8
Increase in contributors, 1989–1996 (in % of 1989 data)	−25.0	−14.4	−6.6
Percentage distribution of pensioners, by type of pension			
– old-age	53.8	36.0	59.2
– disability	24.7	28.6	17.4
– others[e]	21.5	35.4	23.4
Pension expenditure (in % of GDP)	9.9	14.5	9.0
Budgetary subsidies for public pension scheme[f] (in % of GDP)	0.4	1.9	−0.3

Notes: [a] 60+ years old in % of 20–59 years old
              [b] pensioners in % of contributors
              [c] average pension in % of average wage
              [d] Hungarian data are for 1997
              [e] survivors' pensions, i.e. widow/ers' and orphans' pensions
              [f] Poland: estimate of total pension-related subsidies for ZUS and KRUS

Source: Based on Schrooten, Smeeding and Wagner (1999); own calculations.

Table 7.2   Hungarian, Polish and Czech pension systems: features, 1996 [a]

Characteristics	Hungary	Poland	Czech Republic
Type	mandatory, PAYG	mandatory, PAYG	mandatory, PAYG
Standardised contribution rates[b]	26.5	36.7	23.0
– employees	5.2	–	5.8
– employers	21.3	36.7	17.3
Contribution ceiling	yes	no	no
Separation of pension fund from state budget	yes	yes	no
Structure of pension formula	basic + earnings-related component	basic + earnings-related component	basic + earnings-related component
Qualifying years	20	25/20 (men/women)	25
Relevant years of earnings	all since 1988	best 10 out of last 20 (2000)	last 10 (1996); last 30 (2016)
Retirement age today (men/women)	60/55	65/60	60/53–57
Future retirement age (men/women)	62/62 (2008)	65/60	62/57–61 (2007)
Benefit reduction when retiring early	yes	no	yes
Branch privileges	almost abolished	still in force	abolished

Notes: [a] This table intends to compare the outcomes of the early reform measures. Hence, it does *not* reflect the first-tier restructuring that accompanied systemic reform in Hungary and Poland (see subchapter 7.2).
   [b] On standardisation see chapter 4.

Sources: Chapters 4, 5 and 6.

Table 7.3   Voluntary private pension funds in the Czech Republic and Hungary, 1997

Characteristics	Czech Republic	Hungary
Year of introduction	1994	1994
Type of enterprise	Joint Stock Companies	VMB funds
Financing	IFF	IFF
Nature	voluntary	voluntary
Government incentives	subsidy (40% of contribution payments, up to CZK 120 monthly)	tax credit on contribution payments (50%; up to HUF 200,000 p.a.)
Employers' contribution	out of after-tax profit	tax-exempt
Supervision	Ministry of Finance	specialised authority
Number of funds	44	221
Total assets (US$ million)	675	250
Real interest rate p.a.	−4.0 to 3.5	3.0 to 5.5 (1995)
Number of members (million)	1.6	0.6
Members in % of labour force	33.0	15.3

Sources: Chapters 4 and 6.

However, it was relatively undisputed among social security experts that essential reform measures included the separation of pension schemes from the state budget and from other social insurance plans, the abolition of branch privileges, the raising of the retirement age, the restriction of easy access to early retirement and to invalidity pensions, and the introduction of an employees' contribution.[11] By now, these reform measures have largely been enacted (for an overview see Table 7.2), alongside other steps in the areas of organisation, financing, eligibility and benefits. In all three countries considered, these parametric reforms – notably a higher pension age and the abolition of branch privileges – met with considerable political resistance or have even been blocked by constitutional courts (see Żukowski 1996: 109), inducing policymakers to compromise on the speed and/or scope of the required reform steps.

A far less controversial reform measure was the introduction of supplementary old-age security institutions, the first move towards the pluralisation of pension provision in Central–Eastern Europe: in 1994, voluntary private IFF pension funds were created in Hungary and the Czech Republic. Three years later, 1.6 million Czechs, or 33.0 per cent of the labour force, had joined one of 44 private pension funds. The picture is more fragmented in Hungary: there were no less than 221 VMB pension funds, while the number of participants amounted to only 0.6 million, i.e. 15.3 per cent of the labour force (see Table 7.3). With their strong role for employers, the Hungarian VMB funds – rather than the individualist Czech institutions – boil down to a functional proxy for West European occupational schemes.

Bifurcating Reform Paths in the Mid-1990s

The previous section has shown that, on the grounds of their common legacy, Hungarian, Polish and Czech policymakers faced a largely similar pre-1989 agenda of reforms within the existing public PAYG schemes, which they accomplished to a great extent (see Table 7.2).[12] However, by the mid-1990s, policymakers in Poland, Hungary and the Czech Republic embarked on divergent pension reform courses, which will be outlined below.

The paradigm choice made in the Czech Republic remained well within the boundaries of the Bismarckian–Beveridgean welfare paradigm. Today, the Czech pension system is two-tiered, combining a public mandatory PAYG scheme with a voluntary private funded tier. Even though, in early 1997, a debate arose about the introduction of a mandatory pension fund tier (see Mácha 1999b), the comparatively cautious pension reform path followed by successive Czech governments remained unchanged. The Czech policy choice can be interpreted both as a move towards the West European mainstream (see subchapter 2.2) and as a successful attempt to reinvent the pre-communist welfare state traditions (see Hartl and Večerník 1992: 161).

The cases of Hungary and Poland, on the other hand, show that the institutional legacy did not prove decisive for the reform course to be followed, as the Bismarckian–Beveridgean traditions did not prevent Hungarian and Polish policymakers from embarking on radical reform, i.e. partial pension privatisation. Moreover, the interwar experience concerning fully-funded schemes ending with a loss of reserves was apparently no reason for not introducing a mandatory IFF scheme in either country. However, the subsequent PAYG legacy did engender path dependence in that an instant shift to full privatisation was out of the question in fiscal terms, due to the substantial pension entitlements that are widespread among Hungarians and

Poles. The population expected these acquired rights to be recognised, notwithstanding the historic turning-point marked by the *annus mirabilis* of 1989 (see Fox 1997: 377; Brabant 1998: 330).

In the remainder of this chapter, the divergent policy choices in the three Central–Eastern European country cases will be analysed. In particular, it will be asked what accounts for the feasibility of radical pension reform in Hungary and Poland. The following subchapter will provide a comparative analysis of the paradigm choice made in both countries, focusing on conceptual and political economy aspects of the mixed model approach. Because of its particular relevance in the context of this study, the Latin American-style reform path followed in Poland and Hungary will be treated in a separate subchapter, whereas the Czech experience will only be taken up as a contrasting case in the concluding subchapter that examines the differing reform paths from an actor-centred institutionalist perspective.

7.2   RADICAL REFORM IN HUNGARY AND POLAND: CONCEPTUAL AND POLITICAL ECONOMY ASPECTS

The Way Towards Pension Privatisation

By the mid-1990s, in both Hungary and Poland a polarised debate had arisen about the pension reform strategy to be followed (see Ferge 1997c; Golinowska 1999), reflecting the international pension controversy (see subchapter 2.4). The one side, following the traditional Bismarckian–Beveridgean pension paradigm (see subchapter 2.2) and formed by the respective Welfare Ministries, held that a radical regime change in old-age security was neither desirable nor necessary.[13] The other side, the advocates of Latin American-style pension privatisation (see subchapter 2.3), notably the Ministries of Finance, argued that a private IFF pension scheme represented the only appropriate alternative to the financially inviable public old-age security system. It is interesting to note that in Hungary most social security experts tended to back the Bismarckian–Beveridgean faction, while in Poland this was only true for Professors of Social Insurance Law, while most economists dealing with social security were in favour of partial or full pension privatisation.

In both Poland and Hungary, the stalemate between the Ministries of Finance and Welfare on the issue of pension reform was settled in 1996.[14] The compromises that were worked out exhibit a substantial bias towards the privatisation faction. Subsequently, small task forces were set up in both countries to work out the draft legislation (see Nelson 1998: 8–9), thereby bypassing the Welfare Ministry's exclusive competences in pension reform. These special committees were actively supported by the World Bank, with its internationally well-known stance in the pension issue. In the Polish case, the pension reform task force was even headed by a World Bank economist, granting the Bank a pivotal channel to advise Polish pension reformers.

Negotiations with potential opponents preceded the passing of the pension reform laws in both countries, but the reformers were only willing to compromise on the scope of first-tier reforms, while their basic paradigm choice was not put up for discussion with secondary pension reform actors, such as trades unions. Eventually, the Hungarian pension reform laws were enacted by parliament in July 1997 and came into force on 1 January 1998, whereas the Polish reform was scheduled to start in early 1999, after the relevant legislation was passed by the Sejm in two tranches (in summer 1997 and autumn 1998).[15] In both countries, the new pension system is of a mixed type, combining a mandatory public PAYG tier with a partially mandatory IFF system.

The new two-tier scheme offers a purely public as well as a mixed pension option on a mandatory basis.[16] The first, PAYG tier, to be financed by employers' and part of employees' contributions, is mandatory for all insured, at least as first tier. The public pension scheme will cover acquired pension claims by paying some sort of compensatory pension, to be topped up by post-reform pension claims if the insured decides to stick to the purely public pension option. The second, IFF tier consists of a newly created pension fund system.[17] Membership in the IFF tier is obligatory for young people, complementing the first tier (mixed pension path): while joining a pension fund will be mandatory for all new entrants to the labour market in Hungary, everybody under 30 would be required to do so according to the Polish pension reform draft. Those already working (in Poland: those above age 30) are free to choose between the purely public and the mixed pension path. If they opt for the latter, private pension funds will replace part of the first tier: one-fifth (Poland) to one-quarter (Hungary) of mandatory contributions will go to the private pension fund tier. In Poland, those above age 50 cannot enter the IFF scheme, but have to stay in the public system (purely public pension path). The Hungarian reform draft originally provided for an age threshold of 47, which had to be dropped on constitutional grounds in the final version of the pension reform legislation.[18]

The Polish-Hungarian approach to pension reform involves a significant reprioritisation between public and private old-age provision (see Charlton, McKinnon and Konopielko 1998: 1423). Even if the lion's share of Hungarian and Polish old-age security will still be provided by the public PAYG tier, the reform amounts to a partial privatisation of the existing public pension scheme, following the Argentine precedent (see Holzmann 1997b: 9).

This paradigm shift constitutes a radical departure from local social insurance traditions, dating back to the turn of the century.[19]

Differences Between the Hungarian and Polish Reforms

Although the overall set-up of the Hungarian and Polish pension reforms is strikingly similar, it should be noted that both reforms differ in many details (see Simonovits 1999; Żukowski 1999). Here, I will focus on the two most important differences – the range of first-tier reforms and the corporate constitution of second-tier institutions.

Polish first-tier reforms are more sweeping than the ones enacted in Hungary. The introduction of the NDC approach (see subchapter 2.1) will fundamentally change the rules within the public tier, reflecting the involvement of a Swedish advisory team (see Office 1997). Benefit calculation will be based exclusively on the total amount of paid contributions, divided by the average life expectancy at retirement, thereby adopting the Swedish–Latvian pension formula (see subchapter 2.2). Holzmann (1997a: 6) interprets the NDC approach, followed in a number of recent pension reforms, as a 'close analogue' to the Chilean-style paradigm shift, as it appropriates the vocabulary and mimics the logic of IFF schemes.[20] Reportedly, the Polish reformers chose this first-pillar design, that involved a fundamental departure from the redistributive character of the old pension formula, because it seemed to be inconsistent with branch privileges and was therefore thought to facilitate their eventual abolition, one of the most difficult tasks on the Polish pension reform agenda (see Nelson 1998: 15).

As regards the second-tier institutions in both countries, private pension funds in Poland are being created as joint stock companies, that is, financial intermediaries of a commercial type, similar to the ones to be found in the Anglo-Saxon world. By comparison, the Hungarian second-tier institutions have been set up as voluntary mutual benefit (VMB) funds and thus have a co-operative-like corporate constitution (see Palacios and Rocha 1997: 24). VMB funds are non-profit organisations that are self-governed and owned by fund members. At the annual general meeting the principle 'one member, one vote' holds. Corporate governance in co-operative-like financial intermediaries of reasonable size has rarely been a success story, however, as there are too few incentives to exercise ownership rights instead of resorting to free-riding (see Krahnen and Schmidt 1993).[21] However, the *sui generis* corporate structure of the Hungarian pension funds is likely to have been instrumental in making these new financial institutions politically palatable, as it enabled recurrent reference to 'solidarity' as one of the basic principles of these second and third tier institutions, alongside 'self-provision' (see e.g. Ministry of Finance 1994: 9; Pénztarfelügyelet 1997a: 65).

The Relevance of the Latin American Precedents

As far as underlying role models are concerned, it is obvious that the pension reforms enacted in Poland and Hungary are not identical replications of the radical Chilean reform (see subchapter 2.3), since privatisation of old-age security is only partial. Rather, with their mixed set-up, they closely resemble its democratic version – the 'Argentine model', that reflected two years of political bargaining in the Argentine parliament when it came into force in 1994 (see subchapter 2.3).

Though following the basic traits of the Argentine reform as well as its major deviations from the Chilean precedent, Polish and Hungarian reformers did not copy all Argentine design features. They did not establish extremely strict entitlement conditions for public-tier benefits, that effectively limit the recognition of acquired pension claims, and hence create incentives to switch to the mixed scheme. Neither did they opt for granting *all* insured, including new entrants to the labour market, a choice between the mixed and the purely public pension path. Moreover, Polish and Hungarian policymakers refrained from following the Argentine move to introduce a universal basic pension. Earlier opinion polls commissioned by pension reformers in both countries had revealed that such a benefit conflicted with the prevailing notion of justice, being far less popular than an earnings-related approach (see Golinowska 1999: 181; TÁRKI 1995: 8–9). Hence, Central–Eastern European pension reformers opted for a means-tested minimum pension guarantee instead.[22]

As pointed out in chapters 4 and 5, the new pension orthodoxy and, more tangibly, World Bank advice were the main transmission mechanisms between the Southern experiences and the Polish and Hungarian reformers. The inclination towards Latin American role models was aided by Argentine and Chilean advisors involved in the Hungarian and Polish pension reform process. Moreover, the World Bank and USAID sponsored trips to Argentina and Chile, attended by Polish social security experts, journalists, trade unionists and MPs in order to obtain first hand information.

At this point, attentive pundits of West European pension schemes may point to the fact that mixed models are no Latin American peculiarity, considering, e.g., the Swiss, the British and the Dutch old-age systems. However, even though these non-mainstream European pension schemes were certainly not ignored altogether by the Polish and Hungarian reformers, their impact as role models in the recent Central–Eastern European pension reforms can be dismissed on conceptual grounds: the Polish–Hungarian reforms bear considerably more resemblance to the Argentine set-up than to either of the mixed European precedents. This assessment is further supported by the genesis of the respective mixed schemes: while in the non-mainstream

West European cases the introduction of private pension schemes was both gradual and supplementary, Latin American pension reformers had decided to pursue a one-shot transition from a monolithic public PAYG scheme – a literal *privatisation* of previously public old-age provision. Replacing an existing public PAYG scheme by a mandatory private IFF tier, if only partially, results in the frequently mentioned transition costs caused by the recognition of acquired pension claims (see subchapter 2.4). Contrary to this, the supplementary policy path followed in the Netherlands and Switzerland avoided this fiscal implication. The policy problem faced by Central European policymakers resembled that of their Latin American counterparts, hence the relevance of the experiences of the latter in the region. It is thus no coincidence but rather a result of a *sui generis* institutional transfer from the South to the East that the privatisation of old-age security has followed similar patterns in both regions.

This reasoning does not, however, imply that a *de facto* inclination towards Latin American role models resulted in explicit reference to the underlying reform paradigms. Central–Eastern European policymakers soon became aware of the fact that, in the eyes of their compatriots, Latin America carried the stigma of being a less developed region (see Orenstein 1998a: 27). Furthermore, it turned out that Chile was ill-suited as an example in public discourse, as the connotations of the 'Chilean model' extended to the dictatorial political rule under which the famous pension reform was carried through. Therefore the reformers resorted to tactical packaging, seeking to distance themselves from the Chilean precedent and to avoid all reference to Latin American reforms (e.g. Rocha 1996: 15; Rutkowski 1998).

Political Economy Advantages of the Mixed Model

Generally speaking, the introduction of mandatory pension funds in transition economies may be interpreted as a 'concept of creating new stakeholders in the private system' (Graham 1997: 397).[23] Moreover, pension privatisation amounts to a 'signalling' – in the sense employed by Rodrik (1998) – of the respective government's general commitment to market-oriented reform: by the mid-1990s, rating agencies included radical pension reform as a point in favour in their country-risk assessments (see Nelson 1998: 6).[24]

The specific rationale of the mixed approach is 'putting the eggs in two baskets' (Queisser 1998b: 27), i.e. its ascribed potential to diversify the 'classical' drawbacks of both public PAYG schemes and private pension funds – demographic and capital market risks (see e.g. Office 1997: iii). There are further reasons why Polish and Hungarian pension reformers, who long found it difficult to obtain political support for *any* kind of pension reform, opted for the mixed, Argentine-type approach. It is argued here that this policy path exhibited substantial political economy advantages over both textbook alternatives – a reform within the PAYG scheme and a full privatisation of old-age security – in the specific reform situation facing Poland and Hungary.

With their paradigm choice, Hungarian and Polish policymakers have, in part, reacted to the failure of their preceding attempts to make the existing PAYG schemes viable by reforms from within. During the first half of the 1990s, consecutive Polish and Hungarian governments had experienced considerable resistance to parametric reforms within the existing PAYG systems. From a conceptual point of view, these reform measures might be characterised as moderate given the paradigmatic alternatives. However, their main drawback in political economy terms is their large blame-generating potential, making them politically sensitive: these reforms easily allow the identification of individual losses, and are perceived as a mere cutback of acquired entitlements – without anything in exchange (see Holzmann 1994: 191). Furthermore, the political unattractiveness of 'PAYG-only' reforms is exacerbated by a credibility problem of policymakers, who cannot make a convincing commitment that the proposed reform is a lasting one (see Breyer 1996: 119; Holzmann 1997a: 6).[25]

By comparison, under the mixed package deal the difficult task of reforming the PAYG system is bundled up with the introduction of a mandatory private tier.[26] This 'obfuscation strategy' (Pierson 1994; see subchapter 3.2) lowers the visibility of the envisaged cutbacks, drawing public attention to the granting of individualised, visible ownership claims, i.e. individual pension accounts with private pension funds, to large segments of the population.[27] This move proved to be popular with Polish and Hungarian citizens, as confidence in the existing old-age security arrangements had been battered: chapters 4.1 and 5.1 have shown that Poles and Hungarians with a full lifetime career could not be sure of receiving a decent pension before 1989. By comparison, '[t]he money accumulated on the [pension fund] accounts is viewed as personal property, which can be withdrawn under specified circumstances' (Hirschler 1996: 11). With its change of constituencies, the bundling strategy also meets the criterion raised by Graham (1997: 393): 'Integral to the sustainability of such reform efforts is altering the political balance … Many of the successful reform efforts have included explicit or implicit efforts to create new stakeholders in reformed systems.'

Yet another political economy advantage of pension privatisation concerns the public perception of the pros and cons of the envisaged reform. 'Shifting to a funded scheme … allows for arguments that all can win, thus abandoning intractable zero-sum games' (Holzmann 1997b: 3). Pierson (1994: 21) has stressed that the political costs of reform can be lowered by increasing its complexity (see subchapter 3.2). The shift to funding seems to be a case in point: in striking contrast to the public perception of retrenchment mentioned above, the risks and transition costs involved in pension privatisation are easy to conceal.[28] Notably, the scope and financing of transition costs were successfully shielded from public debate in both Poland and Hungary. Consequently, the public in both countries had an asymmetric perception of the strengths and weaknesses of the mixed reform path, biased towards its advantages and based, in part, on fiscal illusion.[29]

However, the Argentine-type reform approach followed in Poland and Hungary also exhibits considerable political economy advantages over the full privatisation of old-age security. The following four modifications of the 'Chilean model' by the Hungarian and Polish reformers are out-standing (see Table 2.3), amounting to political compromises that facilitated the acceptance of this mixed approach to pension reform:

First, the public scheme is only partially replaced by the newly created mandatory pension fund tier, while a complete opting-out of public old-age security, as in Chile, is impossible. This makes the reform approach less iconoclastic, helping to avoid the image of an overly radical regime change. It amounts to a compromise between the Bismarckian–Beveridgean faction and the advocates of pension privatisation, engendering the need to integrate social security experts from both groups into the pension reform team. Moreover, it manages to satisfy the egalitarian (the middle-aged upwards) and the anti-egalitarian (the young) part of the Central–Eastern European population simultaneously so that none of these groups would strongly oppose the reform.

Second, employers' contributions are maintained to finance the existing obligations of the public scheme, even if the respective employee chooses the IFF tier. This move contributes to lowering the fiscal burden resulting from the partial regime change from PAYG to fully-funded financing. Maintaining the employers' contribution also pleases the trades unions, who perceive it as more just if the contribution burden is 'shared' between both parties. This move, however, implies that contribution rates remain high, and that one of the reform goals, the reduction of wage costs (see e.g. Office 1997: iii), is being sacrificed.

Third, the mandatory pension fund tier is built up rather slowly: no more than one-quarter of total contributions is directed to the newly created pension funds – and only in the case of new entrants to the labour market (Hungary), or those below 30 (Poland), as well as those insured that choose to enter the private second tier. This slow-track choice seems more adequate in the light of still fragile capital markets and remaining two-digit inflation in Central–Eastern Europe (see Tables 7.4 and 7.5), two factors that might seriously hamper the pension funds' ability to maintain and increase the real value of the capital stock entrusted to them.

Fourth, there are major fiscal differences between the Chilean approach towards acquired pension claims (interest-bearing recognition bonds) and the Argentine–Polish–Hungarian one (compensatory pension arrangement). In Chile, individual AFP accounts are being credited with the respective value of the recognition bonds only upon retirement of the insured, but the bonds start earning a 4 per cent real annual interest the moment the insured joins an AFP, resulting in an additional fiscal burden. Argentine-type compensatory pensions, on the contrary, do not earn any interest, are not necessarily protected against inflation and are payable only upon retirement. Consequently, the compensatory pension arrangement allows fiscal costs to be lowered and postponed, thus mitigating the cash-flow implications of pension reform for the government budget (see Vittas 1995: 7). More importantly, implicit public pension debt is not made explicit right away, as in Chile, but only step by step. This could have major fiscal advantages from the point of view of Central–Eastern European policymakers, eager to comply with the Maastricht criteria in the near future.[30]

Some Caveats

However, an overall assessment of the Argentine-type approach chosen in Hungary and Poland must take additional aspects into account, which add up to a more ambivalent picture. Even though the mixed pension reform gives a government the chance to diversify the drawbacks of both public PAYG schemes and private pension funds, its specific design and local characteristics determine whether this potential can indeed be exploited. It cannot be ruled out that the mixed model may result in a combination of the negative features of both alternatives: in Poland, the highly subsidised Farmers' Social Insurance Fund, KRUS, remained exempt from any changes, while the issue of branch privileges has not been definitely settled by the recent reform.[31] In Hungary, some urgent reforms within the public PAYG system have been postponed for over a decade, a fact that not only exemplifies the local pension reformers' need to compromise with potential opponents of reform, but also their low priority for restoring the public tier's financial viability, *vis-à-vis* the securing of consent for the rapid introduction of the mandatory private tier.

Furthermore, partial privatisation does not avoid all pitfalls of the 'Chilean model': in Central–Eastern Europe, capital market risks are still considerable, and the fiscal burden caused by the recognition of existing pension claims will be substantial, since almost 100 per cent of the economically active population was insured in the past. Moreover, an informed individual choice between the public and the private pension option, as well as among newly created pension funds, presupposes the understanding of complex financial information (see Davis 1998: 13).

In political economy terms, the mixed model may be interpreted as entailing a 'hidden agenda' because, with its secondary effects, it gives rise to path dependence (see subchapter 3.2). As contributions are increasingly being drained away from the public system, it has a built-in mechanism towards shrinking the PAYG tier, making it ever less viable, fiscally as well as politically: 'The "unsustainability" thus may prove a self-fulfilling prophecy' (Augusztinovics 1999: 29). The Argentine experience seems to confirm this assessment. In order to cope with fiscal constraints, benefit rules in the public tier have already been downward adjusted several times since 1994 and are becoming increasingly unfavourable, undermining its political attractiveness (see Queisser 1998b: 47–8). Similar trends are surfacing in Hungary: in early 1999, i.e. only one year after the reform started, the Hungarian government announced benefit cuts in the public pension scheme, as the number of those choosing the mixed system turned out to be so large that the deficit in the public pension scheme exceeded previous projections (see Augusztinovics 1999: 29; Pintér 1999).

Moreover, even when pension privatisation starts off only partially, it results in a strengthening of the constituency in favour of radical reform, comprising those already affiliated to one of the private pension funds as well as fund managers. This implies that, in the medium term, the mixed model may be functional from the viewpoint of the new pension orthodoxy, since it is biased towards a gradual introduction of the 'Chilean model'. These considerations are in line with the World Bank's most recent recommendations for 'tactical sequencing' (see subchapter 2.4) in order to achieve pension privatisation, even if the mixed reform path implies only partial opting-out at first, unlike the substitutive and parallel approach (see subchapter 2.3). The mixed model is, then, a useful intermediate stage rather than the ultimate paradigmatic outcome of pension reform, since it allows for a 'gradual phasing in' (World Bank 1994a: 285) of the new pension orthodoxy's favourite pension privatisation agenda.[32]

7.3   PARADIGM CHOICES, STRUCTURAL SETTINGS AND ACTOR CONSTELLATIONS IN COMPARISON

Poland, Hungary and the Czech Republic share a common legacy in old-age security, that extends to both the interwar period and the decades of socialist rule. According to theories of path dependence, this might have been expected to lock in Polish, Hungarian and Czech policymakers in a similar way (see Pierson 1996: 175). However, in defiance of this hypothesis, Central–Eastern European policymakers opted for markedly different pension paradigms in the mid-1990s: whereas the Czech reform measures remained well within the boundaries of the Bismarckian–Beveridgean pension paradigm, partial privatisation of old-age security has been enacted in Poland and Hungary. The respective paradigm choices might seem particularly puzzling, considering, on the one hand, the neoliberal discourse of the long-standing Klaus government, and, on the other hand, the fact that Poland and Hungary were governed by post-communist parties when radical pension reform was initiated.[33]

Table 7.4 Selected economic indicators: Hungary, 1990–1996

	1990	1991	1992	1993	1994	1995	1996
GDP growth (percentage change)	−3.5	−11.9	−3.1	−0.6	2.9	1.5	1.0
Unemployment (end-year, in % of labour force)	1.9	7.5	12.3	12.1	10.4	10.4	10.5
Consumer prices (percentage change, annual average)	28.9	35.0	23.0	22.5	18.8	28.2	23.6
General government balance (in % of GDP)	0.4	−2.2	−5.5	−6.8	−8.2	−6.5	−3.5
External debt stock – in US$ billions	n.a.	22.6	21.4	24.6	28.5	31.7	27.6
– in % of exports	n.a.	243.0	214.0	303.7	375.0	247.7	194.4
GDP per capita (in US$)	3,179	3,242	3,617	3,748	4,069	4,286	4,357

Source: Based on EBRD (1997); own calculations. All 1996 figures are estimates.

Why was radical pension reform feasible in Poland and Hungary but not in the Czech Republic? While the previous subchapter has pointed to the considerable political economy advantages of the Argentine-type reform path from the point of view of Polish and Hungarian policymakers, these did not seem to apply in the Czech case. In this subchapter, an attempt is made at explaining the bifurcation of pension reform paths in the region (see Figure 7.5). After outlining the differing perceptions of the problems to be tackled, I will proceed to analyse the constellations and interaction of actors involved in Central–Eastern European pension reform within the relevant structural-institutional context (see Figure 7.4), starting from the explanatory framework outlined in subchapter 3.4.

Differing Perceptions of Problem Settings

Post-1989 policymakers in Hungary, Poland and the Czech Republic faced a largely similar agenda of reforms within the existing public PAYG schemes, which they accomplished to a great extent. But although this early reform performance was comparable in all three countries under consideration, in the mid-1990s local perceptions regarding the viability of the public PAYG schemes and the possibility of reforming them from within differed markedly: while a sense of urgency had built up in the Polish and Hungarian pension reform arena, translating into the consideration of more radical reform moves, much the same 'PAYG-only' reform path was generally perceived to be viable and sufficient in the Czech Republic.[34]

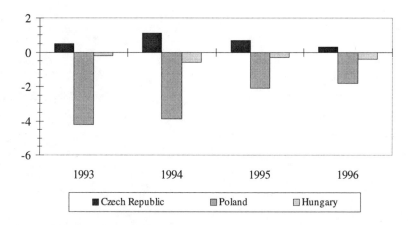

Source: Based on Schrooten, Smeeding and Wagner (1999); own calculations.

Figure 7.2   Financial situation of public pension schemes 1993–1996 (budgetary subsidies in per cent of GDP)

A comparative look at the financial performance of the old-age schemes in Poland, Hungary and the Czech Republic helps to shed light on these different perceptions (see Table 7.1). As noted above, labour market strains had undermined the financial sustainability of the Polish and Hungarian pension schemes, a situation aggravated by liberal access to disability pensions in both countries and, in the Polish case, by a high priority being given to benefit adequacy, reflected in an elevated replacement ratio and average benefit level (see Table 7.1).[35] Contrary to this, the Czech pension scheme, which did not suffer from a comparable slump in the labour market (see Table 7.6), exhibited a permanent surplus. This comparative account points to the relevance of the policy environment in determining the outcomes of early pension reform measures in Central–Eastern Europe (see Figure 7.5). Furthermore, it confirms the notion that the contextual setting may stimulate or restrict the respective actors' perception of available options (Mayntz and Scharpf 1995: 58–60).

Table 7.5   Selected economic indicators: Poland, 1990–1996

	1990	1991	1992	1993	1994	1995	1996
GDP growth (percentage change)	−11.6	−7.0	2.6	3.8	5.2	7.0	6.0
Unemployment (end-year, in % of labour force)	6.3	11.8	13.6	16.4	16.0	14.9	13.6
Consumer prices (percentage change, annual average)	585.8	70.3	43.0	35.3	32.2	27.8	19.9
General government balance (in % of GDP)	3.1	−6.7	−6.6	−3.4	−2.8	−3.6	−3.1
External debt stock							
– in US$ billions	49.0	48.0	47.6	47.2	42.2	43.9	40.4
– in % of exports)	449.5	375.0	340.0	347.1	248.0	191.7	165.6
GDP per capita (in US$)	1,630	2,037	2,197	2,234	2,399	3,055	3,459

Source: Based on EBRD (1997); own calculations. All 1996 figures are estimates.

In accordance with the 'benefit of crises' hypothesis spelt out in chapter 3, it has been argued here that the financial situation of the existing PAYG schemes prepared the ground for the bifurcating policy choices in the mid-1990s, in the sense that the perceived financial inviability of the existing pension schemes was an important precondition for taking radical reform options into account (see Figure 7.5). Other political economy implications of the financial situation of the existing public pension systems will be addressed in the next section, that focuses on the pension-related actor constellations, seeking to gain further insights regarding the different paradigmatic outcomes.

Constellations and Interactions of Main Actors

In order to explain the Central–Eastern European pension reform processes, I will now proceed to identify the relevant actors, whose choices ultimately led to the policy outcome under consideration. As noted in subchapter 3.4, such actors may be individual or corporate.[36] The crucial role extraordinarily committed individuals may play in radical reform has been stressed by scholars of the political economy of policy reform (see Harberger 1993; Rodrik 1994; Williamson 1994a), and such individual actors were certainly not irrelevant in the present country cases, e.g. the former Labour Minister Andrzej Bączkowski, who played a decisive role in initiating radical pension reform in Poland (see Góra and Rutkowski 1998: 23).

The following analysis will, however, focus on corporate actors within and outside government.[37] The actors' perceptions and preferences decide their specific action orientation, influencing the actors' evaluation of the *status quo* and the desirability of a certain course of action. Attention will also be paid to structural-institutional factors that are assumed to stimulate, enable or restrict the strategy options available to the actors involved, as well as determining their relative strength. The actors' perception of the action that needs to be taken is also shaped by this contextual setting (see subchapter 3.4).

A look at the main political actors involved in Polish and Hungarian pension reform on the one hand, and Czech pension reform on the other hand, reveals important differences: whereas, in the Czech Republic, the Welfare Ministry was the only portfolio involved in the reform efforts, in both Poland and Hungary there were three major actors in the pension reform arena: apart from the Welfare Ministry, the Ministry of Finance and the World Bank had a determining influence on the paradigm choice (see Figure 7.5). What accounts for these different actor constellations?

In two of the present country cases, the Welfare Ministry was not the only portfolio shaping pension reform, but there was yet another important intra-governmental actor elaborating reform blueprints and pressing for their implementation – the Ministry of Finance. It might seem puzzling that the Ministry of Finance extended its powers to a genuine social policy area. However, it has been pointed out elsewhere that fiscal crises turn the Ministry of Finance into a potential actor in the pension reform arena (see Alber 1996: 18). A look at Tables 7.4 and 7.5 demonstrates that this condition was undoubtedly met in both Hungary and Poland.[38] More specifically, it was the local PAYG system's dependence on budgetary subsidies (see Tables 4.4 and

5.4) that granted the Finance Ministry an important stake in reforming old-age security. Hence, the 'benefit of crises' hypothesis can, for the Hungarian and Polish cases, be interpreted in such a way that the financial difficulties of both the general government budget and the public old-age scheme can be seen to have resulted in a significant change of the local constellation of actors.[39]

Table 7.6   Selected economic indicators: Czech Republic, 1990–1996

	1990	1991	1992	1993	1994	1995	1996
GDP growth (percentage change)	−1.2	−11.5	−3.3	0.6	2.7	5.9	4.1
Unemployment (end-year, in % of labour force)	0.8	4.1	2.6	3.5	3.2	2.9	3.5
Consumer prices (percentage change, annual average)	10.8	56.6	11.1	20.8	10.0	9.1	8.8
General government balance (in % of GDP)[a]	0.1	−2.0	−3.3	2.7	0.8	0.4	−0.2
External debt stock[b]							
– in US$ billions	6.0	6.7	7.1	8.5	10.7	17.2	20.7
– in % of exports	101.7	80.7	84.5	65.4	76.4	80.0	95.4
GDP per capita (in US$)	3,126	2,466	2,903	3,332	3,853	4,814	5,340

Notes: [a] Please note that 1990–1992 figures refer to Czechoslovakia.
         [b] convertible currency

Sources: EBRD (1994, 1997); own calculations. All 1996 figures are estimates.

The two intra-ministerial actors were not alone in the Hungarian and Polish pension reform arena. They were joined by a major external actor providing conceptual, technical and strategic know-how to pension reformers world-wide – the World Bank (see Mouton 1998: 25–7). The Bank's leverage in Hungary and Poland results largely from both countries' high external debt burden (see Tables 7.4 and 7.5).[40] Figure 7.3 shows the Bank's own financial involvement in all three countries. In the Central–Eastern European pension reform arena, the Bank did not exert its influence through the 'classical' channel, through conditionalities, but first and foremost as an agenda shifter in the local debate, via its local campaign for Latin American-style reforms.

Moreover, the World Bank strengthened the existing reform capacities by offering the local pension reform teams an expert-based knowledge transfer, and by granting loans to finance part of the costs involved in pension privatisation.

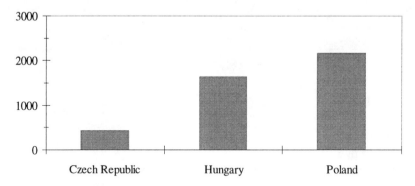

Sources: World Bank (1998a, b, c).

Figure 7.3   Outstanding IBRD loans to Poland, Hungary and the Czech Republic, 1996 (in million US$)

Contrary to the Polish and Hungarian cases, the only portfolio involved in the Czech pension reform efforts was the local Welfare Ministry. As the public pension scheme was financially viable without subsidies from the general budget (see Table 6.4), the Ministry of Finance had no stake in the pension reform issue. Another notable absentee in the Czech case is the World Bank, whose lack of leverage in the Czech Republic coincides with a low level of external debt, compared with the Hungarian and Polish cases (see Table 7.6).[41] This comparative account leads to the conclusion that structural factors – notably the financial situation of the existing public PAYG schemes and the degree of external debt – determine which political actors gain influence on the paradigm choice in old-age security.

In what way are these divergent sets of pension reform actors linked to the observable policy choices? It will be argued here that the cognitive maps and paradigmatic preferences of the potential pension reform actors are so clear-cut that, once the relevant actor constellation is identified, the actors' perceptions of pension reform alternatives and, consequently, the resulting basic paradigm choice in old-age security become predictable.

The underlying reasoning might be considered as naïve on the grounds that pension reformers are unlikely to act in a political vacuum. Thomas and Grindle (1990) have stressed that a policy reform initiative may be altered or reversed at any stage in its life cycle, criticising the extensive focus on the feasibility of decision-making, while little or no attention is paid to implementation. As pointed out in subchapter 3.4, however, in the context of political and economic transformation, the influence of potential opponents – intermediate political actors – proved to be considerably smaller than in a politics-as-usual context with its entrenched vested interests. Consequently, Central–Eastern European policymakers had substantial room for manœuvre in the area of social policy, enabling largely autonomous policymaking (see Götting 1998: 280–1; Mouton 1998: 25).[42]

As to the respective paradigmatic preferences, all three case-studies have shown that the Ministries of Welfare are traditionally inclined towards the Bismarckian–Beveridgean paradigms (see subchapter 2.2), stressing that a pension system should not be designed to bring about macroeconomic desiderata, but to serve the aged. A thorough reform of the existing public PAYG scheme is deemed to be sufficient, while a radical regime change in old-age security is seen as neither desirable nor necessary.

Contrary to this, the respective Ministries of Finance, largely manned with neoliberal economists, joined the ranks of the new pension orthodoxy (see subchapter 2.4), claiming that a private IFF pension scheme represented the only appropriate alternative to the financially inviable public old-age security system, while stressing the favourable macroeconomic effects ascribed to the switch to a funded system. In view of these clear-cut paradigmatic preferences of the two potential intra-governmental actors and the concomitant perceptions of the action that needed to be taken, it comes as no surprise that the Finance and Welfare Ministries in both Poland and Hungary, clashed about the issue of pension reform.

In both countries, the World Bank had sufficient leverage to reinforce the local 'privatisation faction' with its global experience in promoting and assisting pension privatisation (see Figure 7.5). It should be noted that the Polish and Hungarian pension reforms are not tantamount to a full replication of the World Bank's standard agenda (see Mouton 1998: 26).[43] Still, the Bank has actively supported the Hungarian and Polish pension reforms, as they succeeded in creating a precedent for pension privatisation in Central–Eastern Europe (see Palacios and Rocha 1997: 42; Rutkowski 1998).

The above-mentioned breakdown makes it clear that once the Welfare Ministry ceases to be the only relevant actor in the pension reform arena, being joined by the Ministry of Finance and the World Bank, the chosen reform blueprints will include at least a partial switch to an IFF scheme. The Ministry of Finance is generally the stronger of the two portfolios, being reinforced by the World Bank's leverage, thereby outweighing the Welfare Ministry with its typical preference for the Bismarckian–Beveridgean paradigms.[44]

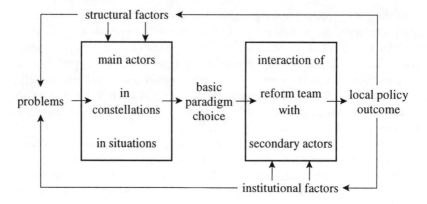

Sources: Mayntz and Scharpf (1995: 45), Scharpf (1997: 44); adapted version of Figure 3.1.

Figure 7.4   An actor-centred institutionalist view on pension reform

This actor-centred analysis stresses the role of ideas over the impact of interests in policymaking.[45] The radical restructuring of the inherited old-age security schemes contrasts conspicuously with the more modest record in other post-1989 social policy areas (see Götting 1998). It is assumed here that the former was facilitated by the existence of a mainstream blueprint for pension reform, comparable to the 'Washington Consensus' for general economic policy (Williamson 1990). The three country cases examined make it clear, however, that in order to be adopted in the local reform arena, the new orthodox template requires both an agent for its transmission (the World Bank) and a local actor ready to adopt neoliberal blueprints (the Ministry of Finance).

Hence, given the actors' paradigmatic preferences and their perception of pension reform alternatives, the constellation of relevant actors defines the basic paradigmatic outcome, whereas the respective contextual setting conditions largely which actors become involved in the pension reform process, as well as their relative strength. Radical pension reform became feasible when those actors inclined towards pension privatisation – the Ministry of Finance and the World Bank – had stakes and leverage in the local reform process. By comparison, pension privatisation did not proceed when the Welfare Ministry was the only relevant pension reform actor. It has also been shown that it is the respective structural-institutional setting – notably the financial situation of the existing public PAYG schemes and the degree of external debt – that conditions whether 'privatisation advocates' will gain sufficient leverage for a determining influence on the paradigm choice.[46]

The Role of Secondary Actors

While the constellations of the main pension reform actors and the relevant structural-institutional context account for the basic paradigm choices made in old-age security, this line of reasoning cannot explain the whole of the local policy outcome: in a second step, the details of the specific local arrangements are produced in an interaction process with secondary actors (see Figure 7.4), including trades unions, pensioners' associations and social security institutions (see below), but also employers' organisations and local financial institutions.[47]

Among these secondary actors, the role of trades unions stands out. Until the mid-1990s, Polish, Hungarian and Czech policymakers experienced strong resistance from the 'grey lobby' – represented, first and foremost, by local trades unions – when trying to introduce relatively modest parametric changes. It is interesting to note that, nowadays, unions in all three countries seem to agree with the governments' reform plans, even when they are as radical as in Hungary and Poland. The trades unions' varying position on the pension reform issue may be explained by the heterogeneous interests they stand for. Since many of their members are pensioners, trades unions in post-communist countries have been dubbed 'pensioners' parties'. Central–Eastern European unions must seek to reconcile the interests of contributors as well as beneficiaries to the scheme, giving rise to shifting and sometimes inconsistent positions on pension reform, which is, after all, no core issue of trades union policy.

In Hungary, the MSZOSZ's initial position was to defend the *status quo*, opposing any comprehensive pension reform. Consequently, they started to voice considerable opposition to the government's pension reform plans. When the draft law was presented to the tripartite ÉT, the government gave in to some transitory modifications, in exchange for a last-minute reversal of the trades unions' stance towards pension privatisation. In Poland, NSZZ *Solidarność* supported a partial shift to funding even before the Welfare Ministry did, while the post-communist OPZZ turned from a staunch opponent of radical reform to an entrepreneur in the mandatory pension fund business, thereby highlighting the fact that partial pension privatisation entails the possibility of handing out attractive stakes to potential opponents. In the Czech Republic, ČMKOS, once a fierce critic of the government's approach to old-age security, has recently shifted its stance: instead of merely defending acquired rights, it has recently turned into one of the main adversaries of the newly emerged pension privatisation faction, claiming that the existing options to reform the public PAYG scheme have not been exhausted. Interestingly, even an increase of the retirement age, strongly opposed in 1995, is no longer ruled out by the ČMKOS, now that the local perception of reform alternatives has shifted.

Pensioners' organisations, another group of secondary actors, were not nearly as influential in Central–Eastern European pension reforms as one might have assumed according to conventional wisdom. In Poland and the Czech Republic, specialised pensioners' parties had been set up but failed to enter parliament. Being a significant constituency, estimated to account for 40 per cent of voters, local governments succeeded in convincing them that they would not be affected by the envisaged pension reforms, a promise doubted by independent experts (see e.g. Ferge 1999: 243–4).

Overall, Central–Eastern European pension reformers did not opt to override potential reform opponents but tried to enhance the sustainability of reform by entering into a dialogue with these groups. They ended up making some relatively minor concessions, largely concerning the scope and speed of envisaged retrenchment measures, in order to win them over. In the country cases where the mixed reform path had been chosen pension reformers were only willing to compromise on first-tier reforms, while their basic paradigm choice – i.e. partial pension privatisation – was not put up for discussion with secondary pension reform actors.

Hence, secondary actors were in no political position to veto the basic paradigmatic course of pension reform in any of the three countries considered. Tripartite bodies ensured that Hungarian, Polish and Czech trades unions, the most important group among the secondary actors, were consulted on the pension reform issue. They were not, however, vested with formal institutional veto powers, as tripartite resolutions were not binding for local policymakers. The non-interference of the Polish and Czech pension insurance institutions in the local pension reform debates can be explained by a lack of institutional autonomy. But even in the Hungarian case, where the institutional setting granted extensive powers to the Pension Fund's self-government – a staunch opponent to pension privatisation alongside the Welfare Ministry – the basic paradigm choice taken by the main pension reform actors remained unshaken.

Yet when the substantial opposition against the comparatively moderate pension reform attempts in the first half of the 1990s is recalled, it becomes clear that the weakness of secondary actors and the lack of veto powers granted to them is an insufficient explanation for the fact that Polish and Hungarian pension reformers managed to overcome resistance to radical reform. Opposition was kept low in the first place, due to tactical moves employed by reformers and the strategic potentialities of the Argentine-type reform path, that are in striking contrast to the political economy drawbacks of 'PAYG-only' reforms.

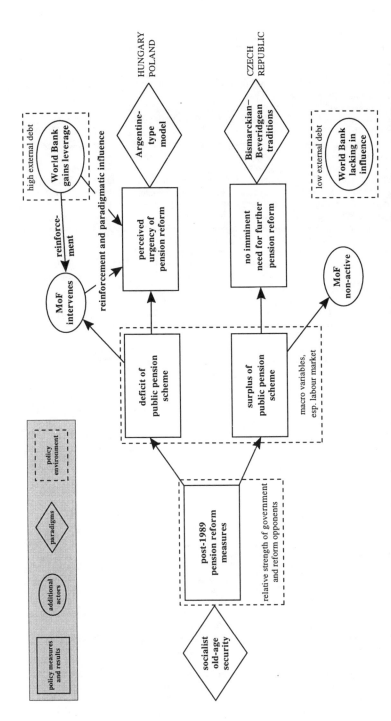

Figure 7.5 Pension reform paths in comparison: interdependence of problem settings, policy environment and actor constellations

175

NOTES

1. Contrary to its counterparts in Hungary and Czechoslovakia, the Polish interwar pension scheme was not self-governed.
2. The Polish Pension Fund was separated from the state budget in 1968.
3. Employees' contributions existed until 1952 in Czechoslovakia, from 1968 to 1972 in Poland and from 1954 in Hungary.
4. In Poland, old-age pensions and disability benefits remained exempt from this move. In Hungary, the pension scheme returned under state administration in 1984.
5. Only in Poland the regular retirement age was higher – 65 for men and 60 for women.
6. In Hungary, the benefit level fully depended on employment incomes and service years. There were no 'work categories', but the special pension supplements for the *nomenklatura* and artists may similarly be interpreted as branch privileges (see Adam 1983).
7. The creation of this *de facto* extra labour supply was functional in the context of the socialist economies, where labour hoarding by enterprises resulted in an excess demand for labour on a macro-level (see Götting 1998: 64–6).
8. It is expected that, in the future, population ageing will affect the region, but to a lesser extent than Western, Northern or even Southern Europe (see Prinz 1997; Légaré 1999).
9. In 1993, the EU-12 average of expenditures for old-age and survivors' pensions amounted to 11.9 per cent of GDP (see Döring 1998: 36).
10. The World Bank recommended the latter – 'reducing and flattening benefits' provided by public pension schemes in transition countries (World Bank 1994a: 285), which is not surprising in the context of the overall pension strategy of this international organisation, reviewed in subchapter 2.4.
11. Even if dividing the contribution burden is largely irrelevant in economic terms, Central–Eastern pension reformers have stressed the psychological importance of introducing individualised contributions (see e.g. Markiewicz 1998: 25).
12. Notable exceptions include the failure to abolish branch privileges and to introduce an employees' contribution in Poland, the unwillingness to separate the Czech pension fund from the budget and the cautious raising of the retirement age in Hungary and the Czech Republic (see Table 7.2). As to the latter, it should be noted that age 65 has emerged as a standard in West European pension systems, at least for males (see Steinmeyer 1996: 37).
13. Strictly speaking, the respective Ministry is called 'Welfare Ministry' in Hungary, 'Ministry of Labour and Social Policy' in Poland and 'Ministry of Labour and Social Affairs' in the Czech Republic. In the following, they will be universally referred to as 'Welfare Ministries' for short.
14. While the Hungarian Welfare Ministry reportedly changed its stance after an intervention by the Prime Minister, in Poland the inconvenient Welfare Minister was removed from his post following a cabinet reshuffle.
15. The considerable delay between the passing of the first and the second tranche of pension reform laws in Poland was due to parliamentary elections, held in September 1997 and resulting in a change of government.
16. Following World Bank terminology, there are four pillars in Poland and Hungary, as the mandatory PAYG and IFF tiers (pillar 1 and 2) are supplemented by both a 'zero' basic pension tier and a third pillar, consisting of voluntary savings for old age.
17. The new mandatory pension funds in Hungary were set up parallel to the already existing voluntary funds. A separation of both systems was necessary because mandatory pension funds require stricter government supervision than voluntary ones.
18. See Palacios and Whitehouse (1998) for a general discussion of switching strategies.
19. For the underlying notion of radical reform see subchapter 3.1.
20. Advantages of the NDC approach include adjusting endogenously to an increase in life-expectancy, providing incentives for formal employment as well as late retirement and, last but not least, allowing a smooth integration with a truly defined-contribution second tier (see Holzmann 1997b: 13).

21. For the case of credit co-operatives, Krahnen and Schmidt (1993: 67) have concluded that their 'corporate constitution ... systematically weakens incentives for internal as well as external control, giving considerable discretionary powers to the employee-managers. As a result, the investment and distribution decisions ... are likely to be suboptimal'.

22. In Argentina, the universal basic pension presupposes a minimum of 30 contributory years, being particularly difficult to obtain for women and informal sector workers. Hence, to prevent old-age poverty, the Polish and Hungarian design appears to be more adequate.

23. Similarly World Bank (1994a: 286) and Fougerolles (1996: 93).

24. James (1998: 185) points to the fact that Hungary's credit rating from Moody's improved after it adopted systemic pension reform, although the reform resulted in an increase in explicit debt.

25. A more differentiated stance is taken up by Diamond (1997: 33): 'Well-chosen repeated legislation is a form of risk sharing. Poorly chosen repeated legislation is a form of risk generation. One way to describe the problem of the design of pension provision is to seek institutions that increase the likelihood of good patterns of legislated changes and decrease the likelihood of bad ones.'

26. In Poland, the original package deal of a simultaneous passage of the politically difficult reforms of ZUS and the fairly popular introduction of private pension funds was abandoned due to time constraints. Instead, Polish policymakers resorted to deliberate sequencing: the laws on the private pension fund tiers were enacted by the outgoing government before the elections, whereas the more intricate part – ZUS reforms – was left to the new government.

27. Cangiano, Cottarelli and Cubeddu (1998: 37) stress the significance of funded schemes in the context of transition economies, given that they provide 'a monitorable track record of the property rights of each individual worker over time – the political system is less likely to take away'.

28. Interestingly, reformers themselves have been claiming to do the opposite: 'This reform will also make the system more transparent and comprehensible' (Office 1997: ii).

29. On the concept of fiscal illusion see e.g. Breyer (1997: 5).

30. The explicit mentioning of the Maastricht criteria in the Hungarian pension reform draft speaks for itself (see Ministry of Welfare and Ministry of Finance 1997: 17).

31. Of late, Polish trades unions have started to express their protest against the government's plans to curtail branch-specific early retirement privileges (see e.g. Solska 1998, 1999; Dziadul 1999).

32. From the new pension orthodoxy's point of view, this is certainly an advantage rather than a caveat.

33. Cukierman and Tommasi (1998a, b) have explained why radical reforms are more likely to be successful if tackled by 'unlikely' administrations, referring to many cases where market-friendly reforms have not been carried out by conservative free marketeers, but rather by left-wing administrations. Rodrik has called this phenomenon 'Nixon-in-China syndrome' (Rodrik 1994: 213). The 'Klaus paradox' has already been discussed in subchapter 6.3.

34. While predominating, these perceptions were not universally shared; see the pension reform controversies outlined in the subchapters 6.4 and 7.2.

35. The average benefit level (see Table 7.1) in Polish old-age security appears elevated *vis-à-vis* the respective pension amounts in Hungary and the Czech Republic – needless to say, in comparison with West European benefit levels, it is rather low. For replacement rates in West European countries see Steinmeyer (1996: 16).

36. Collective actors (see Mayntz and Scharpf 1995: 51) will be left out of consideration here.

37. 'It is appropriate to observe that political institutions can be treated as actors in much the same way we treat individuals as actors' (March and Olsen 1984: 742).

38. See Bönker (1997, 1999) for a comparative analysis of the fiscal performance of Poland, Hungary and the Czech Republic.

39. Similar ideas about the link between crisis and social-sector reforms have been expressed by Nelson (1997: 261–2).

40. Moreover, when compared with other Central and Eastern European countries, 'Hungary and Poland [exhibit] the longest experience in cooperation with the World Bank' (Dąbrowski 1995: 8).

41. Differences regarding the foreign debt burden between Poland and Hungary on the one hand, and the Czech Republic on the other, date back to the pre-1989 era: in the late 1980s, the former countries ranked among the most indebted countries in the world (see Bönker 1997: 6). As regards the post-1989 period, the reluctance of former Prime Minister Klaus about the involvement of foreign advisors is well-known (see Blejer and Coricelli 1995: 63). Unlike in Hungary or Poland, there is no World Bank office in the Czech Republic to allow for institutionalised, permanent contact with local policymakers.
42. However, the impact of secondary pension reform actors on the local policy outcome is discussed below (see also Figure 7.4).
43. This would have included, on the one hand, downgrading any existing public PAYG tier to the limited goal of poverty reduction, and, on the other hand, entrusting the private, funded tier with the whole of the mandatory earnings-related pension business. See, however, subchapter 7.2 for 'tactical sequencing' on behalf of the new pension orthodoxy.
44. Outweighing can take different forms, as subchapters 4.3 and 5.3 have shown. In both Poland and Hungary, the Welfare Ministry clearly lost the intra-governmental conflict on the pension reform course to be followed.
45. For the recent political science and sociological discussion on the role of interests vs. ideas in policy reform see the seminal study by Sikkirk (1991). See Campbell (1998) for a recent contribution.
46. It should be noted that the present case-study methodology does not allow for hypotheses on absolute, let alone universal, thresholds for these crucial structural factors, i.e. the financial situation of the existing public PAYG schemes and the degree of external debt. Still, Tables 4.4, 5.4 and 6.4, as well as 7.4, 7.5 and 7.6 reveal significant differences between Poland and Hungary on the one hand, and the Czech Republic on the other hand.
47. For a similar interpretation of the recent Polish and Hungarian pension reforms see Nelson (1998: 10): 'Both timing and the broad shape of reform were influenced by outside forces. But the more specific design details were outcomes of the analysis and political judgement of the reformers themselves, and of their negotiations and compromises within their governments and with interest groups, watchdog institutions, and legislatures.'

8. Conclusions: The Political Economy of Pension Reform in Central–Eastern Europe

Contrary to conventional wisdom in social policy research, the recent Central–Eastern European experience shows that radical pension reform can indeed be accomplished. The partial privatisation of old-age security in Hungary and Poland, following the Argentine precedent, amounts to a *sui generis* institutional transfer from the South to the East, facilitated by the emergence of the new pension orthodoxy. This study has examined the circumstances that enabled radical pension reform in Poland and Hungary, and held it back in the Czech Republic. The process of paradigm choice in old-age security is not tantamount to an evaluation of the micro- and macroeconomic, distributional and allocational advantages and drawbacks of public PAYG vs. privately run IFF systems. Rather, 'politics matters', when it comes to the determination of the pension reform course to be followed. Thus, political economy considerations prove vital for the understanding of the reform dynamics in the area of old-age security.

Here, an actor-centred institutionalist heuristic was chosen, thereby stressing the importance of actor constellations and the structural-institutional context for different old-age reform paths. As to the structural setting, the financial situation of existing public PAYG schemes – deficit or surplus – makes an impact on the perceived urgency of a radical pension reform. Moreover, it determines whether, apart from the Welfare Ministry, another intra-governmental actor enters the pension reform arena – the Ministry of Finance, with its bias towards a privatisation of old-age security. Within the structural setting, there is yet another crucial factor, i.e. the degree of external debt, that conditions whether an important external actor gets involved – the World Bank, with its policy advice modelled on the Chilean experience. Hence, the respective structural setting determines the set of main pension reform actors, as well as their relative strength.

Given the actors' respective perceptions of pension reform alternatives, the resulting actor constellation conditions the basic paradigm choice in favour or against pension privatisation. Radical pension reform becomes feasible when those actors advocating pension privatisation – the Ministry of Finance and the World Bank – have stakes and leverage in the local reform process, whereas pension privatisation does not proceed when the Welfare Ministry, traditionally inclined towards the Bismarckian–Beveridgean paradigm, is the only relevant pension reform actor.

Pointing to the role of the financial situation of existing public PAYG schemes in co-determining paradigm choice in old-age security is in line with the 'benefit of crises' hypothesis spelt out by scholars of the politics of pension reform and the political economy of policy reform, as well as by the new pension orthodoxy itself. Compared with this, earlier findings on the role of social policy legacies, generating path dependence and locking in policymakers, did not apply in the country cases considered: Poland, Hungary and the Czech Republic share a common legacy in old-age security but opted for markedly different pension paradigms in the mid-1990s.

Regarding the design of old-age security reforms, earlier scholarship had stressed the importance of tactical sequencing, strategic (un)bundling and packaging. Lowering the visibility of cutbacks, e.g. by increasing the complexity of reforms, is another issue in pension reform design. The use of these tactical and strategic devices has been identified in those country cases where policymakers opted for radical reform. Under the Argentine-type package deal chosen in Poland and Hungary, politically sensitive PAYG reforms are bundled up with the popular introduction of individualised, visible ownership claims, amounting to an 'obfuscation strategy' in Pierson's terms, aimed at lowering the political resistance to reform. At the same time, reformers resorted to tactical packaging, distancing themselves from the conspicuous Latin American models and stressing the originality of local reform efforts. In another tactical move, Polish and Hungarian pension reformers refrained from disclosing the expected scope and financing of transition costs that will result from the shift to funding.

As to the timing of pension reforms, they had traditionally been thought unlikely to be pursued shortly before elections, when the hazards of accountability are high. Yet the cases of both Hungary and Poland show that fundamental pension reform was purposely – and successfully – pursued in a pre-electoral period, highlighting that the blame-generating potential of the Argentine-type reform path is outweighed by its perceived attractiveness, thereby differing markedly from the political-economic potentiality of 'PAYG-only' reforms.

The above findings on the factors that drive paradigm choice in Central–Eastern European old-age security are intended as a contribution to the political economy of pension reform, interpreting it as part of a medium-range theory of policy reform. This study may also have laid the comparative-empirical foundations for a formal modelling of the recent moves to privatise old-age security and their political feasibility, to date still a desideratum.

However, the possible generalisation of results and their application to pension reform experiences elsewhere calls for some degree of caution. Even if, by the time the Hungarian, Polish and Czech reforms were passed, the post-1989 'period of extraordinary politics' was over, the policy environment in the three countries considered was still shaped by concomitant political and economic transformation, resulting in the absence of stable institutions and well-established rules of the game. Moreover, Central–Eastern European pension reformers benefited from the weakness of intermediate actors, enabling largely autonomous policymaking. Consequently, a more complex pattern of analysis would probably have to be elaborated to account for the pension reform dynamics in Western industrialised countries with their entrenched vested interests and politics-as-usual context. However, the present explanatory framework may prove useful for the analysis of far-reaching pension reform efforts in other transition countries, particularly Croatia, Latvia, Slovenia and Kazakhstan. Moreover, the radical Latin American reforms are yet to be examined from a political economy perspective, notably those conducted under non-authoritarian regimes (Argentina, Bolivia, Colombia, El Salvador, Mexico and Uruguay). While exhibiting more consolidated political regimes and some well-organised interest groups, the foreign debt problem and the financial imbalances of the public PAYG schemes in these Latin American countries largely paralleled the Hungarian and Polish situation – hence both the Finance Ministry and the World Bank are no strangers to Latin American pension reform arenas. Future research efforts will show the usefulness of the present findings for such cross-regional approaches towards the political economy of pension reform.

As a matter of conclusion, it is expedient to stress that any kind of old-age security reform is but an intermediate stage in an ongoing process. '[I]t seems unlikely that current pension reforms will prove to be one-and-for-all, single, distinct acts, which unambiguously mark out the path towards a predetermined pension system in the distant future. ... How to maintain stability, confidence and how to avoid haphazard injuries to the interest of various groups and cohorts along the route – remains a problem to be solved' (Augusztinovics and Johnson 1997: 270).

References

Aaron, Henry J. (1966), 'The Social Insurance Paradox', *Canadian Journal of Economics and Political Science*, **32**, 371–4.

Adam, Jan (1983), 'The Old Age Pension System in Eastern Europe: A Case Study of Czechoslovak and Hungarian Experience', *Osteuropa-Wirtschaft*, **28** (4), 276–96.

Adam, Jan (1991), 'Social Contract', in Jan Adam (ed.), *Economic Reforms and Welfare Systems in the USSR, Poland and Hungary. Social Contract in Transformation*, London: Macmillan, pp. 1–25.

Adam, Jan (1996), 'Social Costs of Transformation in the Czech Republic', *MOCT-MOST*, **6** (2), 163–83.

Adam, Jan (1998), 'Reform of the Pension and the Health Care System in the Czech Republic', *Osteuropa-Wirtschaft*, **43** (3), 280–94.

A.F.T. (1996), 'Przyszłe emerytury i renty – Obowiązkowe i dobrowolne emerytalne fundusze kapitałowe', *Rzeczpospolita*, 17 October 1996, 2.

A.F.T. (1997), 'Sondaż "Rzeczpospolitej": Ubezpieczenia społeczne – zapobiegliwość wyprzedza reformę', *Rzeczpospolita*, 3 February 1997: http://www.rzeczpospolita. pl.

A.F.T. (1998a), 'Ubezpieczenia Społeczne – Zagrożenia dla reformy', *Rzeczpospolita*, 16 June 1998: http://www.rzeczpospolita.pl.

A.F.T. (1998b), 'Wcześniejsze emerytury: Wyjątki potwierdzające regułę', *Rzeczpospolita*, 27 November 1998: http://www.rzeczpospolita.pl.

A.F.T. (1998c), 'Z prac komisji: Emerytura i pensja bez ograniczeń', *Rzeczpospolita*, 17 October 1998: http://www.rzeczpospolita.pl.

Alber, Jens (1987), *Vom Armenhaus zum Wohlfahrtsstaat. Analysen zur Entwicklung der Sozialversicherung in Westeuropa*, Frankfurt/Main and New York: Campus.

Alber, Jens (1996), *Towards a Comparison of Recent Welfare State Developments in Germany and the United States*, Paper presented at Yale University, New Haven, CT, mimeo.

Antal, Kálmánné, János Réti and Miklós Toldi (1995), 'Pension Outlay and Changes in the Pension System in the Nineties', in Éva Ehrlich and Gábor Révész (eds), *Human Resources and Social Stability During Transition in Hungary*, San Francisco: International Centre for Growth, pp. 193–209.

Apolte, Thomas and Lilianna Chomiuk (1995), 'Die Reform der Rentenversicherung in Polen', in Kornelia van der Beek and Peter Weiss (eds), *Sozialpolitik im Transformationsprozeß*, Berlin and New York: de Gruyter, pp. 131–54.

Arenas de Mesa, Alberto (1997), *Learning from the Privatization of the Social Security Pension System in Chile: Macroeconomic Effects, Lessons and Challenges*, Doctoral Thesis at University of Pittsburgh, mimeo.

Arenas de Mesa, Alberto and Fabio Bertranou (1997), 'Learning from Social Security Reforms: Two Different Cases, Chile and Argentina', *World Development*, **25** (3), 329–48.

Arrau, Patricio (1992), 'El Nuevo Régimen Previsional Chileno', in FAUS-CIID-FESCOL (eds), *Regímenes Pensionales*, Santa Fé de Bogotá: Tercer Mundo, pp. 37–65.

Arrau, Patricio (1998), *The Chilean Pension System: 1981–1997*, Presentation held at the Conference 'Reforming the Social Security System: An International Perspective', 16–17 March 1998, Rome, mimeo.

Arrau, Patricio and Klaus Schmidt-Hebbel (1993), *Macroeconomic and Intergenerational Welfare Effects of a Transition from Pay-as-you-go to Fully-funded Pension Systems*, Santiago de Chile and Washington, DC, mimeo.

Arrau, Patricio and Klaus Schmidt-Hebbel (1994), 'Pension Systems and Reform. Country Experiences and Research Issues', *Revista de Análisis Económico*, **9** (1), 3–20.

Arthur, W. Brian (1989), 'Competing Technologies, Increasing Returns, and Lock-in by Historical Events', *The Economic Journal*, **99** (March 1989), 116–31.

Augusztinovics, Mária (1993), 'The Social Security Crisis in Hungary', in István P. Székely and David M. G. Newbery (eds), *Hungary: An Economy In Transition*. Cambridge, UK: Cambridge University Press, pp. 296–320.

Augusztinovics, Mária (1995), 'The Long-term Financial Balance of the Pension System – Macrosimulations', in Éva Ehrlich and Gábor Révész (eds), *Human Resources and Social Stability During Transition in Hungary*, San Francisco: International Center for Growth, pp. 210–28.

Augusztinovics, Mária (1999), *Pension Systems and Reforms in the Transition Economies*, Paper prepared for the UN/ECE Spring Seminar 'The Economic Implications of Population Ageing in the ECE Region', 3 May 1999, Geneva, mimeo.

Augusztinovics, Mária et al. (1997), *Pension Systems and Reforms – Britain, Hungary, Italy, Poland, Sweden*, Phare ACE Research Project P95-2139-R, Final Report, Budapest, mimeo.

Augusztinovics, Mária and Paul Johnson (1997), 'Concluding Remarks: System and Reform Design', in Mária Augusztinovics et al., *Pension Systems and Reforms – Britain, Hungary, Italy, Poland, Sweden*, Phare ACE Research Project P95-2139-R, Final Report, Budapest, mimeo, pp. 257–70.

Augusztinovics, Mária and Béla Martos (1996), 'Pension Reform: Calculations and Conclusions', *Acta Oeconomica*, **48** (1–2), 119–60.

Autonóm Szakszervetek et al. (1996), *Closing Declaration of International Conference on Employee Responsibility in Security of Pensions*, 26–28 September 1996, Budapest, mimeo.

AWS and UW (1997), *Umowa koalicyjna zawarta pomiędzy Akcją Wyborczą Solidarność i Unią Wolności*, 10 November 1997, Warsaw, mimeo.

Axelrod, Robert (ed.) (1976), *Structure of Decision: The Cognitive Maps of Political Elites*, Princeton: Princeton University Press.

Bagdy, Gábor (1995), 'The Social Protection System of Hungary', in Michael Cichon (ed.), *Social Protection in the Visegrád Countries: Four Country Profiles*, ILO-CEET Report 13, Budapest: ILO-CEET, pp. 39–56.

Baker, Dean (1996), 'The Assumptions Are Too Pessimistic', *Challenge*, (November-December 1996), 31–2.

Balcerowicz, Leszek (1994), 'Poland', in John Williamson (ed.), *The Political Economy of Policy Reform*, Washington, DC: Institute for International Economics, pp. 153–77.

Baldwin, Sally and Jane Falkingham (eds) (1994), *Social Security and Social Change. New Challenges to the Beveridge Model*, New York: Harvester Wheatsheaf.

Banco Nacional de Comercio Exterior (ed.) (1996), 'Reforma previsional en América Latina', *Comercio Exterior*, **46** (9), México, DF.

Barbone, Luca (1997), 'Reforma systemu emerytalnego w Polsce w opinii Banku Światowego', in IPiSS (ed.), *Eksperci Banku Światowego o reformach emerytalnych w Polsce i na świecie. Propozycje, wzory, kontrowersje*, Warsaw: IPiSS, pp. 26–36.

Barr, Nicholas (1992), 'Economic Theory and the Welfare State: A Survey and Interpretation', *Journal of Economic Literature*, **XXX** (June 1992), 741–803.

Barr, Nicholas (1993a), *The Economics of the Welfare State*, London: Weidenfeld and Nicholson.

Barr, Nicholas (1993b), 'Retirement Pensions', in Nicholas Barr and David Whynes (eds), *Current Issues in the Economics of Welfare*, London: Macmillan, pp. 45–62.

Barr, Nicholas (1994a), 'Income Transfers: Social Insurance', in Nicholas Barr (ed.), *Labor Markets and Social Policy in Central and Eastern Europe. The Transition and Beyond*, Washington, DC: Oxford University Press, pp. 192–225.

Barr, Nicholas (ed.) (1994b), *Labor Markets and Social Policy in Central and Eastern Europe. The Transition and Beyond*, Washington, DC: Oxford University Press.

Barreto de Oliveira, Francisco E. (1997), 'Reforma de los sistemas de seguridad social en las sociedades en transición', *Estudios de la Seguridad Social*, **81**, 55–63.

Beattie, Roger and Warren McGillivray (1995), 'A Risky Strategy: Reflections on the World Bank Report "Averting the Old Age Crisis"', *International Social Security Review*, **48** (3–4), 5–22.

Becker, Gary S. (1996), 'A Social Security Lesson from Argentina', *Business Week*, 21 October 1996, 9.

Becker-Neetz, Gerald (1995), 'Der Weltbankbericht über die Krise der Alterssicherungssysteme', *Deutsche Rentenversicherung*, (4/95), 201–13.

Benio, Marek and Zoya Mladenova (1997), 'Transforming Social Security Systems in Bulgaria and Poland. Common Problems', *EMERGO*, **4** (2), 135–44.

Berríos, Rubén (1995), 'Economic Transition in Poland: The Relevance of the Latin-American Experience', *Revista de Economia Política*, **15** (4), 112–33.

Bery, Suman K. (1990), 'Economic Policy Reform in Developing Countries: The Role and Management of Political Factors', *World Development*, **18** (8), 1123–31.

Beveridge, William H. (1942), *Social Insurance and Allied Services: Report by Sir William Beveridge*, London: HMSO.

Beyer, Jürgen and Jan Wielgohs (1999), *Postsozialistische Unternehmensprivatisierung und die Anwendungsgrenzen für Pfadabhängigkeitstheorien*, Berlin, mimeo.

Bikont, Anna (1997), 'Emeryci emerytom', *Gazeta Wyborcza*, 17 September 1997, 18–19.

Bite, Inara (1998), *Transformation of Old-Age Security in Latvia*, Riga, mimeo.

Biuro Pełnomocnika Rządu do Spraw Reformy Zabezpieczenia Społecznego (1996), *Emerytura 2000*, Warsaw, mimeo.

Biuro Pełnomocnika Rządu do Spraw Reformy Zabezpieczenia Społecznego (1997), *Bezpieczeństwo dzięki różnorodności*, Warsaw, mimeo.

Blejer, Mario I. and Fabrizio Coricelli (1995), *The Making of Economic Reform in Eastern Europe. Conversations with Leading Reformers in Poland, Hungary and the Czech Republic*, Aldershot, UK and Brookfield, US: Edward Elgar.

Bobinski, Christopher (1997), 'Reformer Picked as Polish Finance Chief', *Financial Times*, 5 February 1997, 3.

Bod, Péter (1995a), 'For the Pension System and Reform', in Éva Ehrlich and Gábor Révész (eds), *Human Resources and Social Stability During Transition in Hungary*, San Francisco: International Center for Growth, pp. 173–4.

Bod, Péter (1995b), 'Formation of the Hungarian Social Insurance Based Pension System', in Éva Ehrlich and Gábor Révész (eds), *Human Resources and Social Stability During Transition in Hungary*, San Francisco: International Center for Growth, pp. 175–83.

Boller, Eberhard (1997), 'Aufbau von Altersversorgungssystemen im Transformationsprozeß der Reformstaaten Polen, Ungarn und Tschechien', FfW, Studien des Forschungsinstituts für Wirtschaftspolitik an der Universität Mainz No. 55, Mainz.

Bönker, Frank (1994), 'External Determinants of the Patterns and Outcomes of East European Transitions', *EMERGO*, **1** (1), 34–54.

Bönker, Frank (1995), 'The Dog That Did Not Bark? Politische Restriktionen und ökonomische Reformen in den Visegrád-Ländern', in Hellmut Wollmann, Helmut Wiesenthal and Frank Bönker (eds), *Transformation sozialistischer Gesellschaften: Am Ende des Anfangs*, Opladen: Westdeutscher Verlag, pp. 180–206.

Bönker, Frank (1997), *The Political Economy of Fiscal Adjustment in Eastern Europe: A Comparative Analysis of Hungary, Poland, and the Czech Republic*, Frankfurt (Oder), mimeo.

Bönker, Frank (1999), *The Political Economy of Fiscal Reform in Eastern Europe*. Doctoral Thesis submitted to Humboldt University, Berlin, mimeo.

Bonoli, Giuliano (1997), 'Classifying Welfare States: a Two-dimension Approach', *Journal of Social Policy*, **26** (3), 351–72.

Borowczyk, Ewa (1996), 'Polonia ¿Qué reforma es conveniente para el sistema de seguro social?', *Revista Internacional de Seguridad Social*, **49** (3), 89–95.

Börsch-Supan, Axel (1997), 'Sozialpolitik', in Jürgen von Hagen, Paul J. J. Welfens and Axel Börsch-Supan (eds), *Springers Handbuch der Volkswirtschaftslehre*, vol. II, Berlin: Springer, pp. 181–234.

Börsch-Supan, Axel (1998), 'Germany: A Social Security System on the Verge of Collapse', in Horst Siebert (ed.), *Redesigning Social Security*, Tübingen: Mohr, pp. 129–59.

Bos, Ellen (1994), 'Die Rolle von Eliten und kollektiven Akteuren in Transitionsprozessen', in Wolfgang Merkel (ed.), *Systemwechsel*, vol. I, Opladen: Leske & Budrich, pp. 81–109.

Bosworth, Barry P. and Gary Burtless (1998), 'Social Security Reform and Capital Formation', in Horst Siebert (ed.), *Redesigning Social Security*, Tübingen: Mohr, pp. 35–56.

Bovenberg, A. Lans (1998), 'Comment on Martin Feldstein', in Horst Siebert (ed.), *Redesigning Social Security*, Tübingen: Mohr, pp. 316–25.

Bowdler, Neil (1997/98), 'NIFs Part Three – An Uncanny Resemblance', *Business Central Europe*, December 1997/January 1998, 36.

Brabant, Jozef M. van (1998), *The Political Economy of Transition. Coming to Grips with History and Methodology*, London and New York: Routledge.

Breyer, Friedrich (1990), *Ökonomische Theorie der Alterssicherung*, Munich: Vahlen.

Breyer, Friedrich (1994), 'The Political Economy of Intergenerational Redistribution', *European Journal of Political Economy*, **10**, 61–84.

Breyer, Friedrich (1996), 'Zur Kombination von Kapitaldeckungs- und Umlageverfahren in der deutschen Rentenversicherung', in GVG (ed.), *Die Alterssicherungssysteme vor der demographischen Herausforderung. Das Säulen-Modell der Weltbank als Lösungsansatz*, Bonn: I. Vollmer, pp. 117–38.

Breyer, Friedrich (1997), 'Wirtschaftspolitik und Public Choice', in Jürgen von Hagen, Paul J. J. Welfens and Axel Börsch-Supan (eds), *Springers Handbuch der Volkswirtschaftslehre*, vol. II, Berlin: Springer, pp. 1–38.

Breyer, Friedrich (1998), 'The Economics of Minimum Pensions', in Horst Siebert (ed.), *Redesigning Social Security*, Tübingen: Mohr, pp. 273–94.

Breyer, Friedrich and Klaus Stolte (1999), 'The Political Feasibility of Pension Reform in the Light of Demographic Change', in Katharina Müller, Andreas Ryll and Hans-Jürgen Wagener (eds), *Transformation of Social Security: Pensions in Central–Eastern Europe*, Heidelberg: Physica, pp. 79–90.

Browning, Edgar K. (1975), 'Why the Social Insurance Budget Is Too Large in a Democracy', *Economic Inquiry*, **13** (3), 373–88.

Browning, Edgar K. (1983), '"The Economic and Politics of the Emergence of Social Security": A Comment', *The Cato Journal*, **3** (2), 381–4.

Bruno, Michael (1993), *Crisis, Stabilization and Economic Reform: Therapy by Consensus*, New York: Oxford University Press.

Brusis, Martin (1992), 'Systemwechsel und institutionelle Umgestaltung: Die Reform der ungarischen Sozialversicherung', *Südosteuropa*, **41** (9), 528–45.

Brusis, Martin (ed.) (1998), *Central and Eastern Europe on the Way into the European Union: Welfare State Reforms in the Czech Republic, Hungary, Poland and Slovakia*, Munich: Centre for Applied Policy Research.

Buchanan, James M. (1983), 'Social Security Survival: A Public-Choice Perspective', *The Cato Journal*, **3** (2), 339–53.

Burns, Tom R., Thomas Baumgartner and Philippe Deville (1985), *Man, Decisions, Society: The Theory of Actor-System Dynamics for Social Scientists*, New York: Gordon and Breach.

Butler, Stuart and Peter Germanis (1983), 'Achieving a "Leninist" strategy', *The Cato Journal*, **3** (2), 547–56.

Campbell, John (1998), 'Institutional Analysis and the Role of Ideas in Political Economy', *Theory and Society*, **27** (3), 377–409.

Cangiano, Marco, Carlo Cottarelli and Luis Cubeddu (1998), 'Pension Developments and Reforms in Transition Economies', IMF, Fiscal Affairs Department WP/98/151, Washington, DC.

Castello Branco, Marta de (1998), 'Pension Reform in the Baltics, Russia, and other Countries of the Former Soviet Union (BRO)', IMF, European II Department WP/98/11, Washington, DC.

CCET – Centre for Co-operation with the Economies in Transition (1995), *Social and Labour Market Policies in Hungary*, Paris: OECD.

Central Statistical Office (1997), *Statistical Pocket-Book of Hungary '96*, Budapest: KSH.

Charlton, Roger, Roddy McKinnon and Łukasz Konopielko (1998), 'Pensions Reform, Privatisation and Restructuring in the Transition: Unfinished Business or Inappropriate Agendas?', *Europe-Asia Studies*, **50** (8), 1413–46.

Chu, Ke-young and Sanjeev Gupta (1996), 'Social Protection in Transition Countries: Emerging Issues', IMF, PPAA/96/5, Washington, DC.

Chung, Eun Sung (1993), 'Private Pension Reform in Hungary: Issues and Strategies', *The Journal of East and West Studies*, **22** (1), 67–89.

Chwila, Krystyna (1997), 'Uwłaszczenie: Marzenie milionów – Tabliczka dzielenia', *POLITYKA*, 22 November 1997, 83–4.

Cichon, Michael (ed.) (1995), *Social Protection in the Visegrád Countries: Four Country Profiles*, ILO-CEET Report 13, Budapest: ILO-CEET.

Cichon, Michael (1997), 'El debate sobre el envejecimiento en la seguridad social: ¿se sigue el camino equivocado?', *Estudios de la Seguridad Social*, **81**, 109–128.

Cichon, Michael and Krzysztof Hagemejer (1995), 'The Social Protection System of Slovakia', in Michael Cichon (ed.), *Social Protection in the Visegrád Countries: Four Country Profiles*, ILO-CEET Report 13, Budapest: ILO-CEET, pp. 81–98.

ČMKOS (1994a), *Opinion of the Czech and Moravian Chamber of Trades Unions on the Pension Insurance Bill*, Prague, mimeo.

ČMKOS (1994b), *The Ten Demands of the ČMKOS to the Draft Law on Pension Insurance*, 13 December 1994, Prague, mimeo.

Congleton, Roger D. and William F. Shughart (1990), 'The Growth of Social Security: Electoral Push or Political Pull?', *Economic Inquiry*, **28** (1), 109–132.

Cornia, Giovanni Andrea (1996), 'Public Policy and Welfare Conditions During the Transition: An Overview', *MOCT-MOST*, **6** (1), 1–17.

Corsetti, Giancarlo and Klaus Schmidt-Hebbel (1997), 'Pension Reform and Growth', in Salvador Valdés-Prieto (ed.), *The Economics of Pensions. Principles, Policies, and International Experience*, Cambridge, UK: Cambridge University Press, pp. 127–59.

Coulter, Fiona, Christopher Heady, Colin Lawson and Stephen Smith (1997), 'Social Security Reform for Economic Transition: The Case of the Czech Republic', *Journal of Public Economics*, **66** (2), 313–26.

Crawford, Keith (1998), 'The Merits of a Grand Coalition', *The Prague Post*, 10 June 1998: http://www.praguepost.cz.

Csaba, Iván and András Semjén (1997), 'Welfare Institutions and the Transition: In the Search for Efficiency and Equity', KTI-IE, Discussion Paper 47, Budapest. Forthcoming in: László Halpern and Charles Wyplosz (eds), *Hungary Towards a Market Economy*, Cambridge, UK: Cambridge University Press.

Csontos, László, János Kornai and István György Tóth (1997), 'Tax-awareness and the Reform of the Welfare State – Results of a Hungarian Survey', Collegium Budapest, Institute for Advanced Studies, Discussion Papers 37, Budapest.

Cukierman, Alex and Mariano Tommasi (1998a), 'Credibility of Policymakers and of Economic Reforms', in Federico Sturzenegger and Mariano Tommasi (eds), *The Political Economy of Reform*, Cambridge, MA and London: MIT Press, pp. 329–47.

Cukierman, Alex and Mariano Tommasi (1998b), 'When Does It Take a Nixon to Go to China?', *American Economic Review*, **88** (1), 180–97.

Czada, Roland (1995), 'Kooperation und institutionelles Lernen in Netzwerken der Vereinigungspolitik', in Renate Mayntz and Fritz W. Scharpf (eds), *Gesellschaftliche Selbstregelung und politische Steuerung*, Frankfurt/Main and New York: Campus, pp. 299–326.

Czajka, Stanisław (1985), *Renten und Pensionen in Polen*, Dresden: Zentrales Forschungsinstitut für Arbeit.

Czechowska, Maria (1998), 'Formy, w jakich mogą być realizowane pracownicze programy emerytalne', *Przegląd Ubezpieczeń Społecznych*, **32** (10), 7–12.

Czepulis-Rutkowska, Zofia (1999), 'The Polish Pension System and Its Problems', in Katharina Müller, Andreas Ryll and Hans-Jürgen Wagener (eds), *Transformation of Social Security: Pensions in Central–Eastern Europe*, Heidelberg: Physica, pp. 143–58.

Czibere, Károly (1998), 'Pension System and Pension Reform', in Martin Brusis (ed.), *Central and Eastern Europe on the Way into the European Union: Welfare State Reforms in the Czech Republic, Hungary, Poland and Slovakia*, Munich: Centre for Applied Policy Research, pp. 29–35.

Czúcz, Ottó (1993), 'Das Rentensystem in Ungarn – Leistungsarten, Voraussetzungen ihrer Liquidierung und Hauptgründe der notwendigen Umgestaltung des Systems', *Deutsche Rentenversicherung*, (11/93), 737–50.

Czúcz, Ottó and Mária Pintér (1996), *The Development and Timely Issues of the Hungarian Pension System in the Years Since the Change of the Political System (1989–1995)*, Budapest, mimeo.

Czúcz, Ottó and Mária Pintér (1998), *Transformation of Old-Age Security in Hungary*, Budapest, mimeo.

Dąbrowski, Marek (1995), *Western Aid Conditionality and the Post-Communist Transition*, CASE Studies & Analyses 37, Warsaw: CASE.

Danecki, Jan (1994), 'Social Costs of System Transformation in Poland', in Stein Ringen and Claire Wallace (eds), *Societies in Transition. East-Central Europe Today*, Aldershot: Avebury, pp. 47–60.

Dangerfield, Martin (1997), 'Ideology and the Czech Transformation: Neoliberal Rhetoric or Neoliberal Reality?', *East European Politics and Societies*, **11** (3), 436–69.

David, Paul A. (1985), 'Clio and the Economics of QWERTY', *American Economic Review*, **75** (2), 332–7.

Davis, E. Philip (1995), *Pension Funds. Retirement-Income Security, and Capital Markets – An International Perspective*, Oxford: Clarendon Press.

Davis, E. Philip (1998), 'Policy Implementation Issues in Reforming Pension Systems', EBRD, Working Paper 31, London.

Deacon, Bob (1992), 'Eastern European Welfare: Past, Present and Future in Comparative Context', in Bob Deacon et al. (eds), *The New Eastern Europe. Social Policy Past, Present and Future*, London: Sage Publications, pp. 1–29.

Deacon, Bob and Michelle Hulse (1997), 'The Making of Post-communist Social Policy: The Role of International Agencies', *Journal of Social Policy*, **26** (1), 43–62.

De Deken, Johan Jeroen (1994), 'Social Policy in Postwar Czechoslovakia. The Development of Old-Age Pensions and Housing Policies During the Period 1945–1989', European University Institute, EUI Working Paper SPS 94/13, Florence.

De Deken, Johan Jeroen (1995), *The Politics of Solidarity and the Structuration of Social Policy Regimes in Postwar Europe – The Development of Old-Age Pensions and Housing Policies in Belgium, Czechoslovakia, and Sweden*, Doctoral Thesis at European University Institute, San Domenico di Fiesole, mimeo.

Desai, Raj M. and Mitchell Orenstein (1996), 'Business Associations and the State in the Czech Republic', *EMERGO*, **3** (2), 29–41.

Deutsch, Antal (1996), *The Economics and Politics of Pension Reform in Hungary*, Montreal and Budapest, mimeo.

Deutsch, Antal (1997), 'Hungary's "In Vivo" Pension Reform Experience', *Transition*, **8** (6), 19–20.

Deutsche Bank Research (1998), 'Deutschland braucht attraktive Pensionsfonds', DB Research Bulletin 'Aktuelle Wirtschafts- und Währungsfragen', 2/1998, Frankfurt/Main.

Deutsche Rentenversicherung (1998), 'Rentenreformgesetz 1999', *Deutsche Rentenversicherung*, (1–2/98), special edition.

Dewatripont, Mathias and Gérard Roland (1998), 'The Design of Reform Packages under Uncertainty', in Federico Sturzenegger and Mariano Tommasi (eds), *The Political Economy of Reform*, Cambridge, MA and London: MIT Press, pp. 243–67.

Diamond, Peter (1994), 'Pension Reform in a Transition Economy: Notes on Poland and Chile', in Olivier J. Blanchard, Kenneth A. Froot and Jeffrey D. Sachs (eds), *The Transition in Eastern Europe*, vol. II, Chicago and London: University of Chicago Press, pp. 71–103.

190 The Political Economy of Pension Reform in Central–Eastern Europe

Diamond, Peter (1997), 'Insulation of Pensions from Political Risk', in Salvador Valdés-Prieto (ed.), *The Economics of Pensions. Principles, Policies, and International Experience*, Cambridge, UK: Cambridge University Press, pp. 33–57.

Diamond, Peter A., David C. Lindeman and Howard Young (eds) (1996), *Social Security – What Role for the Future?*, Washington, DC: National Academy of Social Insurance.

Disney, Richard (1998), *Social Security Reform in the UK: A Voluntary Privatisation*, Paper prepared for the Conference 'Reforming the Social Security System: An International Perspective', 16–17 March 1998, Rome, mimeo.

Disney, Richard and Paul Johnson (1998), 'The United Kingdom: A Working System of Minimum Pensions?', in Horst Siebert (ed.), *Redesigning Social Security*, Tübingen: Mohr, pp. 207–32.

Dixit, Avinash (1996), *The Making of Economic Policy: A Transaction-Cost Politics Perspective*, Cambridge, MA and London: MIT Press.

Döhler, Marian and Philip Manow (1995), 'Staatliche Reformpolitik und die Rolle der Verbände im Gesundheitssektor', in Renate Mayntz and Fritz W. Scharpf (eds), *Gesellschaftliche Selbstregelung und politische Steuerung*, Frankfurt/Main and New York: Campus, pp. 140–68.

Döring, Diether (1997), *Soziale Sicherheit im Alter? Rentenversicherung auf dem Prüfstand*, Berlin: Aufbau.

Döring, Diether (1998), *Alterssicherungssysteme in der Europäischen Union*. Presentation held at Institut für Wirtschaftsforschung Halle, mimeo.

Drazen, Allan and Vittorio Grilli (1993), 'The Benefit of Crises for Economic Reforms', *American Economic Review*, **83** (3), 598–607.

Drost, André (1997), 'Verhandlungen über die Rentenversicherung und das Bildungswesen', *Finanzarchiv*, **54** (1), 89–103.

Dziadul, Jan (1999), 'Emerytalna farsa – O co chodziło w strajku górników?', *POLITYKA*, 2 January 1999, 17.

Eatwell, John (1999), *The Macroeconomics of Pension Reform*, Paper prepared for the UN/ECE Spring Seminar 'The Economic Implications of Population Ageing in the ECE Region', 3 May 1999, Geneva, mimeo.

EBRD (1994), *Transition Report 1994: Economic Transition in Eastern Europe and the Former Soviet Union*, London: European Bank for Reconstruction and Development.

EBRD (1997), *Transition Report 1997: Enterprise Performance and Growth*, London: European Bank for Reconstruction and Development.

Edwards, Sebastian (1998), 'Chile: Radical Change towards a Funded Pension System', in Horst Siebert (ed.), *Redesigning Social Security*, Tübingen: Mohr, pp. 233–63.

E.L. (1998), 'Drugi filar: Winterthur i Dom dostały licencje', *Rzeczpospolita*, 27 November 1998: http://www.rzeczpospolita.pl.

Elliott, Geoff (1995), 'Europe's Other Pensions Crisis', *Institutional Investor*, **XX** (4), 73–5.

Esping-Andersen, Gøsta (1985), *Politics Against Markets: The Social Democratic Road to Power*, Princeton: Princeton University Press.

Esping-Andersen, Gøsta (1990), *The Three Worlds of Welfare Capitalism*, Princeton: Princeton University Press.

Esping-Andersen, Gøsta (1996), 'After the Golden Age? Welfare State Dilemmas in a Global Economy', in Gøsta Esping-Andersen (ed.), *Welfare States in Transition. National Adaptations in Global Economies*, London: Sage Publications, pp. 1–31.

Fandrejewska, Aleksandra (1998a), 'Reforma emerytalna: Badania opinii społecznej', *Rzeczpospolita*, 22 June 1998: http://www.rzeczpospolita.pl .

Fandrejewska, Aleksandra (1998b), 'Wiano na dobry początek', *Rzeczpospolita*, 27 November 1998: http://www.rzeczpospolita.pl.

Feldstein, Martin (1995), 'Would Privatizing Social Security Raise Economic Welfare?', NBER, Working Paper 5281, Cambridge, MA.

Feldstein, Martin (1996), 'The Missing Piece in Policy Analysis: Social Security Reform', *American Economic Review – Papers and Proceedings*, **86** (2), 1–14.

Feldstein, Martin (1998), 'Transition to a Fully Funded Pension System: Five Economic Issues', in Horst Siebert (ed.), *Redesigning Social Security*, Tübingen: Mohr, pp. 299–315.

Fenge, Robert (1997), *Effizienz der Alterssicherung*, Heidelberg: Physica.

Ferge, Zsuzsa (1991), 'Recent Trends in Social Policy in Hungary', in Jan Adam (ed.), *Economic Reforms and Welfare Systems in the USSR, Poland and Hungary. Social Contract in Transformation*, London: Macmillan, pp. 132–55.

Ferge, Zsuzsa (1992), 'Social Policy Regimes and Social Structure Hypotheses about the Prospects of Social Policy in Central and Eastern Europe', in Zsuzsa Ferge and Jon Eivind Kolberg (eds), *Social Policy in a Changing Europe*, Frankfurt/Main: Campus, and Boulder, CO: WestviewPress, pp. 201–22.

Ferge, Zsuzsa (1994), 'Zur Reform der Sozialpolitik in den posttotalitären Ländern: Anmerkungen zu verschiedenen Reformstrategien', in International Social Security Association (ed.), *Umstrukturierung der sozialen Sicherheit in Mittel- und Osteuropa. Trends – Politiken – Optionen*, Geneva: ISSA, pp. 15–32.

Ferge, Zsuzsa (1995), 'Social policy', in Zsuzsa Ferge, Endre Sik, Péter Róbert and Fruzsina Albert, *Social Costs of Transition. International Report*, Institute for Human Sciences, SOCO Working Paper, Vienna, pp. 181–218.

Ferge, Zsuzsa (1996), 'Freiheit und soziale Sicherheit', *Transit*, (12), 62–80.

Ferge, Zsuzsa (1997a), 'Frauen: Die Verliererinnen der Wohlfahrtsreform', *Transit*, (14), 176–85.

Ferge, Zsuzsa (1997b), 'Social Policy Challenges and Dilemmas in Ex-Socialist Systems', in Joan Nelson, Charles Tilly and Lee Walker (eds), *Transforming Post-Communist Political Economies*, Washington, DC: National Academies Press, pp. 299–321.

Ferge, Zsuzsa (1997c), *The Actors of the Hungarian Pension Reform*, Vienna, mimeo.

Ferge, Zsuzsa (1999), 'The Politics of the Hungarian Pension Reform', in Katharina Müller, Andreas Ryll and Hans-Jürgen Wagener (eds), *Transformation of Social Security: Pensions in Central-Eastern Europe*, Heidelberg: Physica, pp. 231–46.

Ferge, Zsuzsa, Endre Sik, Péter Róbert and Fruzsina Albert (1995), *Social Costs of Transition. International Report*, Institute for Human Sciences, SOCO Working Paper, Vienna.

Fernandez, Raquel and Dani Rodrik (1998), 'Resistance to Reform: Status Quo Bias in the Presence of Individual-Specific Uncertainty', in Federico Sturzenegger and Mariano Tommasi (eds), *The Political Economy of Reform*, Cambridge, MA and London: MIT Press, pp. 61–76.

Ferrara, Peter (1982), *Social Security: Averting the Crisis*, Washington, DC: Cato Institute.

Flakierski, Henryk (1991), 'Social Policies in the 1980s in Poland: A Discussion of New Approaches', in Jan Adam (ed.), *Economic Reforms and Welfare Systems in the USSR, Poland and Hungary. Social Contract in Transformation*, London: Macmillan, pp. 85–109.

Florek, Ludwik (1986), 'Einführung zum Gesetz über die Rentenversorgung der Arbeitnehmer und ihrer Familien', *Jahrbuch für Ostrecht*, **XXVII** (2), 396–408.

Florek, Ludwik (1993), 'Entwicklungsgeschichte sozialer Sicherheit aus östlicher Sicht – das Beispiel Polen', in Bernd von Maydell and Eva-Maria Hohnerlein (eds), *Die Umgestaltung der Systeme sozialer Sicherheit in den Staaten Mittel- und Osteuropas. Fragen und Lösungsansätze*, Berlin: Duncker & Humblot, pp. 39–51.

Flowers, Marilyn R. (1983), 'The Political Feasibility of Privatizing Social Security', *The Cato Journal*, **3** (2), 557–61.

Fontaine, Juan Andrés (1997), 'Are there (Good) Macroeconomic Reasons for Limiting External Investments by Pension Funds? The Chilean Experience', in Salvador Valdés-Prieto (ed.), *The Economics of Pensions. Principles, Policies, and International Experience*, Cambridge, UK: Cambridge University Press, pp. 251–74.

Förster, Michael F. and István György Tóth (1997), *Poverty and Inequalities: Hungary and the Visegrad Countries Compared*, Paris and Budapest, mimeo.

Fougerolles, Jean de (1996), 'Pension Privatization in Latin America – Lessons for Central and Eastern Europe', *Russian and East-European Finance and Trade*, **32** (3), 86–104.

Fox, Louise (1997), 'Pension Reform in the Post-Communist Transition Economies', in Joan Nelson, Charles Tilly and Lee Walker (eds), *Transforming Post-Communist Political Economies*, Washington, DC: National Academies Press, pp. 370–83.

Friedman, Milton J. (1972), 'Second Lecture', in Wilbur J. Cohen and Milton J. Friedman (eds), *Social Security: Universal or Selective?*, Washington, DC: American Enterprise Institute, pp. 21–49.

Gadomski, Witold and Ewa Adamczewska (1997), 'Emeryci boją się reformy', *Nowy Tygodnik Popularny*, 28 September 1997, 4.

Gál, Róbert I. (1996), *The Hungarian Pension Reform: Trends and Issues*, Budapest, mimeo.

Gál, Róbert I. (1999), 'Hungarian Old Age Security Prior to the 1998 Reform', in Katharina Müller, Andreas Ryll and Hans-Jürgen Wagener (eds), *Transformation of Social Security: Pensions in Central–Eastern Europe*, Heidelberg: Physica, pp. 201–10.

Genschel, Philipp (1995), 'Dynamische Verflechtung in der internationalen Standardisierung', in Renate Mayntz and Fritz W. Scharpf (eds), *Gesellschaftliche Selbstregelung und politische Steuerung*, Frankfurt/Main and New York: Campus, pp. 233–65.

Gerencsér, László (1997), *Die ungarische Rentenreform – Kurze Information*, Budapest, mimeo.

Gesell, Rainer, Katharina Müller and Dirck Süß (1998), 'Social Security Reform and Privatisation in Poland: Parallel Projects or Integrated Agenda?', FIT, Discussion Paper 8/98, Frankfurt (Oder).

Główny Urząd Statystyczny (1997), *Mały Rocznik Statystyczny 1997*, Warsaw: GUS.

Golinowska, Stanisława (ed.) (1997), 'Reforma Systemu Emerytalno-Rentowego', CASE , Raporty CASE No. 6, Warsaw.

Golinowska, Stanisława (1999), 'Political Actors and Reform Paradigms in Old-Age Security in Poland', in Katharina Müller, Andreas Ryll and Hans-Jürgen Wagener (eds), *Transformation of Social Security: Pensions in Central–Eastern Europe*, Heidelberg: Physica, pp. 173–99.

Golinowska, Stanisława and Maciej Żukowski (1998), *Transformation of Old-Age Security in Poland*, Warsaw and Poznań, mimeo.

Golinowska, Stanisława, Zofia Czepulis-Rutkowska and Maria Szczur (1997), 'The Case of Poland', in Mária Augusztinovics et al., *Pension Systems and Reforms – Britain, Hungary, Italy, Poland, Sweden*, Phare ACE Research Project P95-2139-R, Final Report, Budapest, mimeo, pp. 107–31.

Gonzalez, Eduardo (1996), *How to Finance the Transition from a Pay-as-You-Go to a Fully Funded Pension System*, Trento, mimeo.

Góra, Marek and Michał Rutkowski (1998), *The Quest for Pension Reform: Poland's Security through Diversity*, Warsaw: Office of the Government Plenipotentiary for Social Security Reform.

Götting, Ulrike (1994), 'Destruction, Adjustment, and Innovation: Social Policy Transformation in East Central Europe', ZeS, Arbeitspapier No. 2/94, Bremen.

Götting, Ulrike (1995), 'Welfare State Development in Post-Communist Bulgaria, Czech Republic, Hungary, and Slovakia', in Victor A. Pestoff (ed.), *Reforming Social Services in Central and Eastern Europe: An Eleven Nation Overview*, Cracow: Cracow Academy of Economics and Friedrich Ebert Stiftung, pp. 349–93.

Götting, Ulrike (1996), 'A New Social Contract? In Defence of Welfare: Social Protection and Social Reform in Eastern Europe', European University Institute, EUI Working Paper RSC 96/42, Florence.

Götting, Ulrike (1998), *Transformation der Wohlfahrtsstaaten in Mittel- und Osteuropa. Eine Zwischenbilanz*, Opladen: Leske & Budrich.

Götting, Ulrike and Stephan Lessenich (1998), 'Sphären sozialer Sicherheit. Wohlfahrtsstaatliche Regimeforschung und gesellschaftliche Transformation', in Stephan Lessenich and Ilona Ostner (eds), *Welten des Wohlfahrtskapitalismus. Der Sozialstaat in vergleichender Perspektive*, Frankfurt/Main and New York: Campus, pp. 271–319.

Gough, Ian (1979), *The Political Economy of the Welfare State*, London: Macmillan.

Gough, Ian (1989), 'Welfare State', in John Eatwell, Murray Milgate and Peter Newman (eds), *The New Palgrave: Social Economics*, London: Macmillan, pp. 276–81.

Graham, Carol (1996), *Strategies for Addressing the Social Costs of Market Reforms: Lessons for Transition Economies in East Asia and Eastern Europe*, Washington, DC, mimeo.

Graham, Carol (1997), 'From Safety Nets to Social Policy: Lessons for the Transition Economies from the Developing Countries', in Joan Nelson, Charles Tilly and Lee Walker (eds), *Transforming Post-Communist Political Economies*, Washington, DC: National Academies Press, pp. 385–99.

Grande, Edgar (1995), 'Regieren in verflochtenen Verhandlungssystemen', in Renate Mayntz and Fritz W. Scharpf (eds), *Gesellschaftliche Selbstregelung und politische Steuerung*, Frankfurt/Main and New York: Campus, pp. 327–68.

Groenewegen, Peter (1991), '"Political Economy" and "Economics"', in John Eatwell, Murray Milgate and Peter Newman (eds), *The New Palgrave: The World of Economics*, London: Macmillan, pp. 556–62.

Grootaert, Christiaan (1995), 'Poverty and Social Transfers in Poland', World Bank, Policy Research Working Paper 1440, Washington, DC.

Grootaert, Christiaan (1997), 'Poverty and Social Transfers in Hungary', World Bank, Policy Research Working Paper 1770, Washington, DC.

GVG – Gesellschaft für Versicherungswissenschaft und -gestaltung (ed.) (1994), *Soziale Sicherung in West-, Mittel- und Osteuropa*, Baden-Baden: Nomos.

Haberlová, Věra (1998), *Old-Age Security Reform Basis in the Czech Republic. Summary Analysis of the Public Opinion*, Prague: RILSA and STEM.

Hagemejer, Krzysztof (1998), 'System emerytalny: Reforma dla naszych dzieci', *Rzeczpospolita*, 17 July 1998: http://www.rzeczpospolita.pl.

Haggard, Stephan and Robert R. Kaufman (1995), *The Political Economy of Democratic Transitions*, Princeton: Princeton University Press.

Haggard, Stephan and Steven B. Webb (1993), 'What Do We Know about the Political Economy of Economic Policy Reform?', *The World Bank Research Observer*, **8** (2), 143–68.

Halásek, Dušan (1995), 'The Czech Republic – Qualitative Aspects of Institutional Change in Social Services', in Victor A. Pestoff (ed.), *Reforming Social Services in Central and Eastern Europe: An Eleven Nation Overview*, Cracow: Cracow Academy of Economics and Friedrich–Ebert–Stiftung, pp. 135–48.

Hancock, Ruth and Stephen Pudney (1997), 'The Welfare of Pensioners During Economic Transition: An Analysis of Hungarian Survey Data', *Economics of Transition*, **5** (2), 395–426.

Handelsblatt (1998), 'Korrekturgesetz – Ungeschmälerte Rentenanpassung und volle Lohnfortzahlung für kranke Arbeitnehmer', *Handelsblatt*, 11–12 December 1998, 5.

Hansson, Ingemar and Charles Stuart (1989), Social Security as Trade Among Living Generations, *American Economic Review*, **79** (5), 1182–95.

Harberger, Arnold C. (1993), 'Secrets of Success: A Handful of Heroes', *American Economic Review – Papers and Proceedings*, **83** (2), 342–50.

Hartl, Jan and Jiří Večerník (1992), 'Economy, Policy and Welfare in Transition', in Zsuzsa Ferge and Jon Eivind Kolberg (eds), *Social Policy in a Changing Europe*, Frankfurt/Main: Campus, and Boulder, CO: WestviewPress, pp. 161–75.

Hausner, Jerzy (1997), *Security Through Diversity – Conditions for the Successful Reform of the Pension System in Poland*. Paper prepared for the Fifth Central European Forum 'The Politics of Welfare: Between Governmental Policy and Local Initiative', 24–26 October 1997, Vienna, mimeo.

Hausner, Jerzy (1998), 'Security through Diversity: Conditions for Successful Reform of the Pension System in Poland', Collegium Budapest, Discussion Paper 49, Budapest.

Hausner, Jerzy, Ove K. Pedersen and Karsten Ronit (eds) (1995), *Evolution of Interest Representation and Development of the Labour Market in Post-Socialist Countries*, Cracow: Cracow Academy of Economics and Friedrich Ebert Stiftung.

Heady, Christopher and Stephen Smith (1995), 'Tax and Benefit Reform in the Czech and Slovak Republics', in David M. G. Newbery (ed.), *Tax and Benefit Reform in Central and Eastern Europe*, London: CEPR, pp. 19–48.

Heinrich, Georges (1997), 'Pension Reforms in Central and Eastern Europe: Yet Another Transition...?', Heriot-Watt University, CERT Discussion Paper 97/5, Edinburgh.

Heinrich, Ralph P. (1996), *Pension Reform in Transition Economies – Containing Short-Term Problems*, Kiel, mimeo.

Heinrich, Ralph P. et al. (1996), *Sozialpolitik im Transformationsprozeß Mittel- und Osteuropas*, Kieler Studien No. 273, Tübingen: Mohr.

Heller, Peter S. (1998), 'Rethinking Public Pension Reform Initiatives', IMF, Fiscal Affairs Department WP/98/61, Washington, DC.

Hemming, Richard (1998), 'Should Public Pensions be Funded?', IMF, Fiscal Affairs Department WP/98/35, Washington, DC.

Hill, Michael (1990), *Social Security Policy in Britain*, Aldershot, UK and Brookfield, US: Edward Elgar.

Hills, John, John Ditch and Howard Glennerster (eds) (1994), *Beveridge and Social Security. An International Retrospective*, Oxford: Clarendon Press.

Hirschler, Richard (1996), 'Reforming the Pension System in Hungary', *Central European Banker*, December 1996, 5–12.

Hirschman, Albert O. (1963), *Journeys Toward Progress. Studies of Economic Policy-Making in Latin America*, New York: The Twentieth Century Fund.

Hirschman, Albert O. (1970), 'The Search for Paradigms as a Hindrance to Understanding', *World Politics*, **22** (3), 329–43.

Hirschman, Albert O. (1991), *The Rhetoric of Reaction: Perversity, Futility, Jeopardy*, Cambridge, MA: Harvard University Press.

Hiršl, Miroslav, Jiří Rusnok and Martin Fassmann (1995), 'Market Reforms and Social Welfare in the Czech Republic: A True Success Story?', UNICEF, Innocenti Occasional Papers, EPS 50, Florence.

Hirte, Georg and Reinhard Weber (1997), 'Pareto Improving Transition from a Pay-as-you-go to a Fully Funded System – is it Politically Feasible?', *Finanzarchiv N.F.*, **54** (3), 303–30.

Hochman, Harold M. and James D. Rodgers (1969), 'Pareto Optimal Redistribution', *American Economic Review*, **59** (4), 542–57.

Hock, Martin (1998), 'Transformation der Wirtschaftsordnung und politisches System – Anspruch und Wirklichkeit der Wirtschaftsreformen in Ungarn 1968–1996', FfW, Studien des Forschungsinstituts für Wirtschaftspolitik an der Universität Mainz No. 58, Mainz.

Holzmann, Robert (1994), 'Funded and Private Pensions for Eastern European Countries in Transition?', *Revista de Análisis Económico*, **9** (1), 183–210.

Holzmann, Robert (1996), 'Pension Reform, Financial Market Development and Economic Growth: Preliminary evidence from Chile', IMF, Working Paper WP/96/94, Washington DC.

Holzmann, Robert (1997a), *A World Bank Perspective on Pension Reform*, Washington, DC, mimeo.

Holzmann, Robert (1997b), 'On Economic Benefits and Fiscal Requirements of Moving from Unfunded to Funded Pensions', Universität of Saarland, Forschungsbericht 9702, Saarbrücken.

Homburg, Stefan (1988), *Theorie der Alterssicherung*, Berlin: Springer.

Homburg, Stefan (1997), 'Old-Age Pension Systems: A Theoretical Evaluation', in Herbert Giersch (ed.), *Reforming the Welfare State*, Berlin: Springer, pp. 233–46.

Hřích, Ján and Kristina Larischová (1998), 'Das System der sozialen Sicherung in der Tschechischen Republik', in Martin Brusis (ed.), *Central and Eastern Europe on the Way into the European Union: Welfare State Reforms in the Czech Republic, Hungary, Poland and Slovakia*, Munich: Centre for Applied Policy Research, pp. 69–79.

Hujo, Katja (1997), *Soziale Sicherung im Kontext von Stabilisierung und Strukturanpassung: Die Reform der Rentenversicherung in Argentinien*, Berlin, mimeo.

Hujo, Katja (1999), 'Paradigmatic Change in Old Age Security: Latin American Cases', in Katharina Müller, Andreas Ryll and Hans-Jürgen Wagener (eds), *Transformation of Social Security: Pensions in Central–Eastern Europe*, Heidelberg: Physica, pp. 121–39.

ILO-CEET (1995), 'Social Expenditure in Central and Eastern Europe Under Challenge: Financing A Decent Society Or Cutting Corners?', *ILO-CEET Newsletter*, (June 1995), 8–10.

Immergut, Ellen M. (1992), *Health Politics – Interests and Institutions in Western Europe*, Cambridge, UK: Cambridge University Press.

Institut für Iberoamerika-Kunde (ed.) (1997), 'Rentenreformen in Lateinamerika – Lehren für Europa', *Lateinamerika, Analysen-Daten-Dokumentation*, **14** (36), Hamburg: IIK.

IPiSS (ed.) (1995), 'Dyskusja wokół rządowego programu ubezpieczeń społecznych', IPiSS, Ekspertyzy – Informacje No. 5, Warsaw.

IPiSS (ed.) (1997), *Eksperci Banku Światowego o reformach emerytalnych w Polsce i na świecie. Propozycje, wzory, kontrowersje*, Warsaw: IPiSS.

IPiSS and Institute for East West Studies (eds) (1995), 'Tworzenie prywatnych funduszy emerytalnych w Polsce', IPiSS, IPiSS Zeszyt 1 (401), Warsaw.

Isuani, Ernesto Aldo and Jorge A. San Martino (1995), 'El nuevo sistema previsional argentino ¿Punto final a una larga crisis?' Primera parte, *Boletín Informativo Techint*, (281), 41–56; Segunda parte, *Boletín Informativo Techint*, (282), 43–67.

Iyer, Subramaniam N. (1993), 'Pension Reform in Developing Countries', *International Labour Review*, **132** (2), 187–207.

Jacoby, Wade (1998), *Talking the Talk: The Cultural and Institutional Effects of Western Models*, Berkeley, CA, mimeo.

James, Estelle (1996), 'Protecting the Old and Promoting Growth. A Defense of "Averting the Old Age Crisis"', World Bank, Policy Research Working Paper 1570, Washington, DC.

James, Estelle (1997), 'New Systems for Old Age Security. Theory, Practice, and Empirical Evidence', World Bank, Policy Research Working Paper 1766, Washington, DC.

James, Estelle (1998), 'New Models for Old Age Security: Experiments, Evidence, and Unanswered Questions', *The World Bank Research Observer* **13** (2), 271–301.

Janoski, Thomas and Alexander M. Hicks (1994), 'Conclusion: *Quo Vadis* Political Economy? Theory and Methodology in the Comparative Analysis of the Welfare State', in Thomas Janoski and Alexander M. Hicks (eds), *The Comparative Political Economy of the Welfare State*, Cambridge, UK: Cambridge University Press, pp. 365–80.

Janowitz, Morris (1976), *Social Control of the Welfare State*, Chicago: University of Chicago Press.

Jędrasik-Jankowska, Inetta (1998), 'Projekt ustawy o emeryturach i rentach z Funduszu Ubezpieczeń Społecznych – Zawieszanie prawa do świadczeń', *Rzeczpospolita*, 24 August 1998: http://www.rzeczpospolita.pl.

Jelínek, Tomáš and Ondřej Schneider (1997a), *Pension System Reform in the Czech Republic – Liberální Institut Project Proposal*, Prague, mimeo.

Jelínek, Tomáš and Ondřej Schneider (1997b), 'Time for Pension Reform in the Czech Republic', *Transitions*, **4** (1), 77–81.

Jelínek, Tomáš and Ondřej Schneider (1999), 'An Analysis of the Voluntary Pension Fund System in the Czech Republic', in Katharina Müller, Andreas Ryll and Hans-Jürgen Wagener (eds), *Transformation of Social Security: Pensions in Central–Eastern Europe*, Heidelberg: Physica, pp. 259–72.

Jończyk, Jan (1997), 'Reforma emerytur: Kosztowna prywatyzacja ryzyka starości', *Rzeczpospolita*, 23 April 1997, 17.

Johnson, Paul and Jane Falkingham (1994), 'Is there a Future for the Beveridge Pension Scheme?', in Sally Baldwin and Jane Falkingham (eds), *Social Security and Social Change. New Challenges to the Beveridge Model*, New York: Harvester Wheatsheaf, pp. 255–70.

Johnson, Paul and Katherine Rake (1997), 'The Case of Britain', in Mária Augusztinovics et al., *Pension Systems and Reforms – Britain, Hungary, Italy, Poland, Sweden*, Phare ACE Research Project P95-2139-R, Final Report, Budapest, mimeo, pp. 25–50.

Jones, Thomas W. (1996), 'A Strategy to Maintain Social Security Benefits', *Challenge*, (November-December 1996), 25–7.

Kabele, Jiří and Martin Potůček (1995), 'The Formation and Implementation of Social Policy in the Czech Republic as a Political Process', START, Research Paper 5, Prague.

Kabilka, Zdeněk (1998), *Údaje o penzijním připojištění*, Prague, mimeo.

Kalina-Prasznic, Urszula (1997), 'Uwagi o reformowaniu systemu emerytalnego', *Praca i Zabezpieczenie Społeczne*, (9), 2–6.

Kavalsky, Basil G. (1998), 'System emerytalno-rentowy – Reforma jest po prostu niezbędna', *Rzeczpospolita*, 27 October 1998: http://www.rzeczpospolita.pl.

Kingson, Eric and John Williamson (1996), 'Undermining Social Security's Basic Objectives', *Challenge*, (November–December 1996), 28–9.

Klaus, Václav (1991), 'We Need an Untainted Market Economy, and We Need it Now', *Transition*, **2** (8), 8–9.

Klimentová, Jana (1994), 'The Development of Pension Schemes in the Czech Republic', in Stein Ringen and Claire Wallace (eds), *Social Reform in the Czech Republic*. Prague Papers on Social Responses to Transformation, vol. II., Prague, pp. 21–4.

Klimentová, Jana (1997a), 'Důchodové systémy zemí Střední a Východní Evropy v období transformace', *Sociální Politika*, (10), 2–3.

Klimentová, Jana (1997b), 'Důchodový systém v Chile', *Sociální Politika*, (2), 10–11.

Klimentová, Jana (1997c), 'Nové trendy ve financování důchodovych systémů', *Sociální Politika*, (4), 2–4.

Klimentová, Jana and Milan Polívka (1997), 'Doporučení se liší: Reforma penzijního systému (1)', *Ekonom* (42), 40.

Kohl, Jürgen (1994), *Alterssicherung im internationalen Vergleich. Analysen zu Strukturen und Wirkungen der Alterssicherungssysteme in fünf westeuropäischen Ländern*, Habilitation thesis, submitted to the Faculty of Sociology at the University of Bielefeld, Bielefeld, mimeo.

Kohler, Berthold (1998), 'Die tschechische Rentnerpartei könnte über die nächste Regierung mitbestimmen', *Frankfurter Allgemeine Zeitung*, 9 June 1998, 8.

Kołodko, Grzegorz (1996), 'Continuity and Change in the Polish Transformation 1993–2000', *EMERGO*, **3** (2), 58–69.

Kołodko, Grzegorz (1999), 'Ten Years of Post-Socialist Transition Lessons for Policy Reform', World Bank, Policy Research Working Paper 2095, Washington, DC.

Kondratowicz, Andrzej and Marek Okolski (1993), 'The Polish Economy on the Eve of the Solidarity Take-over', in Henryk Kierzkowski, Marek Okolski and Stanisław Wellisz (eds), *Stabilization and Structural Adjustment in Poland*, London and New York: Routledge, pp. 7–28.

Kopits, George (1994), 'Soziale Sicherheit in Volkswirtschaften im Übergang', in International Social Security Association (ed.), *Umstrukturierung der sozialen Sicherheit in Mittel- und Osteuropa. Trends – Politiken – Optionen*, Geneva: ISSA, pp. 69–87.

Koral, Jolanta (1996a), 'Pakiet Bączkowskiego – co będzie z reformami społecznymi?', *Gazeta Wyborcza*, 12 November 1996, 2.

Koral, Jolanta (1996b), 'Trzy filary emerytur – Minister Bączkowski chce uchwalenia reformy emerytalnej przed wyborami', *Gazeta Wyborcza*, 17 October 1996, 3.

Koral, Jolanta (1998), 'Filar numer 1', *Gazeta Wyborcza*, 27 November 1998: http://www.gazeta.pl.

Kornai, János (1995), *Highways and Byways. Studies on Reform and Post-Communist Transition*, Cambridge, MA and London: MIT Press.

Kornai, János (1996), 'Bürger und Staat. Die Reform des Wohlfahrtssystems', *Transit*, (12), 29–47.

Kornai, János (1997a), 'Reforming the Welfare State in Postsocialist Societies', *World Development*, **25** (8), 1183–6.

Kornai, János (1997b), 'Reform of the Welfare Sector in the Post-Communist Countries: A Normative Approach', in Joan Nelson, Charles Tilly and Lee Walker (eds), *Transforming Post-Communist Political Economies*, Washington, DC: National Academies Press, pp. 272–97.

Korpi, Walter (1980), 'Social Policy and Distributional Conflict in the Capitalist Democracies: a Preliminary Comparative Framework', *West European Politics*, (3), 296–316.

Kotlikoff, Laurence J. (1989), 'Social Security', in John Eatwell, Murray Milgate and Peter Newman, (eds), *The New Palgrave: Social Economics*, London: Macmillan, pp. 231–42.

Kotlikoff, Laurence J. (1996), 'Rescuing Social Security', *Challenge*, (November-December 1996), 21–2.

Kotlikoff, Laurence J., Kent A. Smetters and Jan Walliser (1998a), 'Social Security: Privatization and Progressivity', *American Economic Review – Papers and Proceedings*, **88** (2), 137–41.

Kotlikoff, Laurence J., Kent A. Smetters and Jan Walliser (1998b), 'The Economic Impact of Privatizing Social Security', in Horst Siebert (ed.), *Redesigning Social Security*, Tübingen: Mohr, pp. 327–48.

Krahnen, Jan Pieter and Reinhard H. Schmidt (1993), *Development Finance as Institution Building*, Gießen and Frankfurt/Main: mimeo.

Král, Jiří (1995), 'Czech Republic', in Michael Cichon and Lenia Samuel (eds), *Making Social Protection Work – The Challenge of Tripartism in Social Governance for Countries in Transition*, Budapest and Nicosia: ILO, pp. 173–9.

Král, Jiří and Martin Mácha (1998), *Transformation of Old-Age Security in the Czech Republic*, Prague, mimeo.

Krueger, Anne O. (1993), 'Virtuous and Vicious Circles in Economic Development', *American Economic Review – Papers and Proceedings*, **83** (2), 351–5.

Krumm, Kathie, Branko Milanovic and Michael Walton (1995), 'Transfers and the Transition From Central Planning', *Finance & Development*, (September 1995), 27–30.

Kruse, Agneta (1997), 'The Case of Sweden', in Mária Augusztinovics et al., *Pension Systems and Reforms – Britain, Hungary, Italy, Poland, Sweden*, Phare ACE Research Project P95-2139-R, Final Report, Budapest, mimeo, pp. 133–57.

Kudlová, Marie, Daniela Skývová and Rene Pechar (1995), 'The Social Protection System of the Czech Republic', in Michael Cichon (ed.), *Social Protection in the Visegrád Countries: Four Country Profiles*, ILO-CEET Report 13, Budapest: ILO-CEET, pp. 13–35.

Kurtán, Sándor (1994), 'Der Rat für Interessenabstimmung – Portrait einer tripartistischen Institution im ungarischen Transformationsprozeß', *INITIAL. Zeitschrift für sozialwissenschaftlichen Diskurs*, (5), 17–24.

Ladó, Mária (1995), 'Representation of Workers' and Employers' Interests in Changing Industrial Relations in Hungary', in Jerzy Hausner, Ove K. Pedersen and Karsten Ronit (eds), *Evolution of Interest Representation and Development of the Labour Market in Post-Socialist Countries*, Cracow: Cracow Academy of Economics and Friedrich Ebert Stiftung, pp. 285–336.

Ladó, Mária (1997), *The Changing Role of Tripartism in Hungary*, Budapest, mimeo.

Langenkamp, Daniel (1997a), 'After Reforms, Pension Fund Boom Looms', *Budapest Business Journal*, 17–23 November 1997, 10-A.

Langenkamp, Daniel (1997b), 'Pension Funds Gear Up for Hard-sell Campaign', *Budapest Business Journal*, 17–23 November 1997, 8.

Lavigne, Marie (1995), *The Economics of Transition – From Socialist Economy to Market Economy*, London: Macmillan.

Légaré, Jacques (1999), *The Demographics of Ageing in relation to Social Security Programs Reforms in UN/ECE Countries*, Paper prepared for the UN/ECE Spring Seminar 'The Economic Implications of Population Ageing in the ECE Region', 3 May 1999, Geneva, mimeo.

Leven, Bozena (1996), 'Distributional Effects of Poland's Transition: The Status of Pensioners', *Comparative Economic Studies*, **38** (4), 121–35.

Lewicka, Ewa, Bogusław Koc, Zbigniew Kruszyński and Jerzy Ptaszyński (1996), 'Projekt NSZZ "Solidarność"', in IPiSS, Nowe Życie Gospodarcze and Klub 500 (eds), *Modele Reformy Systemu Emerytalno-Rentowego i Ścieżki Dojścia*, Warsaw: IPiSS, pp. 53–67.

Łoboda, Alina and Leokadia Szałkiewicz-Zaradzka (1998), 'Zur Reform des Rentenversicherungssystems in Polen', *Wirtschaft und Recht in Osteuropa*, **7** (4), 128–30.

Lodahl, Maria (1997), 'Renten im Transformationsprozeß: Zur Lage in Ungarn, Tschechien und der Slowakei', *DIW-Wochenbericht*, **64** (41), 763–70.

Lodahl, Maria and Mechthild Schrooten (1998), 'Transformation des polnischen Rentensystems', *Osteuropa-Wirtschaft*, **43** (3), 269–79.

Lo Vuolo, Rubén M. (1996), 'Reformas previsionales en América Latina: el caso argentino', *Comercio Exterior*, **46** (9), 692–702.

Lundholm, Michael (1991), *Compulsory Social Insurance. A Critical Review*. Economic Studies 1991: 1, Uppsala: Uppsala University.

Lütz, Susanne (1995), 'Politische Steuerung und die Selbstregelung korporativer Akteure', in Renate Mayntz and Fritz W. Scharpf (eds), *Gesellschaftliche Selbstregelung und politische Steuerung*, Frankfurt/Main and New York: Campus, pp. 169–96.

McClune, Emma (1997), 'Hard Times Ahead for the Average Czech Family', *The Prague Post*, 18 June 1997: http://www.praguepost.cz.

Mácha, Martin (1999a), *Is the Voluntary Second Pillar Becoming Mandatory in the Czech Republic?* Presentation at the ZeS Workshop 'Old-age Security in Central and Eastern Europe – Public and/or Private?', 13–16 May 1999, Héviz.

Mácha, Martin (1999b), 'Political Actors and Reform Paradigms in Czech Old Age Security', in Katharina Müller, Andreas Ryll and Hans-Jürgen Wagener (eds), *Transformation of Social Security: Pensions in Central–Eastern Europe*, Heidelberg: Physica, pp. 247–57.

McKelvey, Richard D. (1976), 'Intransitivities in Multidimensional Voting Models and Some Implications for Agenda Control', *Journal of Economic Theory*, **12** (3), 472–82.

Mackenzie, George A., Philip Gerson and Alfredo Cuevas (1997), 'Kann eine Rentenreform die gesamtwirtschaftliche Ersparnis erhöhen?' *Finanzierung & Entwicklung*, (December 1997), 44–7.

Maltby, Tony (1994), *Women and Pensions in Britain and Hungary. A Cross-national and Comparative Case Study of Social Dependency*, Aldershot: Avebury.

Manow, Philip (1998), 'Individuelle Zeit, institutionelle Zeit, soziale Zeit. Das Vertrauen in die Sicherheit der Rente und die Debatte um Kapitaldeckung und Umlage in Deutschland', *Zeitschrift für Soziologie*, **27** (3), 193–211.

March, James G. and Johan P. Olsen (1984), 'The New Institutionalism: Organizational Factors in Political Life', *American Political Science Review*, **78** (3), 734–49.

Mareš, Petr, Libor Musil and Ladislav Rabušic (1994), 'Values and the welfare state in Czechoslovakia', in Christopher G. A. Bryant and Edmund Mokrzycki (eds), *The New Great Transformation? Change and Continuity in East-Central Europe*, London and New York: Routledge, pp. 78–98.

Maret, Xavier and Gerd Schwartz (1994), 'Polonia: Protección social y el sistema de pensiones durante la transición', *Revista Internacional de Seguridad Social*, **47** (2), 61–82.

Markiewicz, Wojciech (1998), 'Z wora na konta – ZUS czeka prawdziwa rewolucja', *POLITYKA*, 12 September 1998, 24–5.

Marquardt, Marko and Wolfgang Peters (1998), *Collective Madness. How Ageing Influences Majority Voting on Public Pensions*, Frankfurt (Oder), mimeo.

Marsh, Virginia (1997), 'Hungary Spreads the Pension Load – Looming Contribution Crisis is Forcing Painful Adjustment', *Financial Times*, 22 January 1997, 2.

Martinelli, César and Mariano Tommasi (1998), 'Sequencing of Economic Reforms in the Presence of Political Constraints', in Federico Sturzenegger and Mariano Tommasi (eds), *The Political Economy of Reform*, Cambridge, MA and London: MIT Press, pp. 285–304.

Martos, Béla (1995), 'Point system of individual pensions: Setup and operation' in Éva Ehrlich and Gábor Révész (eds), *Human Resources and Social Stability During Transition in Hungary*, San Francisco: International Center for Growth, 229–41.

Mayntz, Renate and Fritz W. Scharpf (1995), 'Der Ansatz des akteurzentrierten Institutionalismus', in Renate Mayntz and Fritz W. Scharpf (eds), *Gesellschaftliche Selbstregelung und politische Steuerung*, Frankfurt/Main and New York: Campus, pp. 39–72.

Mayntz, Renate and Volker Schneider (1995), 'Die Entwicklung technischer Infrastruktursysteme zwischen Steuerung und Selbstorganisation', in Renate Mayntz and Fritz W. Scharpf (eds), *Gesellschaftliche Selbstregelung und politische Steuerung*, Frankfurt/Main and New York: Campus, pp. 73–100.

Mazur, Marek (1996), 'Cele i uwarunkowania reformy systemu ubezpieczeń społecznych – Projekt przygotowany w Ministerstwie Finansów', in IPiSS, Nowe Życie Gospodarcze and Klub 500 (eds), *Modele Reformy Systemu Emerytalno-Rentowego i Ścieżki Dojścia*, Warsaw: IPiSS, pp. 22–52.

Mazur, Marek (1997), 'Social Insurance System', in World Economy Research Institute (ed.), *Poland – International Economic Report 1996/97*, Warsaw: Warsaw School of Economics, pp. 217–24.

Merkel, Wolfgang (1994), 'Struktur oder Akteur, System oder Handlung: Gibt es einen Königsweg in der sozialwissenschaftlichen Transformationsforschung?', in Wolfgang Merkel (ed.), *Systemwechsel*, vol. I, Opladen: Leske & Budrich, pp. 303–31.

Merton, Robert K. (1948), 'Discussion', *American Sociological Review*, **14** (1), 164–8.

Mesa-Lago, Carmelo (1978), *Social Security in Latin America. Pressure Groups, Stratification, and Inequality*, Pittsburgh: University of Pittsburgh Press.

Mesa-Lago, Carmelo (1991), 'Social Security and Prospects for Equity in Latin America', World Bank, Discussion Paper 140, Washington, DC.

Mesa-Lago, Carmelo (1992), 'Protection for the Informal Sector in Latin America and the Caribbean by Social Security or Alternative Means', in Víctor E. Tokman (ed.) (1992), *Beyond Regulation. The Informal Economy in Latin America*, Boulder, CO and London: Lynne Rienner, pp. 169–206.

Mesa-Lago, Carmelo (1993), 'Soziale Sicherheit und Rentenreform in Lateinamerika: Bedeutung und Evaluierung von Privatisierungsansätzen', *Zeitschrift für internationales Arbeits- und Sozialrecht*, **7** (3), 159–208.

Mesa-Lago, Carmelo (1996), 'Pension System Reforms in Latin America: The Position of the International Organizations', *CEPAL Review*, (60), 73–98.

Mesa-Lago, Carmelo (1997a), 'Die Reform der Renten in Lateinamerika und die Position der internationalen Organisationen', *Zeitschrift für ausländisches und internationales Arbeits- und Sozialrecht*, **11** (3), 161–274.

Mesa-Lago, Carmelo (1997b), 'Social Welfare Reform in the Context of Economic-Political Liberalization: Latin American Cases', *World Development*, **25** (4), 497–517.

Mesa-Lago, Carmelo (1998), 'The Reform of Social Security Pensions in Latin America: Public, Private, Mixed and Parallel Systems', in Franz Ruland (ed.), *Verfassung, Theorie und Praxis des Sozialstaats. Festschrift für Hans F. Zacher zum 70. Geburtstag*, Heidelberg: Müller, pp. 609–33.

Mesa-Lago, Carmelo and Alberto Arenas de Mesa (1997), 'Fünfzehn Jahre nach der Privatisierung des Rentensystems in Chile: Evaluation, Lehre und zukünftige Aufgaben', *Deutsche Rentenversicherung*, (7/97), 405–27.

Mesa-Lago, Carmelo and Kristin Kleinjans (1997), 'Die internationale Renten-reformdebatte – Annahmen und Realität der lateinamerikanischen Reformen', *Lateinamerika, Analysen-Daten-Dokumentation*, (36), 33–50.

Milanovic, Branko (1993), 'Social Costs of Transition to Capitalism: Poland 1990–91', World Bank, Research Paper 2, Washington, DC.

Miller, Petr et al. (1992), *Development in the Sphere of Labour, Wages and Social Affairs since December 1989 and Other Perspectives*, Bratislava, mimeo.

Ministère Fédéral du Travail et des Affaires Sociales (1980), *Le régime des pensions en Tchécoslovaquie*, Prague, mimeo.

Ministry of Finance (1982), 'The Social Insurance System', Public Finance in Hungary 5, Budapest.

Ministry of Finance (1992), 'Social Security (Insurance) in Hungary', Public Finance in Hungary 105, Budapest.

Ministry of Finance (1994), 'Act on the Voluntary Mutual Benefit Funds', Public Finance in Hungary 128, Budapest.

Ministry of Finance (1997), *Pension Reform*, Budapest, mimeo.

Ministry of Health and Social Affairs (1998), *Pension Reform in Sweden – A Short Summary*, Stockholm, mimeo.

Ministry of Labour and Social Affairs (1996a), *Old-age, Disability, Survivor's Pensions – Basic Information*, Prague: MPSV.

Ministry of Labour and Social Affairs (1996b), *Pension System in the Czech Republic*, Prague, mimeo.

Ministry of Labour and Social Policy (1993), *Workers' Pensions. Chances and Threats – Construction of a System*, Warsaw, mimeo.

Ministry of Labour and Social Policy (1995a), *Program reformy ubezpieczeń społecznych*, April 1995, Warsaw, mimeo.

Ministry of Labour and Social Policy (1995b), *Program reformy ubezpieczeń społecznych*, December 1995, Warsaw, mimeo.

Ministry of Labour, Wages and Social Affairs (1983), *Pension Security in Polish People's Republic*, Warsaw, mimeo.

Ministry of Welfare and Ministry of Finance (1996), *Proposal for a Compositely Financed Pension System and Conditions of the Introduction of System*, Report discussed on May 9, 1996, by the Government and accepted as the ground of further work, Budapest, mimeo.

Ministry of Welfare and Ministry of Finance (1997), *Prospectus on the Proposed New Pension System and Related Regulations*, Budapest, mimeo.

Mishra, Ramesh (1977), *Society and Social Policy. Theoretical Perspectives on Welfare*, London: Macmillan.

Mitchell, Olivia and Joseph Quinn (1996), 'The Hard Facts About Social Security', *Challenge*, (November–December 1996), 16–18.

Mitchell, Olivia and Steven Zeldes (1996), 'Social Security Privatization: A Structure For Analysis', NBER, Working Paper 5512, Cambridge, MA.

Mlada Fronta Dnes (1998), 'Vyšší odvody mají spasit penzijní systém', *Mlada Fronta Dnes*, 5 September 1998, 12.

Mortkowitz, Siegfried (1998), 'Pensioners Flex Political Muscle', *The Prague Post*, 15 April 1998: http://www.praguepost.cz.

Mouton, Pierre (1998), 'State of the Reforms in Central and Eastern Europe', in ISSA (ed.), *Evaluation and Prospects of Social Security Reforms*, Geneva: ISSA, pp. 9–38.

MSZOSZ (1997), *Information of the National Confederation of Hungarian Trade Unions*, February 1997, Budapest, mimeo.

Mueller, John (1998), 'The Stock Market Won't Beat Social Security', *Challenge*, (March–April 1998), 95–117.

Müller, Katharina (1997a), 'Pension Reform in the Czech Republic, Hungary, and Poland: A Comparative View', in Nada Stropnik (ed.), *Social and Economic Aspects of Ageing Societies: An Important Social Development Issue*, Ljubljana: IUCISD, pp. 224–34.

Müller, Katharina (1997b), 'Pensions: The "Chilean Model" for Central–Eastern Europe?' In: Maria Sławińska (ed.), *From Plan To Market – Selected Problems of the Transition*, Poznań: Akademia Ekonomiczna, pp. 59–68.

Müller, Katharina (1997c), 'The "New Pension Orthodoxy" and Beyond: Transforming Old Age Security in Central–Eastern Europe', FIT, Discussion Paper 16/97, Frankfurt (Oder).

Müller, Katharina (1998a), 'Blueprints of Pension Reform in Hungary and Poland', in Witold Jurek (ed.), *From Plan To Market – Selected Problems of the Transition*, Proceedings of Łagów '97, Poznań: Akademia Ekonomiczna, pp. 90–8.

Müller, Katharina (1998b), 'Postsozialistische Sozialpolitik: Der Fall der Alterssicherung', *INITIAL. Zeitschrift für sozialwissenschaftlichen Diskurs*, **9** (2/3), 159–69.

Müller, Katharina (1998c), 'Shall We Forget the Latin American Precedents?', *Transition*, **9** (5), 29.

Müller, Katharina (1998d), 'The "New Pension Orthodoxy" and Beyond: Transforming Old Age Security in Central–Eastern Europe', KOPINT-DATORG, Discussion Paper 50, Budapest.

Müller, Katharina (1998e), 'Vom Staat zum Markt? Rentenreformen in Mittelosteuropa', *Staatswissenschaften und Staatspraxis*, **9** (2), 161–87.

Müller, Katharina (1999a), 'Pension Reform Paths in Comparison: The Case of Central–Eastern Europe', *Czech Sociological Review* **VII** (1), 51–66.

Müller, Katharina (1999b), 'Structural Settings, Political Actors and Paradigmatic Outcomes in Central–Eastern European Pension Reforms', in Katharina Müller, Andreas Ryll and Hans-Jürgen Wagener (eds), *Transformation of Social Security: Pensions in Central–Eastern Europe*, Heidelberg: Physica, pp. 291–305.

Myers, Robert (1996), 'The Social Security Sky Is Not Falling', *Challenge*, (November-December 1996), 23–4.

Myles, John (1984), *Old Age in the Welfare State: The Political Economy of Public Pensions*, Boston: Little, Brown.

Myles, John and Paul Pierson (1997), 'Friedman's Revenge: The Reform of "Liberal" Welfare States in Canada and the United States', European University Institute, EUI Working Paper RSC 97/30, Florence.

Nawacki, Lesław (1995), 'Poland: Tripartite Negotiations on Social Protection Reform', in Michael Cichon and Lenia Samuel (eds), *Making Social Protection Work – The Challenge of Tripartism in Social Governance for Countries in Transition*, Budapest and Nicosia: ILO, pp. 50–3.

Nelson, Joan M. (1994), 'Panel Discussion', in John Williamson (ed.), *The Political Economy of Policy Reform*, Washington, DC: Institute for International Economics, pp. 472–7.

Nelson, Joan M. (1997), 'Social Costs, Social-Sector Reforms, and Politics in Post-Communist Transformations', in Joan Nelson, Charles Tilly and Lee Walker (eds), *Transforming Post-Communist Political Economies*, Washington, DC: National Academies Press, pp. 247–71.

Nelson, Joan M. (1998), *The Politics of Pension and Health Care Delivery Reforms in Hungary and Poland*, forthcoming as Collegium Budapest Discussion Paper, Budapest, mimeo.

Nitsch, Manfred (1996), *The Chilean Model for Social Security Reform in Eastern Europe?*, Berlin, mimeo.

Nitsch, Manfred and Helmut Schwarzer (1996), 'Recent Developments in Financing Social Security in Latin America', ILO, Discussion Paper 'Issues in Social Protection' 1, Geneva.

North, Douglass C. (1990), *Institutions, Institutional Change and Economic Performance*, Cambridge, UK: Cambridge University Press.

Nowakowski, Jerzy (1996), 'The Role of the World Bank in Poland's Transition to a Market Economy', *Eastern European Economics*, **34** (6), 68–79.

O'Connor, James (1973), *The Fiscal Crisis of the State*, New York: St. Martin's Press.

OECD (1996), *Economic Survey Poland 1996–1997*, Paris: OECD.

Offe, Claus (1993), 'The Politics of Social Policy in East European Transitions. Antecedents, Agents, and Agenda of Reform', ZeS, Arbeitspapier No. 2/93, Bremen.

Offe, Claus (1994), *Der Tunnel am Ende des Lichts. Erkundungen der politischen Transformation im Neuen Osten*, Frankfurt/Main and New York: Campus.

Office of the Government Plenipotentiary for Social Security Reform (1997), *Security Through Diversity – Reform of the Pension System in Poland*, Warsaw, mimeo.

Okrasa, Włodzimierz (1987), 'Social Welfare in Poland', in Julian Le Grand and Włodzimierz Okrasa (eds), *Social Welfare in Britain and Poland*, ST/ICERD, Occasional Paper 12, London, pp. 14–23.

Olczyk, Eliza and Jerzy Pilczyński (1998), 'Renty i emerytury po nowemu', *Rzeczpospolita*, 27 November 1998: http://www.rzeczpospolita.pl.

Olson, Mancur (1965), *The Logic of Collective Action: Public Goods and the Theory of Groups*, Cambridge, MA: Harvard University Press.

Olson, Mancur (1983), '"Social Security Survival": A Comment', *The Cato Journal*, **3** (2), 355–9.

OPZZ (1997), *Stanowisko Rady Ogólnopolskiego Porozumienia Związków Zawo-dowych z dnia 24 kwietnia 1997 r. w sprawie prac nad doskonaleniem programu reformy ubezpieczeń społecznych i przedłożonych projektów ustaw przez Biuro Pełnomocnika Rządu do Spraw Reformy Zabezpieczenia Społecznego*, Warsaw, mimeo.

Orenstein, Mitchell (1995a), 'The Czech Tripartite Council and its Contribution to Social Peace', in Jerzy Hausner, Ove K. Pedersen and Karsten Ronit (eds), *Evolution of Interest Representation and Development of the Labour Market in Post-Socialist Countries*, Cracow: Cracow Academy of Economics and Friedrich Ebert Stiftung, pp. 337–60.

Orenstein, Mitchell (1995b), 'Transitional Social Policy in the Czech Republic and Poland', *Czech Sociological Review*, **III** (2), 179–96.

Orenstein, Mitchell (1996), 'The Failures of Neo-liberal Social Policy in Central Europe', *Transition*, 28 June 1996, 16–20.

Orenstein, Mitchell (1998a), *Political and Institutional Impacts on Pension Reform in the Transition Countries*, Syracuse, NY, mimeo.

Orenstein, Mitchell (1998b), 'Václav Klaus: Revolutionary and Parliamentarian', *East European Constitutional Review*, **7** (1), 46–55.

Ostrom, Elinor, Roy Gardner and James Walker (1994), *Rules, Games, and Common-Pool Resources*, Ann Arbor: University of Michigan Press.

Overbye, Einar (1994), 'Convergence in Policy Outcomes: Social Security Systems in Perspective', *Journal of Public Policy*, **14** (2), 147–74.

Palacios, Robert and Roberto Rocha (1997), 'The Hungarian Pension System in Transition', forthcoming in Lajos Bokros and Jean-Jacques Dethier (eds), *Public Finance Reform during the Transition: The Experience of Hungary*, Washington, DC: World Bank.

Palacios, Robert and Edward Whitehouse (1998), *The Role of Choice in the Transition to a Funded Pension System*, World Bank, Washington, DC, mimeo.

Pataki, Judith (1993), 'A New Era in Hungary's Social Security Administration', *RFE/RL Research Report*, **2** (27), 57–60.

Pénztarfelügyelet (1996), *Önkéntes Kölcsönös Biztosító Pénztárak Evkönyve 1996*, Budapest: Önkéntes Biztosító Pénztárak Felügyelete.

Pénztarfelügyelet (1997a), *Önkéntes Kölcsönös Biztosító Pénztárak Evkönyve 1997*, Budapest: Önkéntes Biztosító Pénztárak Felügyelete.

Pénztarfelügyelet (1997b), *Pénztárak főbb adatai*, Budapest, mimeo.

Perraudin, William and Thierry Pujol (1994), 'Framework for the Analysis of Pension and Unemployment Benefit Reform in Poland', *IMF Staff Papers*, **41** (4), 643–74.

Persson, Mats (1998a), 'Reforming Social Security in Sweden', in Horst Siebert (ed.), *Redesigning Social Security*, Tübingen: Mohr, pp. 169–85.

Persson, Mats (1998b), *Social Security Reform: The Case of Sweden*. Presentation held at the Conference 'Reforming the Social Security System: An International Perspective', 16–17 March 1998, Rome, mimeo.

Pestoff, Victor A. (1995a), 'Reforming Social Services in Central and Eastern Europe: Meso-Level Institutional Change', in Victor A. Pestoff (ed.), *Reforming Social Services in Central and Eastern Europe: An Eleven Nation Overview*, Cracow: Cracow Academy of Economics and Friedrich–Ebert–Stiftung, pp. 395–418.

Pestoff, Victor A. (ed.) (1995b), *Reforming Social Services in Central and Eastern Europe – An Eleven Nation Overview*, Cracow: Cracow Academy of Economics and Friedrich Ebert Stiftung.

Pestoff, Victor A. (1998), 'Reforming Social Services in Central and Eastern Europe: Shifts in the Welfare Mix and Meso-Level Institutional Change', *EMERGO*, **5** (1), 15–42.

Peters, Wolfgang (1990), 'Reform oder Privatisierung der Alterssicherung – Spielraum der Umlagefinanzierung und Chancen des Kapitaldeckungsverfahrens', in Bernhard Gahlen et al. (eds), *Theorie und Politik der Sozialversicherung*, Tübingen: Mohr, pp. 103–32.

Pierson, Paul (1993), 'When Effect Becomes Cause: "Policy Feedback" and Political Change', *World Politics*, **45** (4), 595–628.

Pierson, Paul (1994), *Dismantling the Welfare State? Reagan, Thatcher, and the Politics of Retrenchment*, Cambridge, UK: Cambridge University Press.

Pierson, Paul (1996), 'The New Politics of The Welfare State', *World Politics*, **48** (2), 143–79.

Pierson, Paul and R. Kent Weaver (1993), 'Imposing Losses in Pension Policy', in R. Kent Weaver and Bert A. Rockman (eds), *Do Institutions Matter? Government Capabilities in the United States and Abroad*, Washington, DC: The Brookings Institution, pp. 110–50.

Piñera, José (1996), *Bez obawy o przyszłość*, Warsaw: Centrum im. Adama Smitha and Fundacja im. Hugona Kollątaja.

Pintér, Mária (1999), *The Mandatory 'Second Pillar'*, Presentation at the ZeS Workshop 'Old-age Security in Central and Eastern Europe – Public and/or Private?', 13–16 May 1999, Héviz, mimeo.

Piskorski, Marcin (1997), 'Zdążyć z reformą ubezpieczeń: Zieliński przejmie wrażliwość Kuronia i fachowość Bączkowskiego', *Nowa Europa*, 11–12 January 1997, 2.

Poganietz, Witold-Roger (1997), 'Vermindern Transferzahlungen den Konflikt zwischen Gewinnern und Verlierern in einer sich transformierenden Volkswirtschaft?', Institut für Agrarentwicklung in Mittel- und Osteuropa, IAMO Discussion Paper 7, Halle.

Polívka, Milan (1997), 'Nedobytné rezervy: Reforma penzijního systému (2)', *Ekonom*, (43), 38.

Potůček, Martin (1994), 'Quo Vadis, Social Policy in Czechoslovakia?', in Stein Ringen and Claire Wallace (eds), *Societies in Transition: East-Central Europe Today*, Aldershot: Avebury, pp. 129–35.

Prinz, Christopher (1997), 'Population Ageing: A Three-Level Perspective', in Nada Stropnik (ed.), *Social and Economic Aspects of Ageing Societies: An Important Social Development Issue*, Ljubljana: Institute for Economic Research, pp. 9–26.

Przedstawicielstwo Fundacji im. Friedricha Naumanna w Polsce and Instytut Badań nad Demokracją i Przedsiębiorstwem Prywatnym (eds) (1996), *Ubezpieczenia Społeczne – Zagrożenie dla Finansów Publicznych?*, Warsaw: FNS/IBDPP.

Queisser, Monika (1993), *Vom Umlage- zum Kapitaldeckungsverfahren: Die chilenische Rentenreform als Modell für Entwicklungsländer?*, ifo forschungsberichte der abteilung entwicklungsländer No. 79, Munich: Weltforum.

Queisser, Monika (1995), 'Después de Chile: la segunda generación de reformas en América Latina', *Revista Internacional de Seguridad Social*, **48** (3–4), 29–48.

Queisser, Monika (1996), 'Pensions in Germany', World Bank, Policy Research Working Paper 1664, Washington, DC.

Queisser, Monika (1998a), 'Die Rente mit Kapital unterlegen. Der Blick nach Lateinamerika und Osteuropa zeigt: Eine grundlegende Reform der Alters-sicherung ist möglich und finanzierbar', *Frankfurter Allgemeine Zeitung*, 24 January 1998, 17.

Queisser, Monika (1998b), *The Second-Generation Pension Reforms in Latin America*, Paris: OECD.

Ragin, Charles C. (1994), 'A Qualitative Comparative Analysis of Pension Systems', in Thomas Janoski and Alexander M. Hicks (eds), *The Comparative Political Economy of the Welfare State*, Cambridge, UK: Cambridge University Press, pp. 320–45.

Réti, János (1996a), *A nyugdíjreform megalapozó számításai: a reform mozgástere*, Budapest, mimeo.

Réti, János (1996b), *Die Berechnungen zur Fundierung der Rentenreform: der Spielraum der Reform*, Budapest, mimeo.

Rey, Michael (1996), 'Polish Pension Reform: Political Death Wish?', *Business Central Europe*, February 1996, 18–19.

Reynaud, Emmanuel (1995), 'Financiamiento de las jubilaciones: reparto y capitalización en la Unión Europea', *Revista Internacional de Seguridad Social*, **48** (3–4), 49–68.

Ribhegge, Hermann (1990), 'Denkfehler zur Alterssicherung. Kapitaldeckungs-versus Umlageverfahren', *Jahrbuch für Sozialwissenschaft*, **41**, 359–76.

Ribhegge, Hermann (1998), 'Sozialpolitische Reformen in demokratischen Systemen', in Eckhard Knappe and Norbert Berthold (eds), *Ökonomische Theorie der Sozialpolitik. Bernhard Külp zum 65. Geburtstag*, Heidelberg: Physica, pp. 299–318.

Ribhegge, Hermann (1999), 'The Controversy between the Pay-As-You-Go System and the Fully-Funded System in Old-Age Security', in Katharina Müller, Andreas Ryll and Hans-Jürgen Wagener (eds), *Transformation of Social Security: Pensions in Central–Eastern Europe*, Heidelberg: Physica, pp. 61–77.

Rocha, Roberto (1996), 'The Hungarian Public Must Be Better Informed about the Available Options', *Transition*, **7** (1), 14–15.

Rodrik, Dani (1993), 'The Positive Economics of Policy Reform', *American Economic Review – Papers and Proceedings*, **83** (2), 356–61.

Rodrik, Dani (1994), 'Comment', in John Williamson (ed.), *The Political Economy of Policy Reform*, Washington, DC: Institute for International Economics, pp. 212–15.

Rodrik, Dani (1996), 'Understanding Economic Policy Reform', *Journal of Economic Literature*, **XXXIV** (March 1996), 9–41.

Rodrik, Dani (1998), 'Promises, Promises: Credible Policy Reform via Signalling', in Federico Sturzenegger and Mariano Tommasi (eds), *The Political Economy of Reform*, Cambridge, MA and London: MIT Press, pp. 307–27.

Rose, Richard (1989), 'Welfare: The Public/Private Mix', in Sheila B. Kamerman and Alfred J. Kahn (eds), *Privatization and the Welfare State*, Princeton, NJ: Princeton University Press, pp. 73–95.

RSSG – Rada Strategii Społeczno-Gospodarczej przy Radzie Ministrów (ed.) (1995), *Reforma Systemu Emerytalno-Rentowego*, Raport No. 9, Warsaw: RSSG.

Rusnok, Jiří (1997), 'Hledání optimálního modelu nového důchodového systému', *Hospodářské Noviny*, 23 September 1997, 10.

Rutkowski, Michał (1998), 'A New Generation of Pension Reforms Conquers the East – A Taxonomy in Transition Economies', *Transition*, **9** (4), 16–19.

Rymsza, Marek (1998), 'Reforma ubezpieczeń społecznych w Polsce – Uwagi o pracach w Sejmie nad ustawą o systemie ubezpieczeń społecznych', *Przegląd Ubezpieczeń Społecznych*, **32** (10), 3–6.

Rys, Vladimír (1995), 'Social Security Developments in Central Europe: A Return to Reality', *Czech Sociological Review*, **III** (2), 197–208.

Rzeczpospolita (1998), 'Fundusze emerytalne: Pierwszych sześć licencji', *Rzeczpospolita*, 27 October 1998: http://www.rzeczpospolita.pl.

Sachs, Jeffrey (1994), 'Life in the Economic Emergency Room', in John Williamson (ed.), *The Political Economy of Policy Reform*, Washington, DC: Institute for International Economics, pp. 503–23.

Sachs, Jeffrey (1995), 'Postcommunist Parties and the Politics of Entitlements', *Transition*, **6** (3), 1–4.

Sachs, Jeffrey (1996a), 'Der lange Schatten des Kommunismus: Postkommunistische Staaten stellen weltweit die größten Sozialbudgets', *Süddeutsche Zeitung*, 31 January 1996, VII.

Sachs, Jeffrey (1996b), 'Producing Dynamic Growth is the Task Ahead', *Politická Ekonomie*, (1/96), 3–7.

Sachs, Jeffrey and Andrew M. Warner (1996), 'Achieving Rapid Growth in the Transition Economies of Central Europe', Harvard Institute for International Development, Development Discussion Paper 544, Cambridge, MA.

Scharpf, Fritz W. (1997), *Games Real Actors Play: Actor-Centered Institutionalism in Policy Research*, Boulder, CO: WestviewPress.

Scharpf, Fritz W. and Matthias Mohr (1997), 'Efficient Self-Coordination in Policy Networks – A Simulation Study', Appendix 2 in Fritz W. Scharpf, *Games Real Actors Play: Actor-Centered Institutionalism in Policy Research*, Boulder, CO: WestviewPress, pp. 245–79.

Schimank, Uwe (1995), 'Politische Steuerung und Selbstregulation des Systems organisierter Forschung', in Renate Mayntz and Fritz W. Scharpf (eds), *Gesellschaftliche Selbstregelung und politische Steuerung*, Frankfurt/Main and New York: Campus, pp. 101–39.

Schimank, Uwe and Jürgen Wasem (1995), 'Politische Steuerung und Selbstregulation des Systems organisierter Forschung', in Renate Mayntz and Fritz W. Scharpf (eds), *Gesellschaftliche Selbstregelung und politische Steuerung*, Frankfurt/Main and New York: Campus, pp. 197–232.

Schmähl, Winfried (1981), 'Soziale Sicherung im Alter', in *Handwörterbuch der Wirtschaftswissenschaft*, vol. 6, Stuttgart: Fischer, pp. 645–61.

Schmähl, Winfried (1995), *Die Umgestaltung der Alterssicherung im Transformationsprozeß ost- und mitteleuropäischer Staaten – ein Konzept für eine Analyse aus landesspezifischer und international vergleichender Perspektive*, Bremen, mimeo.

Schmähl, Winfried (1998), 'Comment on the Papers by Axel Börsch-Supan, Edward M. Gramlich, and Mats Persson', in Horst Siebert (ed.), *Redesigning Social Security*, Tübingen: Mohr, pp. 186–96.

Schmähl, Winfried (1999), 'Pension Reforms in Germany: Major Topics, Decisions and Developments', in Katharina Müller, Andreas Ryll and Hans-Jürgen Wagener (eds), *Transformation of Social Security: Pensions in Central–Eastern Europe*, Heidelberg: Physica, pp. 91–120.

Schmidt-Hebbel, Klaus, Luis Servén and Andrés Solimano (1996), 'Saving and Investment: Paradigms, Puzzles, Policies', *The World Bank Research Observer*, **11** (1), 87–117.

Schneider, Ondřej (1996a), 'Pension Reform in the Czech Republic: Gradualistic Czechs', *Central European Banker*, (December 1996), 22–6.

Schneider, Ondřej (1996b), *The Reform of the Czech Pension System – Proposals and Qualifications*, Prague, mimeo.

Schrooten, Mechthild, Timothy M. Smeeding and Gert G. Wagner (1999), 'Distributional and Fiscal Consequences of Social Security Reforms in Central–Eastern Europe', in Katharina Müller, Andreas Ryll and Hans-Jürgen Wagener (eds), *Transformation of Social Security: Pensions in Central–Eastern Europe*, Heidelberg: Physica, pp. 275–89.

Schulthess, Walter and Gustavo Demarco (1995), 'Budowa drugiego filaru systemu emerytalno-rentowego w Argentynie', in IPiSS and Institute for East West Studies (eds), *Tworzenie prywatnych funduszy emerytalnych w Polsce*, IPiSS Zeszyt 1(401), Warsaw: IPiSS, pp. 193–233.

Schulthess, Walter and Gustavo Demarco (1996), *El sistema de jubilaciones y pensiones de Argentina a dos años de la reforma*, Serie Estudios Especiales No. 5, Buenos Aires: SAFJP.

Schulz-Weidner, Wolfgang (1996), 'Das "chilenische Modell" einer Privatisierung der Rentenversicherung – mehr Leistung für weniger Beiträge?', *Deutsche Rentenversicherung*, (3/96), 158–75.

Schwartz, Gerd (1994), 'Social Impact of the Transition', in Liam P. Ebrill et al., *Poland – The Path to a Market Economy*, IMF, Occasional Paper 113, Washington, DC, pp. 80–8.

Schwarzer, Helmut (1998), *Muster der lateinamerikanischen Rentenreformen*, Berlin, mimeo.

Sedlar, Lin (1998), 'Who Will Pay for our Retirement?', *The Prague Tribune*, November 1998: http//www.prague-tribune.cz.

Sell, Katrin (1998a), 'Die ungarischen Gewerkschaften und die Reform des Sozialsystems', *INITIAL. Zeitschrift für sozialwissenschaftlichen Diskurs*, **9** (2/3), 151–8.

Sell, Katrin (1998b), *Konsolidierung zwischen Markt und Staat. Die Bedeutung der Arbeitsbeziehungen für die Demokratisierung in Spanien und Ungarn*, Doctoral Thesis at Humboldt University, Berlin, mimeo.

Siebert, Horst (1998), 'Pay-as-You-Go vs. Capital-Funded Pension Systems: The Issues', in Horst Siebert (ed.), *Redesigning Social Security*, Tübingen: Mohr, pp. 3–33.

Sikkirk, Kathryin (1991), *Ideas and Institutions. Developmentalism in Brazil and Argentina*, Ithaca, NY and London: Cornell University Press.

Simonovits, András (1997), 'The Case of Hungary', in Mária Augusztinovics et al., *Pension Systems and Reforms – Britain, Hungary, Italy, Poland, Sweden*, Phare ACE Research Project P95-2139-R, Final Report, Budapest, mimeo, pp. 51–77.

Simonovits, András (1999), 'The New Hungarian Pension System and Its Problems', in Katharina Müller, Andreas Ryll and Hans-Jürgen Wagener (eds), *Transformation of Social Security: Pensions in Central–Eastern Europe*, Heidelberg: Physica, pp. 211–30.

Singh, Ajit (1995), *Pension Reform, the Stock Market, Capital Formation and Economic Growth: A Critical Commentary on the World Bank's Proposals*, Cambridge, UK, mimeo.

Skocpol, Theda (1985), 'Bringing the State Back In: Strategies of Analysis in Current Research', in Peter B. Evans, Dietrich Rueschemeyer and Theda Skocpol (eds), *Bringing the State Back In*, Cambridge, UK: Cambridge University Press, pp. 3–37.

Skocpol, Theda and Edwin Amenta (1986), 'Did Capitalists Shape Social Security?', *American Sociological Review*, **50**, 572–5.

Skývová, Daniela (1996), *Financing of Social Security in the Czech Republic*, Prague, mimeo.

Solska, Joanna (1998), 'Strajk zamiast składki – Z czyjej kieszeni pójdą pieniądze na emerytury górnicze', *POLITYKA*, 19 December 1998, 16.

Solska, Joanna (1999), 'Tłok na pomoście – Zaostrza się spór o wcześniejsze emerytury', *POLITYKA*, 8 May 1999, 62–4.

Sosenko, Barbara (1995), 'Transformations in the System of Social Insurance in Poland During the Years 1990–93', UCEMET, Working Paper 19, Cracow.

Sowada, Christoph (1996), 'Sozialpolitik im Transformationsprozeß am Beispiel Polens', Potsdam University, Finanzwissenschaftliche Diskussionsbeiträge No. 7, Potsdam.

Śpiewak, Kuba (1997), 'The Polish Gray Panthers?', *Warsaw Voice*, 15 June 1997: http://ww.contact.waw.pl.

Stallings, Barbara (1994), 'Discussion', in John Williamson (ed.), *The Political Economy of Policy Reform*, Washington, DC: Institute for International Economics, p. 46.

Standing, Guy (1996), 'Social Protection in Central and Eastern Europe: A Tale of Slipping Anchors and Torn Safety Nets', in Gøsta Esping-Andersen (ed.), *Welfare States in Transition. National Adaptations in Global Economies*, London: Sage Publications, pp. 225–55.

Standing, Guy (1998), *The Babble of Euphemisms: Re-embedding Social Protection in 'Transformed' Labour Markets*, Geneva, mimeo.

Štangová, Věra (1993), 'Die Rentenversicherung in der Tschechischen Republik (im Rahmen der Sozialreform)', *Deutsche Rentenversicherung*, (11/93), 732–6.

Staniland, Martin (1985), *What Is Political Economy? A Study of Social Theory and Underdevelopment*, New Haven, CT: Yale University Press.

Stark, David (1992), 'Path Dependence and Privatization Strategies in East Central Europe', *East European Politics and Societies*, **6** (1), 17–54.

Stark, David and László Bruszt (1998), *Postsocialist Pathways – Transforming Politics and Property in East Central Europe*, Budapest: Central European University Press.

Steinmeyer, Heinz-Dietrich (1996), 'Basic and Complementary Pension Schemes', in Wouter van Ginneken (ed.), *Finding the Balance: Financing and Coverage of Social Protection in Europe*, Geneva: ILO, pp. 25–49.

Stropnik, Nada (ed.) (1997), *Social and Economic Aspects of Ageing Societies: An Important Social Development Issue*, Ljubljana: Institute for Economic Research.

Strunk, Stefan, Alexander Telyukov, Udo Schulte-Mimberg, Volker Leienbach and Sibylle Angele (1994), 'Die Sozialversicherung in Mittel- und Osteuropa', in GVG (ed.), *Soziale Sicherung in West-, Mittel- und Osteuropa*, Baden-Baden: Nomos, pp. 199–300.

Sturzenegger, Federico and Mariano Tommasi (1998a), 'Introduction', in Federico Sturzenegger and Mariano Tommasi (eds), *The Political Economy of Reform*, Cambridge, MA and London: MIT Press, pp. 1–33.

Sturzenegger, Federico and Mariano Tommasi (eds) (1998b), *The Political Economy of Reform*, Cambridge, MA and London: MIT Press.

Stykow, Petra (1996), 'Organized Interests in the Transformation Processes of Eastern Europe and Russia: Towards Corporatism?', Humboldt University, Arbeitspapiere AG TRAP 96/11, Berlin.

Świątkowski, Andrzej (1993), 'History of Social Security in Poland', *Yearbook of Polish Labour Law and Social Policy*, **4**, 193–208.

Szamuely, László (1997), 'The Social Costs of Transformation in Central and Eastern Europe', KOPINT-DATORG, Discussion Paper 44, Budapest.

Széman, Zsuzsa (1995), 'The Role of NGOs in Social Welfare Services in Hungary', in Victor A. Pestoff (ed.), *Reforming Social Services in Central and Eastern Europe: An Eleven Nation Overview*, Cracow: Cracow Academy of Economics and Friedrich–Ebert–Stiftung, pp. 323–47.

Tanner, Michael (1996), 'It's Time To Privatize Social Security', *Challenge*, (November–December 1996), 19–20.

TÁRKI (1995), *Reform of the Budget, People with a Family and People before Retirement. Research Report for the Ministry of Finance*, Budapest, mimeo.

TÁRKI (1996), *Changes of Attitudes to Pensions and to the Pension Reform. Report No. 1/5 for the Ministry of Finance*, Budapest, mimeo.

Taylor-Gooby, Peter (1997), 'When is an Innovation? Recent Pension Reform in France, Germany, Italy and the UK', forthcoming in *Social Policy and Administration*, **33** (1).

Thomas, John W. and Merilee S. Grindle (1990), 'After the Decision: Implementing Policy Reforms in Developing Countries', *World Development*, **18** (8), 1163–81.

Thompson, Lawrence H. (1983), 'The Social Security Reform Debate', *Journal of Economic Literature*, **XXI** (December 1983), 1425–67.

Thompson, Lawrence (1999), *Forging a New Social Security Consensus*. Paper prepared for the UN/ECE Spring Seminar 'The Economic Implications of Population Ageing in the ECE Region', 3 May 1999, Geneva, mimeo.

Titmuss, Richard M. (1974), *Social Policy. An Introduction*, London: Allen and Unwin.

Tomann, Horst and Oliver Scholz (1996), 'Strukturwandel und soziale Sicherung', in Jens Hölscher et al. (eds), *Bedingungen ökonomischer Entwicklung in Zentralosteuropa*, vol. 4, Marburg: Metropolis, pp. 129–77.

Tomeš, Igor (1991), 'Social Reform: A Cornerstone in Czechoslovakia's New Economic Structure', *International Labour Review*, **130** (2), 191–8.

Tomeš, Igor (1994a), 'Social Policy and Protection in Czechoslovakia since November 1989', in Stein Ringen and Claire Wallace (eds), *Societies in Transition: East-Central Europe Today*, Aldershot: Avebury, pp. 137–47.

Tomeš, Igor (1994b), *Verschwendung und gezielter Mitteleinsatz in der sozialen Sicherheit: Überlegungen zu den Ländern Mittel- und Osteuropas*, Vienna: Internationale Vereinigung für Soziale Sicherheit.

Tommasi, Mariano and Andrés Velasco (1996), 'Where Are We in the Political Economy of Reform?' *Journal of Policy Reform*, **1**, 187–238.

Topińska, Irena (1995), 'The Social Protection System of Poland', in Michael Cichon (ed.), *Social Protection in the Visegrád Countries: Four Country Profiles*, ILO-CEET Report 13, Budapest: ILO, pp. 59–78.

Topiński, Wojciech and Marian Wiśniewski (1991), *Pensions in Poland – Proposals for Reform*, Warsaw, mimeo.

Topiński, Wojciech and Marian Wiśniewski (1995), 'Prywatne programy emerytalne – Propozycje reform', in IPiSS and Institute for East West Studies (eds), *Tworzenie prywatnych funduszy emerytalnych w Polsce*. IPiSS Zeszyt 1 (401), Warsaw: IPiSS, pp. 126–47.

Touraine, Alain (1989), *América Latina – Política y sociedad*, Madrid: Espasa-Calpe.

Toye, John (1994), 'Comment', in John Williamson (ed.), *The Political Economy of Policy Reform*, Washington, DC: Institute for International Economics, pp. 35–43.

Trapp, Manfred (1993), 'Sozialpolitik im Prozeß der Transformation der sozialistischen Systeme Osteuropas', in Günther Lottes (ed.), *Soziale Sicherheit in Europa. Renten- und Sozialversicherungssysteme im Vergleich*, Heidelberg: Physica, pp. 205–14.

Trend/Prognózis Rt. (ed.) (1997), *Nyugdíjreform konferencia*, Budapest: Trend/Prognózis.

Tsebelis, George (1995), 'Decision Making in Political Systems: Veto Players in Presidentialism, Parliamentarism, Multicameralism, and Multipartyism', *British Journal of Political Science* **25**, 289–325.

Turner, John (1998), 'The Contemporary Debate on Social Security Reform', in ILO (ed.), *An Operational Framework for Pension Reform*, Geneva, forthcoming.

Turnovec, František (1995), 'Visegrád Countries – Political Profiles in 1995', CERGE-EI, Discussion Paper 74, Prague.

Turnovec, František (1996), *Political Economy of Social Welfare Reform: 1996 Parliamentary Election in the Czech Republic*, Prague, mimeo.

Tymowska, Katarzyna and Marian Wiśniewski (1993), 'Public Health and Social Security', in Henryk Kierzkowski, Marek Okolski and Stanisław Wellisz (eds), *Stabilization and Structural Adjustment in Poland*, London and New York: Routledge, pp. 219–42.

Vanovska, Inta and Lilita Velde (1997), 'Pension Reform in Latvia', in Nada Stropnik (ed.), *Social and Economic Aspects of Ageing Societies: An Important Social Development Issue*, Ljubljana: Institute for Economic Research, pp. 219–23.

Večerník, Jiří (1996), *Markets and People – The Czech Reform Experience in a Comparative Perspective*, Aldershot: Avebury.

Verbon, Harrie A. A. (1986), 'Altruism, political power, and public pensions', *Kyklos*, **39** (3), 343–58.

Verbon, Harrie A. A., Theo Leers and Lex C. Meijdam (1998), 'Transition towards a Funded System: The Political Economy', in Horst Siebert (ed.), *Redesigning Social Security*, Tübingen: Mohr, pp. 357–72.

Višek, Petr and Jana Klimentová (1996), *About the Social Reform in the Czech Republic*, Prague, mimeo.

Vittas, Dimitri (1993), 'Swiss Chilanpore. The Way Forward for Pension Reform?', The World Bank Country Economics Department, WPS 1093, Washington, DC.

Vittas, Dimitri (1995), *The Argentine Pension Reform and Its Relevance for Eastern Europe*, World Bank, Washington, DC, mimeo.

Vittas, Dimitri (1996), 'Private Pension Funds in Hungary', World Bank, Policy Research Working Paper 1638, Washington, DC: World Bank.

Vittas, Dimitri and Roland Michelitsch (1995), 'Pension Funds in Central Europe and Russia. Their Prospects and Potential Role in Corporate Governance', World Bank, Policy Research Working Paper 1459, Washington, DC: World Bank.

Wadensjö, Eskil (1996), 'Schweden', in Europäische Kommission (ed.), *Die Perspektiven der ergänzenden Altersversorgung angesichts des demographischen, wirtschaftlichen und sozialen Wandels*, Soziales Europa – Beiheft 7/96, Brussels, pp. 225–42.

Wagener, Hans-Jürgen (1997), 'Transformation als historisches Phänomen', *Jahrbuch für Wirtschaftsgeschichte*, 1997/2, 179–91.

Wagener, Hans-Jürgen (1999), 'Social Security – A Second Phase Transformation Phenomenon?', in: Katharina Müller, Andreas Ryll and Hans-Jürgen Wagener (eds), *Transformation of Social Security: Pensions in Central–Eastern Europe*, Heidelberg: Physica, 13–30.

Weaver, Carolyn L. (1983), 'The Economic and Politics of the Emergence of Social Security: Some Implications for Reform', *The Cato Journal*, **3** (2), 361–84.

Weaver, R. Kent (1986), 'The Politics of Blame Avoidance', *Journal of Public Policy*, **6** (October–December 1986), 371–98.

Wei, Shang-Jin (1998), 'Gradualism versus Big-Bang: Speed and Sustainability of Reforms', in Federico Sturzenegger and Mariano Tommasi (eds), *The Political Economy of Reform*, Cambridge, MA and London: MIT Press, pp. 269–84.

Weizsäcker, Robert K. von (1990), 'Population Aging and Social Security: A Politico-Economic Model of State Pension Financing', *Public Finance*, **XXXXV** (3), 491–509.

Werle, Raymund (1995), 'Staat und Standards', in Renate Mayntz and Fritz W. Scharpf (eds), *Gesellschaftliche Selbstregelung und politische Steuerung*, Frankfurt/Main and New York: Campus, pp. 266–98.

Whitehead, Laurence (1990), 'Political Explanations of Macroeconomic Management: A Survey', *World Development*, **18** (8), 1133–46.

Więcław, Eliza (1998a), 'Fundusze emerytalne: Wielki apetyt', *Rzeczpospolita*, 20 November 1998: http://www.rzeczpospolita.pl.

Więcław, Eliza (1998b), 'KPTE Razem: Towarzystwo ma własny sposób na pozyskanie klientów', *Rzeczpospolita*, 27 November 1998: http://www.rzeczpospolita.pl.

Wiesenthal, Helmut (1993), 'Die "Politische Ökonomie" des fortgeschrittenen Transformationsprozesses und die (potentiellen) Funktionen intermediärer Akteure', Humboldt University, Arbeitspapiere AG TRAP 93/1, Berlin.

Wiesenthal, Helmut (1995), 'Preemptive Institutionenbildung: Korporative Akteure und institutionelle Innovationen im Transformationsprozeß postsozialistischer Staaten', Humboldt University, Arbeitspapiere AG TRAP 95/4, Berlin.

Wiesenthal, Helmut (1996), 'Contingencies of Institutional Reform: Reflections on Rule Change, Collective Actors, And Political Governance in Postsocialist Democracies', Humboldt University: Arbeitspapiere AG TRAP 96/10, Berlin.

Wiktorow, Aleksandra (1996), 'System emerytalno-rentowy, przesłanki i możliwości reformowania', Instytut Badań nad Gospodarką Rynkową, Transformacja Gospodarki No. 65, Gdańsk.

Wilczyński, Wacław (1996), 'Uczymy się od Chilijczyków!', in José Piñera, *Bez obawy o przyszłość*, Warsaw: Centrum im. Adama Smitha and Fundacja im. Hugona Kollątaja, pp. 5–7.

Wilde, Klaus (1981), 'Hundert Jahre Sozialversicherung in Deutschland', *Aus Politik und Zeitgeschichte*, (B 47), 3–20.

Wilensky, Harold L. (1975), *The Welfare State and Equality: Structural and Ideological Roots of Public Expenditures*, Berkeley, CA: University of California Press.

Wilensky, Harold L. (1976), *The 'New Corporatism', Centralization, and the Welfare State*, Beverly Hills, CA: Sage Publications.

Williamson, John (ed.) (1990), *Latin American Adjustment: How Much Has Happened?*, Washington, DC: Institute for International Economics.

Williamson, John (1993), 'Democracy and the "Washington Consensus"', *World Development*, **21** (8), 1329–36.

Williamson, John (1994a), 'In Search of a Manual for Technopols', in John Williamson (ed.), *The Political Economy of Policy Reform*, Washington, DC: Institute for International Economics, pp. 9–28.

Williamson, John (ed.) (1994b), *The Political Economy of Policy Reform*, Washington, DC: Institute for International Economics.

Williamson, John B. (1997), 'Should Women Support the Privatization of Social Security?' *Challenge*, (July–August 1997), 97–108.

Williamson, John (1998), 'Latin American Reform: A View from Washington', in Harry Costin and Hector Vanolli (eds), *Economic Reform in Latin America*, Fort Worth: The Dryden Press, pp. 106–11.

Williamson, John and Stephan Haggard (1994), 'The Political Conditions for Economic Reform', in John Williamson (ed.), *The Political Economy of Policy Reform*, Washington, DC: Institute for International Economics, pp. 525–96.

Williamson, John B. and Fred C. Pampel (1993), *Old-Age Security in Comparative Perspective*, New York and Oxford: Oxford University Press.

Working Group on the Implementation of the Pension Reform (1998), *The Pension Reform – Final Report*, Stockholm, mimeo.

World Bank (1992), *Hungary – Reform of Social Policy and Expenditures*, Washington, DC: World Bank.

World Bank (1993), *Poland – Income Support and the Social Safety Net During the Transition*, Washington, DC: World Bank.

World Bank (1994a), 'Averting the Old Age Crisis. Policies to Protect the Old and Promote Growth', Washington, DC: Oxford University Press.

World Bank (1994b), *Poland – Policies for Growth with Equity*, Washington, DC: World Bank.

World Bank (1995), *Hungary – Structural Reforms for Sustainable Growth*, Washington, DC: World Bank.

World Bank (1997), *The State in a Changing World. World Development Report 1997*, Washington, DC: Oxford University Press.

World Bank (1998a), *Czech Republic at a Glance*, Washington, DC, mimeo.

World Bank (1998b), *Hungary at a Glance*, Washington, DC, mimeo.

World Bank (1998c), *Poland at a Glance*, Washington, DC, mimeo.

World Bank (1998d), *Project Information Document – Kazakhstan*, Washington, DC, mimeo.

Wóycicka, Irena (1998), 'Dreisäulenmodell soll Rentensystem vor dem Kollaps retten', *Handelsblatt*, 2 June 1998, 26.

Zabala, Ricardo (1995), 'Fundusze emerytalne w Chile', in IPiSS and Institute for East West Studies (eds), *Tworzenie prywatnych funduszy emerytalnych w Polsce*, IPiSS Zeszyt 1 (401), Warsaw: IPiSS, pp. 184–92.

Zakład Ubezpieczeń Społecznych (1997a), *Zakład Ubezpieczeń Społecznych przed reformą – informacje, fakty*, Warsaw: ZUS.

Zakład Ubezpieczeń Społecznych (1997b), *Ważniejsze informacje z zakresu ubezpieczeń społecznych*, Warsaw: ZUS.

Zecchini, Salvatore (1995), 'The Role of International Financial Institutions in the Transition Process', *Journal of Comparative Economics*, **20** (1), 116–38.

Ziemer, Klaus (1996), *Das Parteiensystem der Republik Polen fünf Jahre nach dem Runden Tisch*, Trier, mimeo.

Żukowski, Maciej (1994), 'Pensions Policy in Poland after 1945: Between "Bismarck" and "Beveridge" Traditions', in John Hills, John Ditch and Howard Glennerster (eds), *Beveridge and Social Security – An International Retrospective*, Oxford: Clarendon Press, pp. 154–70.

Żukowski, Maciej (1996), 'Das Alterssicherungssystem in Polen – Geschichte, gegenwärtige Lage, Umgestaltung', *Zeitschrift für internationales Arbeits- und Sozialrecht*, **10** (2), 97–200.

Żukowski, Maciej (1997), *Wielostopniowe systemy zabezpieczenia emerytalnego w Unii Europejskiej i w Polsce: Między państwem a rynkiem*, Poznań: Wydawnictwo Akademii Ekonomicznej.

Żukowski, Maciej (1999), 'The New Polish Pension Laws', in Katharina Müller, Andreas Ryll and Hans-Jürgen Wagener (eds), *Transformation of Social Security: Pensions in Central–Eastern Europe*, Heidelberg: Physica, pp. 159–72.

Zürn, Michael (1992), *Interessen und Institutionen in der internationalen Politik: Grundlegung und Anwendungen des situationsstrukturellen Ansatzes*, Opladen: Leske & Budrich.

Index

Aaron's rule 26–7
actor 3–5, 7, 40, 49–56, 58, 81, 87–9,
    103, 122–3, 143–5, 157, 166–75,
    177, 179–81
actor-centred institutionalism 6, 49–
    52, 59, 156, 172, 179
actor constellation 5, 7, 50–53, 56,
    88, 113, 122, 144, 164–74, 179
actors
    collective ~ 48, 50–51, 59, 177
    corporate ~ 50–51, 82, 168
    individual ~ 48, 50–51, 59, 111,
        168, 177
    main ~ 53, 80, 113, 168–74, 179
    political ~ 5, 48–55, 58, 72, 80,
        88, 113–4, 144, 168, 170–71
    secondary ~ 52, 54, 89, 123, 157,
        172–4, 178
AFJPs *see* private pension funds,
    Argentine
AFPs *see* private pension funds,
    Chilean
agenda
    reform ~ 2, 28, 42, 45, 49, 57, 63,
        114, 139, 140, 155, 158, 164,
        166, 171
    setter 45, 54, 59
    shifter 54, 59, 76, 88, 140, 144,
        169
Argentina 19, 21–4, 28, 34, 76, 90,
    107, 111, 116, 122, 159, 163–4,
    177, 179, 181

Bączkowski, Andrzej 110–12, 125,
    168
Belka, Marek 111
Beveridge, William 13
Bismarck, Otto von 13, 93

blame
    avoidance 41, 46, 55, 148
    -generating potential 38
Bokros, Lajos 74, 77

Chile 19–24, 30, 32, 34–6, 39, 55, 74,
    76, 90, 104, 107, 125, 159–60,
    163, 179
ČMKOS *see* trades unions, Czech
cognitive map 5, 52, 170
compensation 2, 7, 36, 38, 41, 47, 78,
    90, 117
complexity of reform 41, 53, 88, 162,
    180
conditionality 45, 54, 58, 169
constitutional courts 54, 58, 71, 79,
    103, 115, 154, 157
contribution rate 14–15, 17–18, 20–
    21, 25–6, 42–4, 61, 66, 80, 84,
    89–91, 99, 100–102, 119, 122
costs
    political ~ 40–42, 53, 58, 161
    social ~ 2–3, 8, 18, 47, 138
    transition ~ 11, 25, 31, 38, 78, 85–
        6, 88, 91–2, 104–6, 112, 120–
        21, 123, 126, 141, 143, 160,
        162, 170, 180
coverage 9, 18, 60–62, 89, 93–6, 127,
    132, 149–50
crises, benefit of 46, 55, 58–9, 88,
    122, 167, 169, 180
crisis 6, 16, 18, 24, 26, 29–32, 35,
    40–41, 46, 53, 58, 63, 75, 96–7,
    107, 122, 124–5, 143, 147, 151,
    168, 177

deficit of public pension scheme 32,
    66, 87, 90, 121, 132, 136, 164,
    175, 179